ACE THE BOARDS:
CYTOPATHOLOGY

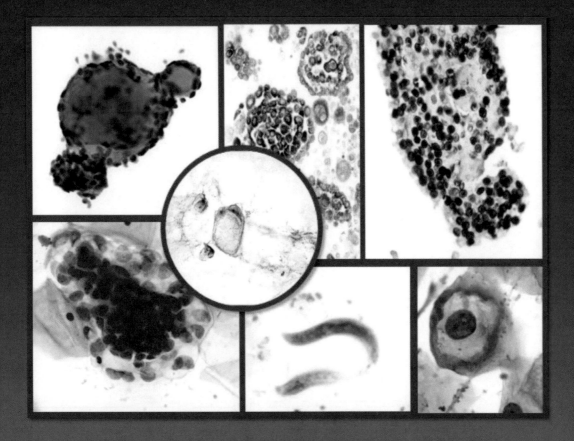

Akanksha Gupta, MD

Swikrity U Baskota, MD; Melissa Hogan, MD;
Binny Khandakar, MD; Abeer M Salama, MD;
Deepa Iyer Kotari, MD; Laila Nomani, MD

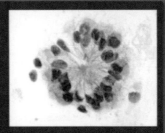

Ace My Path

First Edition

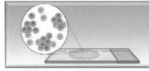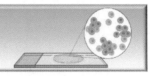
EDITORS

MAIN EDITOR/TEAM LEADER

AKANKSHA GUPTA, MBBS, MD, FASCP, FCAP
Hematopathologist
University of Michigan Health – West, MI
Hematopathology Fellowship
Memorial Sloan Kettering Cancer Center, NY
Renal Pathology Fellowship
University of North Carolina at Chapel Hill, NC
AP/CP Residency, Hartford Hospital, CT

EDITORS AND AUTHORS

MELISSA HOGAN, MD, FASCP
Surgical Pathology Fellow
Cytopathology Fellowship
Vanderbilt University Medical Center
Nashville, TN

SWIKRITY U BASKOTA, MD
Assistant Professor
Cytopathology and Surgical Pathology
Columbia University Irving Medical Center, NY
Cytopathology Fellowship
University of Pittsburgh, PA

BINNY KANDAKAR, MD
Oncologic Surgical Pathology Fellow
Memorial Sloan Kettering Cancer Center
AP/CP Residency,
Icahn School of Medicine/Mount Sinai Health System
New York, NY

ABEER M. SALAMA, MD, MAS
Women's Health Pathology Fellow
NYU Langone Health
Cytopathology Fellowship, MSKCC
New York, NY

DEEPA ANANTHA LAXMI N.V, MBBS, MD
(AKA DEEPA IYER KOTARI)
Practicing Pathologist, Hyderabad, India
AP/CP residency MIMS; MBBS: GMC, Hyderabad, India
Certified training, Dept of Cytopathology, &
Hematopathology, TMH, Mumbai, India
Autopsy pathology- KEM, Mumbai, India
Certified IA-QMS (ISO 15189-NABL 112); PH-GCLP-ME(ICMR)

LAILA NOMANI, MD
Assistant Professor, Medical College of Wisconsin
Hematopathology Fellowship & Residency
Cleveland Clinic, Cleveland, OH
Cytopathology Fellowship
Loyola University Medical Center, IL

TERRANCE J. LYNN, MD, MS
Cytopathology Fellow
Geisinger Medical Center, Danville, PA
Future Molecular Genetic Fellowship
University of Nebraska Medical Center
Omaha, NE

VARUN BHAT, MD
Cytopathology Fellowship
Hartford Hospital
Hartford, CT

SWATI SATTURWAR, MD
Assistant Professor
Department of Pathology
Ohio State University Wexner Medical Center
Columbus, OH

OTHER AUTHORS

SINCHITA ROY-CHOWDHURI, MD, PhD
Associate Professor, Department of Pathology
Medical Director, Molecular Diagnostics Laboratory
The University of Texas MD Anderson Cancer Center
Houston TX

CHARANJEET SINGH, MD
Cytopathologist and Gynecological Oncologic Pathologist
Advent Health Central Florida, Orlando
Adjunct Professor of Pathology
University of Central Florida, Orlando
Director of Pathology and Laboratory
Holmes Regional Medical Center, Melbourne

AJ ROY
ProQMS, Houston, TX

LYNH NGUYEN, MD
Assistant Professor at University of South Florida's
Morsani College of Medicine
Hematopathologist at James A. Haley Veterans'
Hospital, Tampa, FL

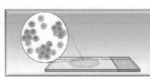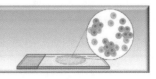

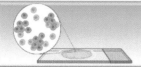
DEEPAK DONTHI, MD, MPH
Gynecologic Pathology Fellow
University of Texas Southwestern Medical Center
Dallas, TX

SAKSHI GUPTA (SAKSHI), MD
Surgical Pathology Fellow
Mayo Clinic, Rochester, MN
Future Cytopathology Fellow 2022
MD Anderson Cancer Center
Houston, TX

SIDDHARTHA DALVI, MBBS, MD, MSc, FRCPC, D(ABMM)
Clinical Lecturer, Pathology Department
University of Alberta
Edmonton, Canada

ABHILASHA NITIN BORKAR MBBS, MD
Resident, AP/CP, UTHSC, TN
Cytopathology fellowship
Loyola University Medical Center, Chicago, IL
Clinical Pathologist, PMC, India
Pathology Residency, TNMC, Mumbai, India

AASTHA CHAUHAN, MD
GI/Liver Fellow
University of Minnesota
Minneapolis, MN

HAYK MELKUMYAN
Cytotechnologist
Vienna, Austria

REVIEWERS

ZARINE KAMALUDDIN, MD
Assistant Professor
University at Buffalo
Jacobs School of Medicine Biomedical Sciences
Cytopathology Fellowship
Ohio State University

JUDITH JEBASTIN THANGAIAH, MD
Assistant Professor
Cytopathology and Bone Soft Tissue Pathology
Mayo Clinic, Rochester, MN

LOPA MODI, MD
Attending Pathologist
Cytopathology
Englewood Health, Englewood, NJ

IMAGE COURTESY

CYTOATLAS APP
BY SINCHITA ROY-CHOWDHURI, MD, PHD
CHARANJEET SINGH, MD, AND AJ ROY

ABEER M. SALAMA, MD
HAYK MELKUMYAN
SYED ALI, MD
NAOMI HARDY, MD
SAMER KHADER, MD
AND MANY OTHER TWITTER FOLKS...

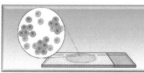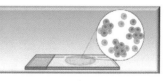

The world of cytopathology: what could be more exciting than piecing together cells to make beautiful pictures that tell a story. "The Ace the Boards: Cytopathology Review" book is a concise, but thorough review of high-yield topics with high quality images that is an essential tool for anyone taking the cytopathology boards. The handy tables, flow-charts, and illustrations make the complex world of cytopathology manageable and even fun for any pathology trainee.

I was contacted by the Ace My Path Team to contribute some of the high-quality images that are part of our mobile app *CytoAtlas*. To me this represented a unique opportunity to collaborate between teaching platforms. I hope the images provided by *CytoAtlas* provide cytomorphologic details that will help the reader familiarize themselves with the various cytologic entities.

The team of authors and editors have worked tirelessly to provide a handy, concise, but comprehensive review that is perfect for medical students, trainees, and anyone looking to brush up on their cytopathology knowledge. Congratulations to the Ace My Path Team for bringing the world of cytopathology into the Ace My Path Series of review books!

SINCHITA ROY-CHOWDHURI, MD, PhD
Associate Professor, Department of Pathology
Medical Director, Molecular Diagnostics Laboratory
The University of Texas MD Anderson Cancer Center
Houston TX

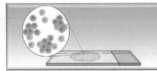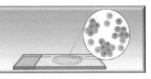

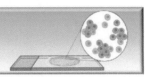

Ace The Boards: Cytopathology is yet another marvelous addition to the series put together by our highly motivated and dedicated team of fellows and practicing cytopathologists at Ace My Path. This book resulted in a quest to provide trainees at various levels with well-illustrated concise, easy-to-read cytopathology content.

The inception of this book began a year ago when some of the authors preparing for their anatomic pathology or cytopathology boards were struggling to find a single, best reliable source for cytopathology. A team of highly motivated then-residents, fellows, and attendings across the US decided to gather in a virtual platform to explore the possibility of a cytopathology book that will be essential to residents, fellows, and practicing pathologists. The rest is history, an exciting journey and we are delighted to bring the final result to you.

The first edition of this book is a comprehensive collection of globally adopted standardized classification systems, cytomorphology, and high-yield facts of each entity in a bulleted format for an easy read, more than 650 high-definition pictures, and brilliant illustrations- all bundled in one.

This book can be resourceful at various levels of training: whether as a medical student interested to know more about cytopathology, residents starting their first rotation in cytopathology, preparing for the resident-in-service examination, or primary anatomic pathology, cytopathology fellow preparing for service work or cytopathology board examination, proficiency testing and as a day-to-day reference handy book by any surgical pathologist at all stages of their clinical career.

We thank all our editors, reviewers, and authors for their relentless hours of devotion and dedication for bringing this well-summarized, beautifully visualized, and easy-to-use resource that we believe will come in handy to every pathologist and is a must-have for their bookshelf. We would also like to thank our image contributors for their amazing quality images.

We welcome valuable thoughts from our cherished readers as we embark on this journey, and we hope to incorporate their feedback in our future editions.

We wish you the greatest success as you study for the Boards and beyond!

-Ace my Path Team

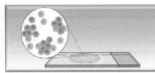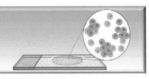

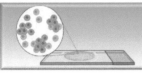 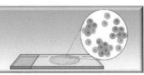

ACKNOWLEGEMENTS

We want to thank God almighty, our families for their love and encouragement, our mentors for their guidance and support, and the amazing path twitter community for their contributions and feedback. This book would not have been possible without the collective efforts of all the above. Furthermore, **CytoAtlas Application by Dr. Sinchita Roy Chowdhury and Charanjeet Singh, MD** has been a phenomenal catalyst in our journey as well!

"To my parents, Maya Gupta and Jugalkishore Gupta, my loving husband, Ashish Gupta, MD, and my darling son, Siddharth Gupta. Keeping our first copy in the feet of Lord Ganesha."
- AKANKSHA GUPTA, MBBS, MD, FASCP, FCAP

"Dedicated to my ever loving and supporting husband Saroj for everything you have done for me, my Dad (baba) and Mom (aama) for what I am today, my always supportive siblings and their better halves Smrity, Nabin, Shristi, Binayak, Bidhisa and my lovely niece Reya"
- SWIKRITY U BASKOTA, MD

"Dedicated to my loving husband, Kevin, who supports me in every endeavor, no matter how crazy and no matter the timing. And to my sweet son Benjamin, who doesn't know it yet, but learned a lot of cytology in his formative first months during the editing of this book. And to my family for always being to loving and supportive"
- MELISSA HOGAN, MD

"Dedicated to my ever-supporting parents, loving sister, amazing friends and great mentors."
- BINNY KHANDAKAR, MD

"Dedicated to my parents A. Saroja & Late.N.V. Venkatraman who lived an inspirational life and always told me "True happiness is being of help to others", to my loving husband Sai S Kotari, MD who supported me in all my endeavors and my little brother Srinath. I am extremely grateful to Dr. Akanksha Gupta, MD for giving me this opportunity and mentoring me through this astounding journey."
- DEEPA IYER KOTARI, MD

"Dedicated to my mother who is my guiding light, forever and always. To my husband and best friend Nisar, for always supporting me in every endeavor.
- LAILA NOMANI, MD

"This work is dedicated to my husband, Abdullah Alhumood, who has been a constant source of support and encouragement during the challenges of school and life. I am truly thankful for having you in my life. This work is also dedicated to the spirit of my dad, Majid, who have always loved me unconditionally and whose good examples have taught me to work hard for the things that I aspire to achieve. My beloved daughter, Dana, and all my family, the symbol of love and giving."
- ABEER M. SALAMA, MD

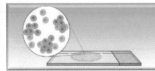 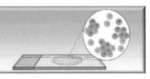

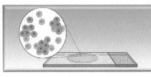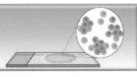
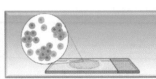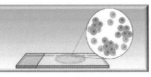

Chapter 1: Introduction

Swikrity U Baskota, MD

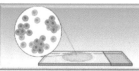
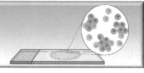

Hayk Melkumyan

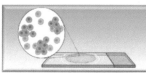
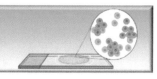

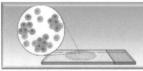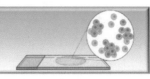
OVERVIEW OF TYPES OF CYTOLOGY SAMPLES

- Cytology samples can be broadly categorized as:
  - Exfoliative cytology
  - Fine Needle Aspiration (FNA) samples
  - Others

EXFOLIATIVE CYTOLOGY

- Exfoliative cytology includes:
  - Cervical and Vaginal cytology (PAP smears)
  - Sputum, bronchial lavage, washing and brushings
  - Urine and bladder cytology
  - Pleural, pericardial, peritoneal fluids and washings
  - Cerebrospinal fluid (CSF)
  - Gastrointestinal tract lavage and brushing

TYPES OF EXFOLIATIVE CYTOLOGY PREPARATIONS

- Conventional Smears
- Liquid-Based Preparations

SPECIMEN COLLECTION (PAP SMEARS)

- The best time for specimen collection is 5 days after menstruation stops
- Sample should be obtained before application of Lugol's iodine/acetic acid
- Speculum can be lubricated with warm water or water-based lubricant
- Excess mucus/discharge should be removed

CONVENTIONAL SMEARS

- Obtained using a combination of spatula and brush
- Plastic spatula is recommended
- Spatula is inserted first and rotated for at least 360^0 and smeared on a slide
- Brush is used next for endocervical sample and usually one-quarter turn is enough for good sampling and smeared on another slide
- Smears are then fixed by using coating fixatives (contains alcohol and polyethylene glycol) or can be immersed directly into 95% ethanol

LIQUID-BASED CYTOLOGY

- ThinPrep® and SurePath™
- No significant difference from conventional smears in the detection of HSIL

ADVANTAGES

- Thinner cell preparation
- Duplicate slides and cell block preparations from residual samples
- Lesser area to screen with minimal cell overlap
- Easier for automated screening devices

- Ability to do aliquoting for ancillary studies (e.g., HPV testing)
- Figure 1: SurePath™ and ThinPrep® Processing Techniques

FINE NEEDLE ASPIRATION (FNA)

- Used for evaluating palpable superficial and deep seated cystic or solid masses
- With or without image-guidance

FINE NEEDLE ASPIRATION SETTINGS AND EQUIPMENT

- Can be done in a pathologist run FNA clinic or inpatient bedside or outpatient specialist clinic
- FNA equipment list is shown in Figure 2.

PERFORMING AN FNA

- Consent should always be taken before the procedure
- Perform a time-out procedure
- Palpate, localize, immobilize the lesion and if needed, use lidocaine injection or spray for pain management
- Sample the lesion adequately with back-and-forth motion for at least 10 seconds once in the lesion
- Do a rapid on-site evaluation/assessment (ROSE/ROSA) of the obtained sample for triage
- Triage the sample for flow cytometry, microbial culture, and ancillary studies as deemed appropriate
- Perform multiple passes (if required)
- Provide post-procedure care instructions to the patient
- Figure 3 depicts the process of performing an FNA and preparing smears from the obtained material

COMPLICATIONS OF FNA

- Very rare except for minor pain, bleeding, and bruising
- Pneumothorax in perithoracic lesions
- Needle tract seedling if >17 G needle (rarely used)

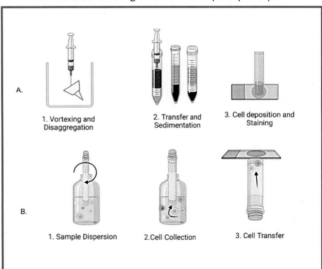

Figure 1: SurePath™ and ThinPrep® Processing Techniques

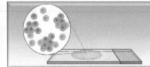

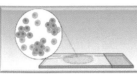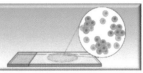
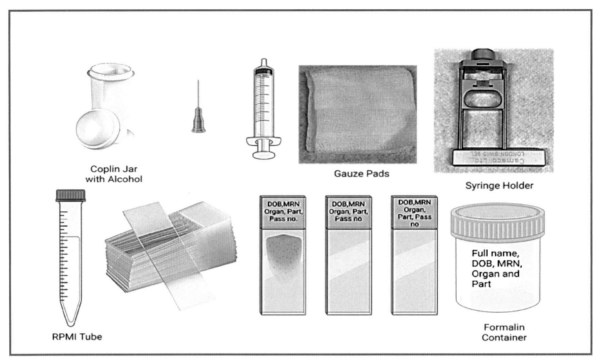

Figure 2: FNA equipment

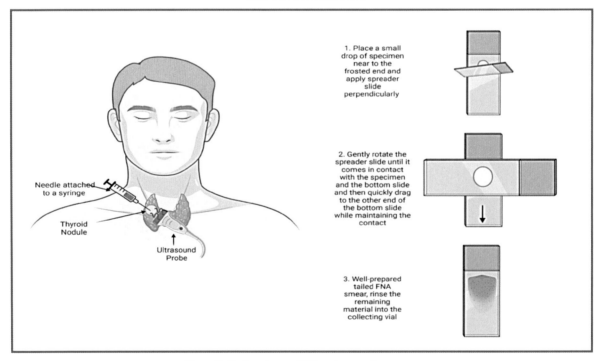

Figure 3: Performing an FNA and preparing a smear

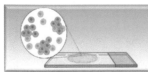

Chapter 2: Cervical and Vaginal Cytology

Abeer M. Salama, MD
Hayk Melkumyan

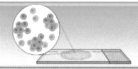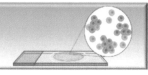

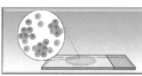

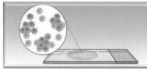 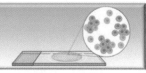
BETHESDA SYSTEM (2014):

REPORTING CERVICAL CYTOLOGY	
I. SPECIMEN TYPE: Conventional vs liquid-based preparation	
II. SPECIMEN ADEQUACY	

SATISFACTORY FOR EVALUATION
 	
 Figure: Field count guide, for assessing specimen adequacy.
 Created by Swikrity U Baskota with BioRender
	• Minimum number of squamous cells
	   ➤ Liquid-based: 5000 cells (10 fields count, starting at the edge to include the center of the slides at 40x)
	   ➤ Conventional: 8000-12000 cells
	 • Note the presence or absence of transformation zone (10 endocervical or metaplastic cells)
	 • Presence or absence of transformation zone is for quality assurance only

UNSATISFACTORY FOR EVALUATION  Obscuring inflammation >75% squamous cells	• Specimen collection issues: Broken slide, missing patient identification, insufficient epithelial cells • Obscuring factors: (RBCs, WBCs, or lubricants) >75% of epithelial cells
III. INTERPRETATION	
NEGATIVE FOR INTRA EPITHELIAL LESION OR MALIGNANCY (NILM)	
A. Organisms	• Trichomonas vaginalis, Candida, bacterial vaginosis, Actinomyces, HSV, CMV
B. Others Atrophy IUD Effect Radiation Atypia	• Atrophy • Glandular cell post hysterectomy • Inflammation, Repair, radiation changes and IUD • Endometrial cells in a woman older than 45 years of age
EPITHELIAL CELL ABNORMALITY	

A. Squamous cell
 	
 LSIL   HSIL   SCC
	• Atypical squamous cells
	   ➤ Of Undetermined significance (ASC-US)
	   ➤ Cannot exclude HSIL (ASC-H)
	 • Low-Grade Squamous Intraepithelial Lesion (LSIL)
	 • High-Grade Squamous Intraepithelial Lesion (HSIL)
	 • Squamous cell carcinoma

B. Glandular cell
 	
 Glandular cell   Favor neoplastic   Adenocarcinoma
	• Atypical
	   ➤ Endocervical cells (NOS)
	   ➤ Endometrial cells (NOS)
	 • Glandular cells
	 • Atypical, favor neoplastic
	   ➤ Endocervical cells, favor neoplastic
	   ➤ Glandular cells, favor neoplastic
	
	 ‣ Endocervical adenocarcinoma in Situ (AIS)
	 ‣ Adenocarcinoma
	   ➤ Endocervical
	   ➤ Endometrial
	   ➤ Not otherwise specified (NOS)

OTHER HIGH YIELD POINTS	• Absent transformation zone is not considered unsatisfactory and does not require a repeat pap • Adding 10% glacial acetic acid increases satisfactory sample % of ThinPrep® pap • ThinPrep® is methanol based and SurePath™ is ethanol-based preparation • NILM can be reported by cytotechnologist (except reactive/repair changes)

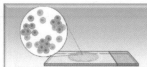 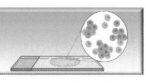

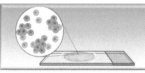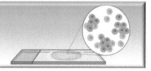

NORMAL PAP SMEAR: CYTOMORPHOLOGY

GENERAL FEATURES (COMPARISION BETWEEN SQUAMOUS AND GLANDULAR CELLS)		
Cell type	SQUAMOUS CELL	GLANDULAR CELL
Groups	• 2D flat sheets, isolated cells, keratin pearls	• 3D, gland with secretion, honeycombs, micro-acini
Cells	• Polyhedral, spindle, intercellular bridges (CB)	• Cuboidal/columnar
Cytoplasm	• Dense, orangeophilic (Pap), blue waxy (DQ)	• Delicate, pale blue, foamy, mucin vacuole
Nucleus	• Central, coarse	• Eccentric, nucleoli
Other high yield points	Optimal PAP smear • Sample should contain ectocervix and endocervix • Sample should be taken before acetic acid application • Sample taken 2 weeks after start of last menstrual period • Avoid vaginal douches, tampons, and intercourse 2-3 days prior procedure	

SQUAMOUS CELLS	Superficial	Intermediate	Basal/Parabasal (Atrophy)	Squamous metaplasia	Hyperkeratosis /Parakeratosis
Age	• Reproductive		• Postpartum, Post menopause	• Any age	• Any age
Nucleus	• Small, pyknotic	• Large, fine granular	• Variable/large	• Interlocking parabasal cells	• Hyperkeratosis: Anucleate squamous cells
Cytoplasm	• Large polygonal, pink cytoplasm	• Scant, round	• Similar to superficial		• Parakeratosis: Pyknotic nucleus, organophilic cytoplasm
Status	• High estrogen		• Low estrogen		• Any chronic irritation/ uterine prolapse
Cytology	 Superficial	 Intermediate	 Basal/Parabasal	 Sq metaplasia	 Parakeratosis
OTHER HIGH YIELD POINTS	• Basal/parabasal / atrophy (low estrogen): Premenarchal, postpartum, post menopause, post-partum, and Turner syndrome • High estrogen: Obesity, post puberty				

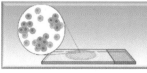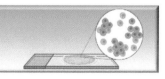

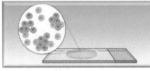
GLANDULAR CELLS	Endocervical	Endometrial	Lower uterine segment
Architecture	• Strips/honeycomb sheets	• 3D Sphere, balls	• Large fragments: glands +stroma
Cytoplasm	• Fine, granular, vacuolated	• Scant, scalloped	
Nucleus	• Eccentric	• Small, dark, molding	• Fine granular
Cytology	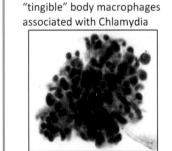	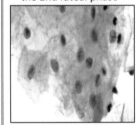	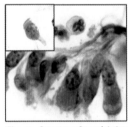

Figure: Courtesy Sean McNair, MD (Twitter: @smcnair0328) |

OTHER BENIGN CHANGES

FOLLICULAR CERVICITIS	LACTOBACILLI	TUBAL METAPLASIA	SYNCYTIOTROPHOBLAST
• Lymphocytes, plasma cells, "tingible" body macrophages associated with Chlamydia	• Gram + rod, reduces PH resulting in "cytolysis" in the 2nd luteal phase	• Ciliated endocervical cells	• Dark, coarse nuclei, multinucleated cells
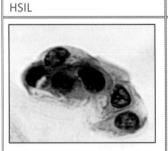		

Figure: Courtesy Saeed Asiry, MD (Twitter: @SaeedAsiry) |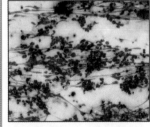

Figure: Courtesy Lucas Massoth, MD (Twitter: @lucasMassoth) |

MIMICS OF EXFOLIATED ENDOMETRIAL CELLS

HSIL	AIS	SQUAMOUS CELL CARCINOMA	SMALL CELL CARCINOMA
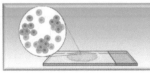		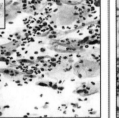

Figure: Courtesy Hayk Melkumyan, MD | |
| • Smaller than endometrial cells in flat aggregates (Sphere in endometrial) | • Mitosis (uncommon in exfoliative endometrium) | • Tumor diathesis | • Darker than endometrial cells with nuclear smudging and smearing |

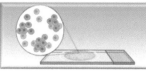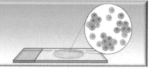
ORGANISMS AND INFECTIONS

BACTERIAL VAGINOSIS	CANDIDA	CMV	HSV
• Shift in normal bacteria flora (no lactobacilli) associated with Gardenalia Vaginalis	• Shish kabab: squamous cells with pseudo hyphae and budding	• Mononuclear, basophilic intranuclear inclusion	• Molding, multinucleation and margination with eosinophilic intranuclear inclusions
		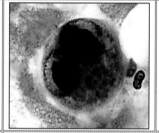	

ACTINOMYCES	TRICHOMONAS VAGINALIS	HIGH YIELD POINTS
• Cotton balls, dark associated with IUD	• Hazy oval nucleus with eosinophilic cytoplasm granules associated with poly-balls (clusters of neutrophils)	Infectious association • Trichomonas vaginalis • Leptothrix often associated with Trichomonas (spaghetti and meatballs) • Bacterial vaginosis: Gardnerella vaginalis (Coccobacilli and absence of lactobacilli)
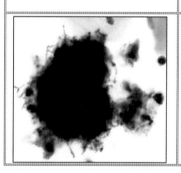	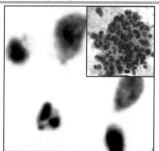	

ARTIFACTS/ CONTAMINATIONS:

COCKLEBUR	CORN FLAKING	GLYCOGENATED	VEGETABLES/ PLANTS	CARPET BEETLE LARVA	COLLAGEN BALL
• Calcium, lipid, and glycogen associated with pregnancy	• Artifact air bubbles				
	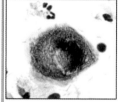	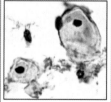		Image Courtesy Hena Khandakadar, MD	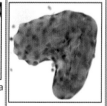

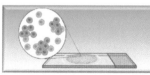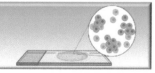

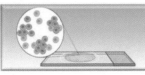
	ATROPHY	RADIATION ATYPIA	HYPERKERATOTIC	PARAKERATOTIC	IUD EFFECT
Nucleus	• Small, round	• Multinucleation, Normal N:C ratio	• Absent "ghost"	• Pyknotic	• Combination of vacuolated cell & small dark cell
Cytoplasm	• Dense	• Cytoplasmic vacuoles (two-tone pink and blue) & streaming sheets	• Organophilic		Figure: Courtesy Tania Iabiano, MD (Twitter: @tlabiano)
Conditions	• Post menopause, post-partum	• Radiation	• Uterine prolapse	• Chronic irritation	

SQUAMOUS INTRAEPITHELIAL LESIONS

A. HPV

- HPV: double stranded DNA virus with early (E) and late (L) genes
- Starts in the basal epithelium
- HPV vaccine: L1 viral protein
- E6 gene binds to P53 inhibit apoptosis
- E7 gene binds Rb inhibit cell cycle arrest (proliferation)

HPV type	Serotypes
Low risk	6,11
High risk	16,18,31,33

- HPV 16: common in cervical adenocarcinoma
- Serology is not accurate
- Most HPV infection are cleared

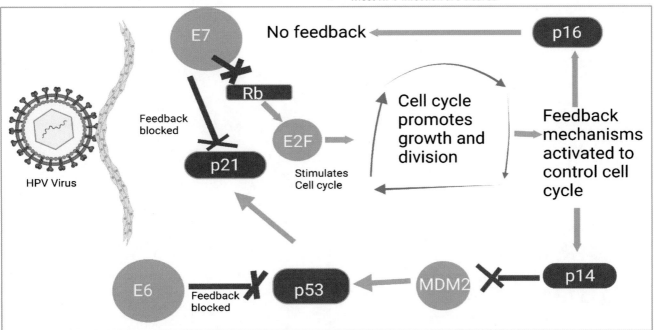

Figure: Mechanism of HPV virus genome of host cell integration. Courtesy of Swikrity U Baskota, MD made using BioRender

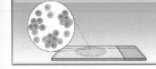

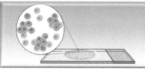 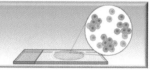
CYTOMORPHOLOGY:

	LSIL	HSIL	SCC
Cell size	• Intermediate to superficial cells	• Parabasal (immature cells): single/ groups	• Marked variation
Nucleus	• Large 3x, irregular, hyperchromatic	• Smaller, marked hyperchromatic, irregular, coarse	• Irregular, dense, macronucleoli
Cytoplasm	• Halo (koilocyte)	• No halo	• Keratinizing, non-keratinizing
Others	• No nucleoli	• High N:C ratio (except in keratinized cytoplasm)	• Tumor diathesis • Fiber cell (tadpoles)
Progression	• 21% progress to HSIL • <1% progress to invasive squamous cell carcinoma (SCC)	• 1.4% progress to invasive squamous cell carcinoma	NA
Morphology	• Koilocytic • Non-koilocytic • Keratinizing	• Syncytium-like • Keratinizing	• Single in keratinizing • Syncytial aggregates are non-keratinizing

DIFFERENTIAL DIAGNOSIS SQUMAOUS INTRAEPITHELIAL LESIONS

DIFFERENTIAL DIAGNOSIS LSIL		DIFFERENTIAL DIAGNOSIS HSIL	
Reactive squamous cells	• School of fish, streaming monolayered with inflammation and prominent nucleoli	Squamous metaplasia	• Even chromatin
Reactive endocervical cells	• Enlarged cells with cytoplasmic vacuoles	Atrophy	• Regular nucleus, fine chromatin

Figure: Courtesy Samer Khader, MD
(Twitter: @SamKhader)

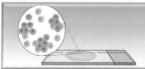

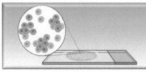
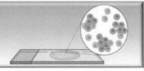
DIFFERENTIAL DIAGNOSIS HSIL			
TRANSITIONAL METAPLASIA 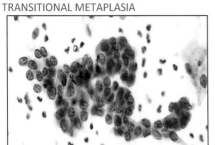	• Coffee bean nucleus	**HISTOCYTES** 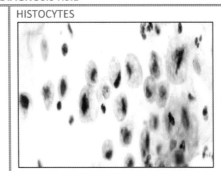	• Fine fluffy cytoplasm
ENDOMETRIAL CELLS 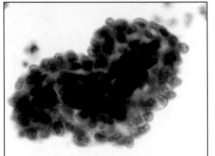 Figure: Courtesy Israh Khan Akhtar, MD (Twitter: @israhkhan)	• 3D sphere, smaller	**IUD ARTIFACT** 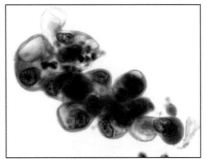 Figure: Courtesy Tania labiano, MD (Twitter: @tlabiano)	• Few, more prominent nucleoli
FOLLICULAR CERVICITIS 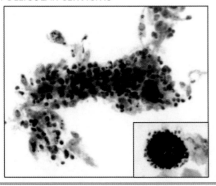	• Small, lymphocytes and plasma cells, tingible - body macrophage	**ADENOCARCINOMA IN SITU** 	• Feathering, rosette formation
SQUAMOUS CELL CARCINOMA 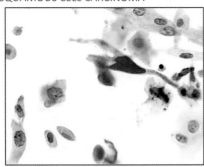	• Tadpoles • Prominent nucleoli • Tumor diathesis	**ASC-H** 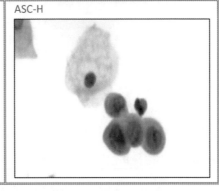	• Single or small groups< 10 cells • Nucleus up to 2.5x normal • N:C ratio of HSIL

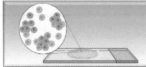
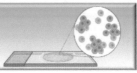

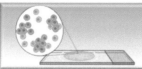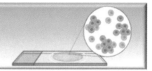
GLANDULAR EPITHELIAL ABNORMALITIES:
ENDOCERVICAL ADENOCARCINOMA IN SITU (AIS)

ENDOCERVICAL ADENOCARCINOMA IN SITU (AIS)	ATYPICAL ENDOCERVICAL CELLS, FAVOR NEOPLASTIC
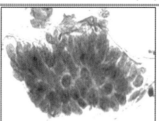	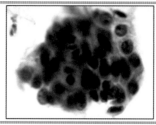
• 3D, feathering, strips ("bird tail" in SurePath™), rosette, pseudo stratification • Nuclear enlargement, high N/C, overlap, hyperchromasia, coarse chromatin, mitosis, Inconspicuous nucleoli • Clean background, No tumor diathesis	• Quantitatively or qualitatively falls short of AIS or adenocarcinoma • Sheets and strips with nuclear crowding, overlap, and/or pseudo-stratification

ADENOCARCINOMA:

	ENDOCERVICAL ADENOCARCINOMA	ENDOMETRIAL ADENOCARCINOMA	EXTRA UTERINE ADENOCARCINOMA
Pictures			
Cellularity	• Hypercellular	• Hypocellular	• Rare few cells, unless direct extension
Architecture	• Flat strips, sheets or single	• 3D, small clusters	• Variable
Background diathesis	• Common	• Absent or thin watery	• Absent unless direct extension
Cell	• Oval to elongated	• Round to irregular	• Variable
Nuclei	• Large, round with clearing	• smaller, round hyperchromatic	• Variable
Nucleoli	• Prominent	• Prominent	• Variable
Cytoplasm	• Abundant, mucin	• Scant with vacuoles, abundant with neutrophils (polys bags)	• Variable
HPV risk	• HPV 18> 16	• Negative	• Negative
Associated with SIL	• >50%	• Absent	• Absent
P16	• Block positivity	• Patchy except in high grade serous	• Variable

OTHERS:
- 25 % AGC cases test positive for hrHPV
- 50 % of AGC cases with hrHPV are associated with higher lesions
- Less than 5% AGC cases without hrHPV are associated with significant lesions
- Most prevalent types of hrHPV are 18/45, followed by 16

- hrHPV-positive AGC is more likely to have positive cervical pathology
- hrHPV-negative AGC is more likely to show cancer of endometrial or extrauterine in origin, or a benign reactive condition
- There is no difference in the management of the disease for women with AIS, than the special populations, such as in pregnancy and in women (21–24 years)

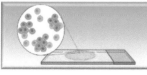

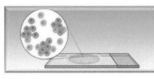
ATYPICAL SQUAMOUS CELL (ASC) INCLUDING ASCUS AND ASC-H

	ASCUS	ASC-H
DEFINITION	• Atypical cells suggestive of LSIL but either quantity or quality are insufficient for LSIL after examining the entire specimen	• Atypical cells suggestive of HSIL but either quantity or quality are insufficient for LSIL after examining the entire specimen
CYTOMORPHOLOGY	• Atypical cells with mature but also immature cytoplasm suggestive of koilocytes • Atypia associated with atrophy • Atypical parakeratosis • Atypical repair	• Immature squamous metaplastic cells with mild - moderate nuclear atypia and membrane irregularity

High Yield:
- ASC/HSIL ratio < 3:1
- Median ASC/AIL ratio 1.5

CERVICAL CANCER SCREENING (ASC 2020)

Population	Screening ASC (2020)
< 25 years	• No screening
25-65 years	• Start cervical cancer screening: 25 years (Primary HPV q 5 years -preferred) • Alternatives: Co-testing q 5 years or cytology alone x3 years (acceptable method and strongly recommended) • Note: Since access to primary HPV testing for primary screening may be limited in some areas, co-testing or cytology testing alone are still acceptable options for screening
>65 years	• Discontinue cervical cancer screening if • Last 25 years: No CIN2 or more AND • Last 10 years: Documented negative screen X10 years period before the age of 65 • Note: If insufficient documentation + patient without limited life conditions continue to screen until criteria is met for cessation
Adequate negative prior screening	• 2 consecutive HPV negative tests, or 2 consecutive negative co-tests, or 3 consecutive negative cytology tests within the past 10 years and having most recent negative test within the past 3-5 years • Note: -These criteria do not apply to patients with abnormal screening results and are under surveillance • Discontinued cervical cancer screening at any age if patient with limited life expectancy
Status post hysterectomy	• Discontinue cervical cancer screening if • No cervix + no history of ≥ CIN2 X past 25 years
HPV vaccinated	• Follow age-specific recommendations (as unvaccinated)

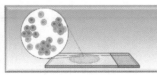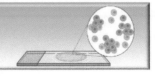

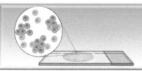
CERVICAL CANCER SCREENING TESTS

TEST	TYPE	FDA approved	Genotype
PAP cytology	• Sample brushing of cervix and test under the microscope for abnormal cells		
Primary HPV	• Detects the DNA (high-risk) HPV taken from PAP smears	• Cobas® HPV (2014)	• HPV 16/18
		• Onclarity HPV (2018)	• HPV 16, 18, 45, 31, 51, 52, 33+58, 35+39+68, 56+59+66
Co-testing (Cytology +HPV)	• Combination of the above	• Digene HC2 (2003	• None
		• Cervista HPV HR (2009)	• None
		• Cervista HPV16/18 (2009)	• HPV 16 /18
		• Aptima HPV (2011)	• No
		• Aptima HPV16 and 18/45 (2012)	• HPV 16/18 and 45
		• Cobas HPV (2011)	• HPV 16/18
		• Onclarity HPV (2018)	• HPV 16, 18, 45, 31, 51, 52, 33+58, 35+39+68, and 56+59+66

MANAGEMENT GUIDELINES (ASCCP 2019):

Changes from previous management guidelines

1) Recommendations now are based on risk and not results
2) Colposcopy can be deferred in HPV-positive LSIL after a negative screen: Recommend repeat HPV testing or co-testing at 1 year
3) Guidance for expedited treatment is now expanded (i.e., treatment without a preceding colposcopy biopsy to include:

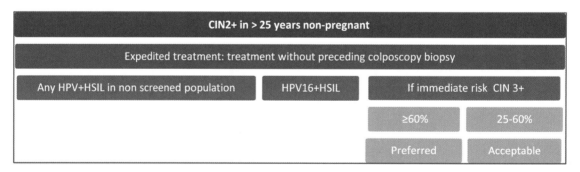

4) Excisional treatment is preferred to ablative treatment in adenocarcinoma in situ (AIS)
5) Observation is preferred over treatment for CIN 1
6) All positive primary HPV screening tests (regardless of genotype) Do additional reflex triage testing from the same PAP specimen (Do reflex cytology PAP)
- Additional testing from the same PAP specimen is recommended because the findings may guide colposcopy (E.g.: HPV-16 positive HSIL will be qualified for expedited treatment)
- HPV 16/18 positive with negative cytology →colposcopy with biopsy even when cytology is negative (because they have the highest risk for CIN 3 and occult cancer)
- If HPV 16 /18 testing is positive, and additional reflex cytology of the same PAP sample is not feasible → proceed to direct colposcopy
7) After treatment of HSIL, CIN 2, CIN 3, or AIS → Continue surveillance with HPV testing or co-testing q3 years x 25 years

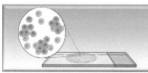

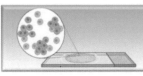
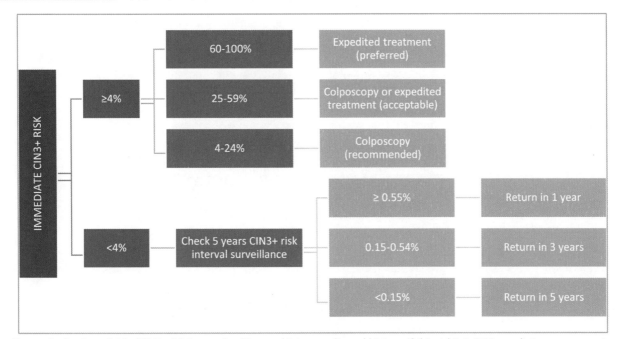

Figure: Evaluation of risk. CIN 3+ risk is examined by combining results and history. If this risk is ≥ 4% immediate management (colposcopy or treatment) is needed. If the immediate risk < 4%, the 5-year CIN 3+ risk is calculated to determine whether patient should return in 1, 3, or 5 years

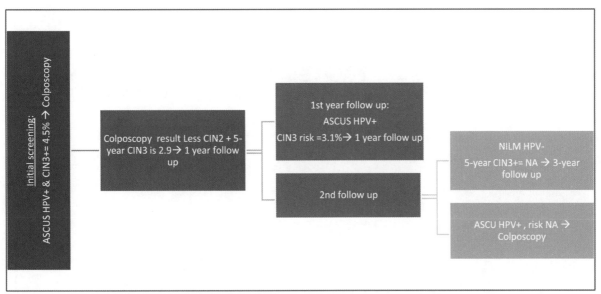

Figure: Management of risk estimates for low-grade screening abnormality (HPV-positive ASC-US)

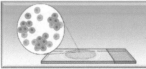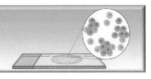

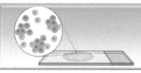 

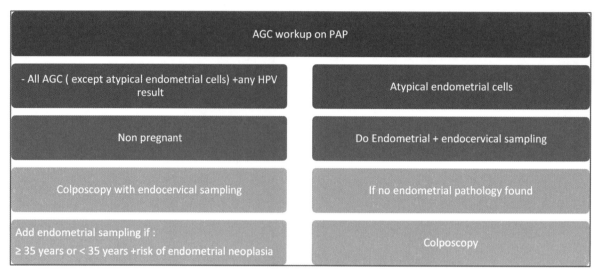

Figure: Initial AGC workup in PAP cytology

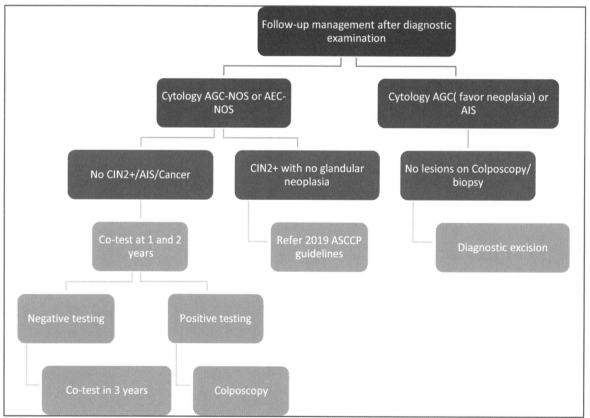

Figure: Follow-up management after pathologic diagnosis from the above figure

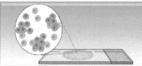 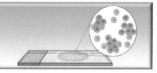

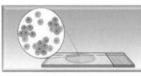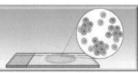
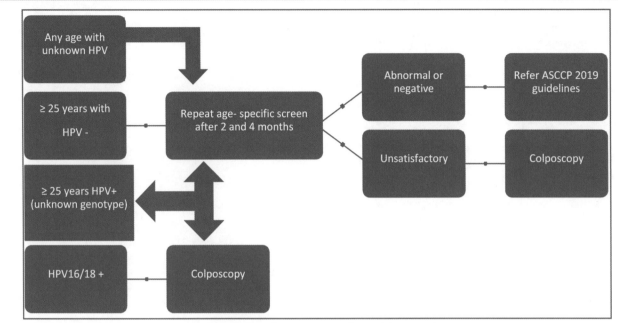

Figure: Clinical management of unsatisfactory PAP

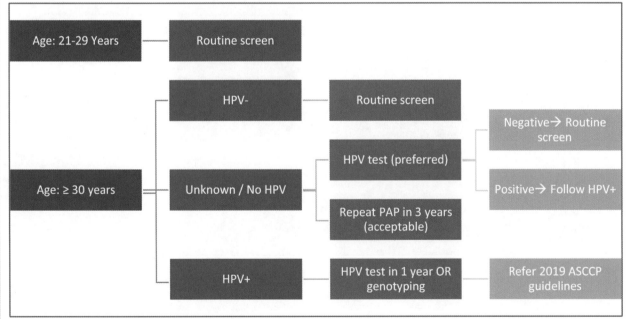

Figure: Clinical management of absent transformation zone in Negative for intraepithelial lesion (NILM)

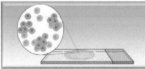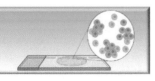

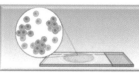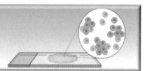
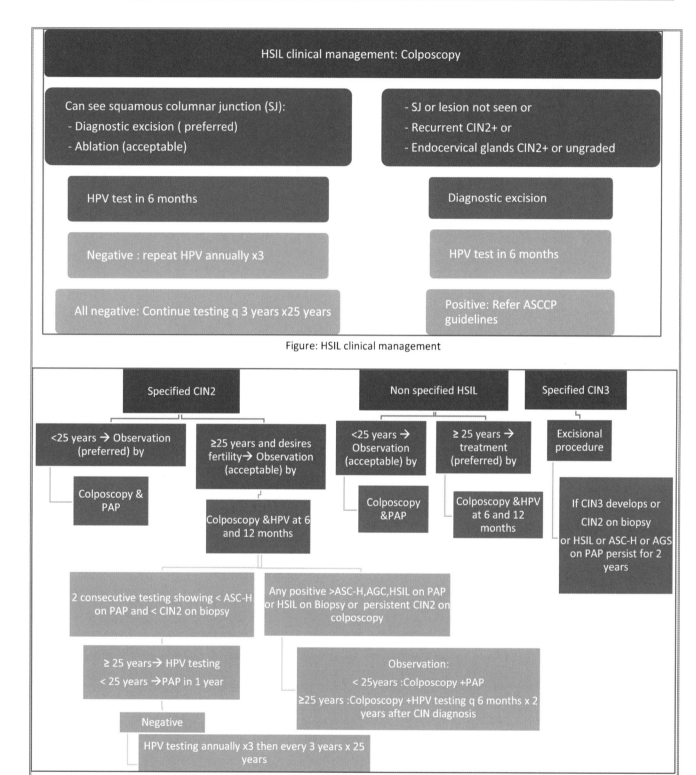

Figure: HSIL clinical management

Figure: Management of CIN2 in patients with fertility concern over cancer and Non specified HSIL diagnosis

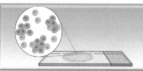

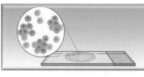

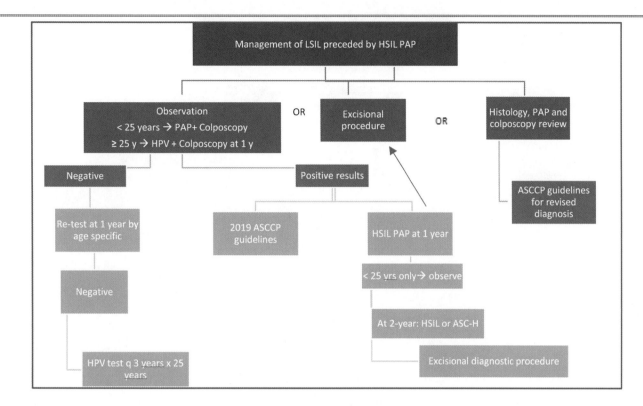

Figure: Management of LSIL preceded by HSIL PAP

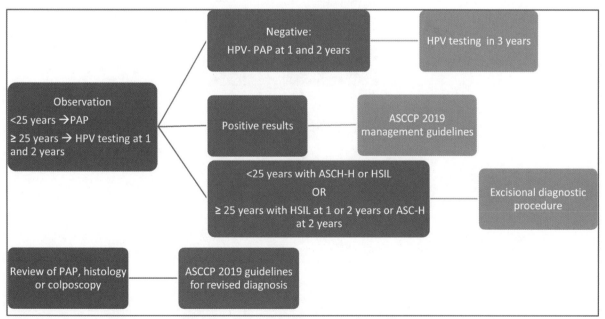

Figure: Management of LSIL preceded by ASC-H PAP

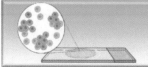
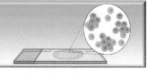

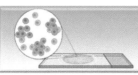
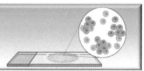

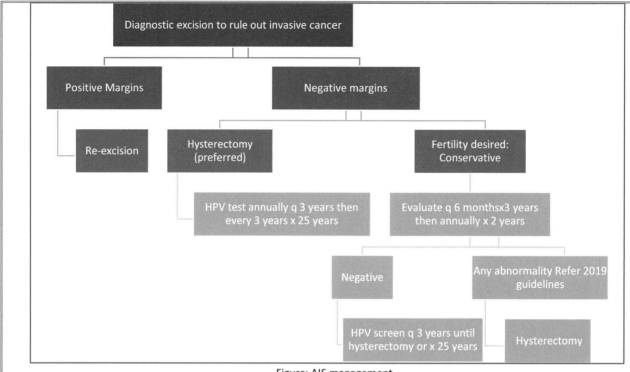

Figure: AIS management

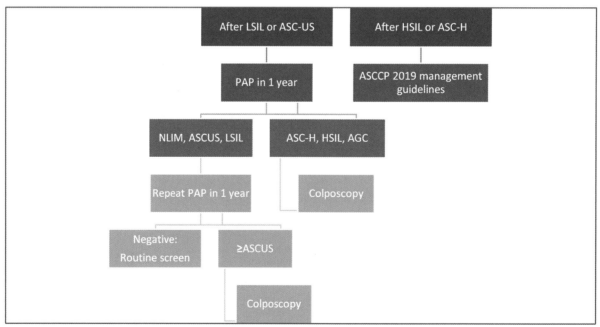

Figure: Individuals < 25 years with abnormal cytology

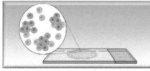
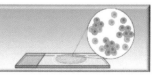

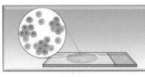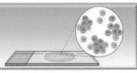

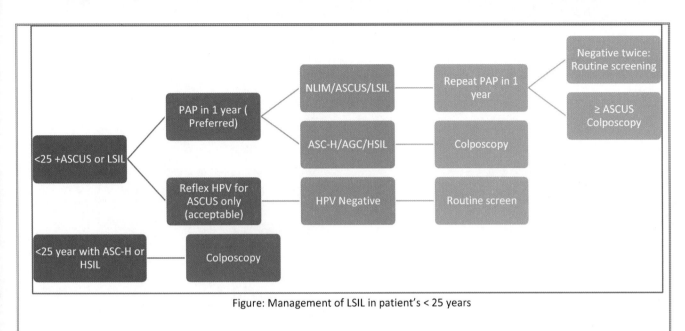

Figure: Management of LSIL in patient's < 25 years

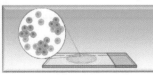

Marie Antoinette

Hayk M.

daughter of Emperor Francis I and Maria Theresa of Austria

Chapter 3: Respiratory Cytology

Varun Bhat, MD

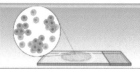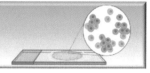

Marie Antoinette

Hayk M.

daughter of Emperor Francis I and Maria Theresa of Austria

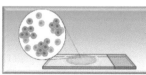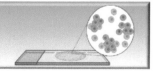

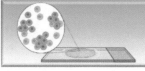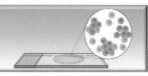
SPUTUM

Contents

- Cellular component:
    - Pulmonary macrophages (contain foamy cytoplasm and anthracotic pigment)
    - Squamous cells
    - Ciliated epithelial cells
    - Organisms
- Acellular mucus

Sample collection

- Portions of fresh sputum with solid tissue fragments and blood are selected for smear preparation ('pick and smear technique')
- Early morning sample is preferred; collecting multiple samples over several days increases sensitivity
- Sputum induction by inhalation of nebulized water or saline increases rates of cancer detection

Adequacy

- Satisfactory sputum specimen must contain abundant pulmonary macrophages, indicating sampling of the lower respiratory tract

BRONCHIAL BRUSHINGS

Sample collection

- Endobronchial lesions are bronchoscopically visualized and a brush is applied to collect cells from the lesion

Utility

- Depending on the location of the lesion within the airways, bronchial brushing can be used as an alternative to bronchoalveolar lavage

BRONCHOALVEOLAR LAVAGE

Sample collection

- Sample obtained by inserting a bronchoscope far into the distal respiratory airway and flushing with sterile saline solution

Utility

- Useful for detecting opportunistic infections in immunocompromised patients such as *Pneumocystis*, *M. Tuberculosis* and atypical mycobacteria, *Histoplasma*, *Cryptococcus*, etc.
- Can also be used to diagnose malignancy

Adequacy

- Presence of abundant neutrophils suggests true infection. Presence of numerous squamous cells suggests oral contamination of the specimen

- False positive: due to atypical type II pneumocytes, usually in cases with a recent history of lung injury

FNA LUNG

Types

- Transbronchial FNA (TBNA)
- Endobronchial Ultrasound (EBUS) guided FNA
- Transesophageal FNA
- Percutaneous FNA

TRANSBRONCHIAL FNA

- A catheter with a retractable (Wang) needle is sent down a bronchoscope and lesional contents are aspirated

Utility

- To assess lung lesions beneath bronchial epithelium
- To assess mediastinal lymph nodes

Contraindications

- Coagulopathy, respiratory failure, uncontrollable coughing

ENDOBRONCHIAL ULTRASOUND-GUIDED (EBUS) FNA

- A bronchoscope with an attached ultrasound probe tip is used to locate and sample the target mass with a 22G needle

Adequacy

- Considered adequate if the sample contains a moderate number of lymphocytes if targeting a lymph node unless atypical cells present
- Presence of pigmented pulmonary macrophages indicates adequate lung mass sampling

Utility

- Minimally invasive
- Lymph node sampling for cancer staging
- Diagnosis of miscellaneous lymph node pathology, such as sarcoidosis, infections, and metastatic disease

TRANSESOPHAGEAL FNA (TE-FNA)

- Sample obtained by endoscopically passing the needle through the esophagus to access mediastinal lymph nodes

Utility

- Assessment of mediastinal lymph nodes that are inaccessible with EBUS-FNA (stations 8 and 9) used in conjunction with EBUS-FNA to improve mediastinal staging

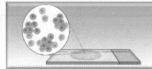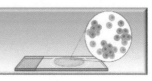

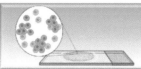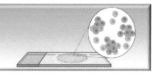
Adequacy
- Same as EBUS guided FNA

PERCUTANEOUS FNA
- Chest lesions are accessed percutaneously under computerized tomography- or ultrasound- guidance

Adequacy
- Presence of lesional material is considered adequate

Contaminants
- Contaminants from the path of the needle: cutaneous squamous cells, muscle and fibroconnective tissue from chest wall, pleural mesothelial cells, and hepatocytes: do not meet adequacy requirements

Complications
- Pneumothorax - most common complication; greater risk with larger needle size, smaller target lesions, and if the needle has to traverse aerated lung en-route to the target lesion
- Hemothorax
- Hemopericardium
- Air embolism
- Tumor seeding

Contraindications
- Lung pathology such as COPD, pulmonary hypertension
- Bleeding diathesis
- Cardiac disease
- Arteriovenous malformations
- Suspected echinococcal cyst (risk of anaphylaxis)

Figure: Diff-Quik stain. Benign bronchial cell with terminal bar and cilia

Figure: PAP stain. Normal/reactive bronchial cells–honeycomb appearance of cells with round/oval nuclei and bland chromatin, cilia are visible.

Figure: PAP stain. Creola body: 3D cluster of reactive bronchial cells. Courtesy Kalyani Bambal, MD @kriyer68

Figure: PAP stain. Curschmann's spiral and Charcot Leyden crystals. Courtesy Sanjay Mukhopadhyay, MD @smlungpathguy

BENIGN BRONCHIAL CELLS
CYTOMORPHOLOGY
- Uniform cuboidal or columnar cells with a terminal bar (darker band at the luminal aspect of the cell)
- Round to oval nuclei with smooth nuclear membranes and inconspicuous nucleoli
- Cilia may or may not be seen (presence of cilia favors benignity)

REACTIVE SQUAMOUS CHANGES
CYTOMORPHOLOGY
- Benign squamous cells can show reactive changes ranging from mild atypia (seen in trauma, infection, inflammation) to markedly atypical changes (associated with lung injury seen in cases with sepsis, diffuse alveolar damage, pulmonary infarction, post-chemoradiation, and adjacent to stomas, cavitary fungal lesions)
- Good clinical history helps avoid over-diagnosing these changes as squamous cell carcinoma

REACTIVE BRONCHIAL CELL CHANGES
CYTOMORPHOLOGY
- Three-dimensional clusters of sloughed off reactive bronchial cells (known as Creola bodies) can be seen in chronic airway diseases such as asthma; other findings that can be seen in asthma and allergic diseases are Curschmann's spirals (spirally coiled, purple-colored mucus casts) and Charcot-Leyden crystals (slender, rhomboid-shaped, orange-red structures with pointed ends, composed of eosinophilic lysophospholipase binding protein Galectin-10)
- Squamous metaplastic changes can be seen in chronic injury (e.g., smoking)
- Cellular changes that mimic carcinoma (e.g., increased N/C ratio, multinucleation, and prominent nucleoli) can be seen after administration of chemo and radiation therapy

OTHER HIGH YIELD POINTS
- Factors favoring benign reactive changes over malignancy:
  - Presence of cilia
  - Lack of a distinct two cell population (i.e., cells show a spectrum of atypical changes ranging from mild to severe)

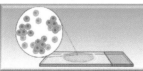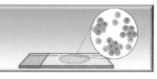

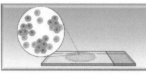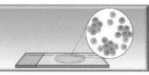
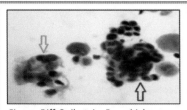 Figure: Diff-Quik stain. Bronchial reserve cell hyperplasia (red arrow) – compare with benign ciliated bronchial cells (green arrow). Courtesy Samer Khader, MD (Twitter: @SamKhader)	**BRONCHIAL RESERVE CELL HYPERPLASIA (RCH)** CYTOMORPHOLOGY • Reserve bronchial cells are tightly packed, cohesive groups of small cells • Are approximately the size of an erythrocyte and show nuclear molding, scant cytoplasm, and dark, smudgy chromatin OTHER HIGH YIELD POINTS • Bronchial reserve cell proliferation is associated with surface epithelium injury • Main differential is small cell carcinoma due to similar features such as nuclear molding and high N/C ratio • Unlike small cell carcinoma, RCH cells show cell-cell cohesion without necrosis or mitoses
	REPAIR RELATED CHANGES CYTOMORPHOLOGY • Can mimic atypia/carcinoma due to the presence of large nuclei with nuclear hyperchromasia, prominent nucleoli, and mitotic figures • Unlike carcinoma, cells displaying reparative changes tend to show greater cohesion and are seen as flat, orderly sheets of cells with ample cytoplasm and lower N/C ratios • Reparative changes tend to be seen during re-epithelialization of an ulcer (associated with trauma, radiation, infections, etc.)
	TYPE II PNEUMOCYTE HYPERPLASIA CYTOMORPHOLOGY • Can be seen as single cells or 3D clusters • Pneumocytes can mimic adenocarcinoma due to the presence of large nuclei with coarse chromatin, prominent nucleoli, and even occasional cytoplasmic vacuolation; considerable diagnostic difficulty can be encountered especially in cases with florid pneumocyte hyperplasia OTHER HIGH YIELD POINTS • Thorough clinical history is essential in diagnosing type II pneumocyte hyperplasia - any history of acute lung injury (including infection, emboli, infarction, chemoradiation, etc.) within the past month can account for such cytologic changes

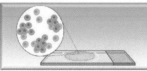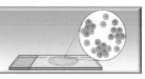

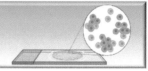

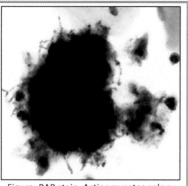

Figure: PAP stain. Actinomycetes colony visualized as a clump of filamentous organisms giving a 'cotton ball' appearance; background neutrophils can be seen.

BACTERIAL AND MYCOBACTERIAL INFECTIONS
BACTERIAL PNEUMONIA
CYTOMORPHOLOGY
- Most commonly is characterized by variable amounts of neutrophilic infiltrates
- Common organisms include Streptococcus pneumoniae (pneumococcus), other streptococci, Staphylococcus aureus, Haemophilus influenza, Klebsiella pneumonia, Pseudomonas sp., Legionella sp., Actinomyces sp., Nocardia sp., and anaerobic bacteria
- The radiating filaments of Actinomyces colonies appear as blue cotton balls on cytology
  - Actinomycetes pneumonia shows bacterial colonies associated with neutrophilic inflammation
  - Actinomyces contaminant from the oral/tonsillar region shows no/rare neutrophils and can show increased number of squamous cells
- Nocardial organisms are thin, filamentous organisms that show a beaded appearance with right-angle branching (Chinese letter pattern) in a background of neutrophils; these organisms are gram-positive, weakly acid-fast, and can be highlighted with silver stains

OTHER HIGH YIELD POINTS
- Pneumonia can display a variety of clinical presentations including broncho-centric consolidation or lobar/lobular pulmonary distribution, and can even mimic malignancy by appearing as well-defined mass lesions in the lung
- Actinomycetes pneumonia is seen in the setting of aspiration of oral contents, extension from a subdiaphragmatic abscess, and in patients with poor dental hygiene; occasionally, yellow sulfur granules can be identified grossly
- Nocardial pneumonia usually occurs in the setting of immunosuppression (e.g., post-transplantation, chemotherapy, steroids administration)

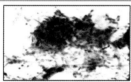

Figure: PAP stain. Non-necrotizing granulomatous inflammation

TUBERCULAR PNEUMONIA
CYTOMORPHOLOGY
- Can show granulomatous inflammation seen as tight aggregates of epithelioid histiocytes, lymphocytes, and Langhans giant cells
- Histiocytes show syncytial arrangement with indistinct cell borders, with curved or elongated nuclei
- Variable amount of necrosis and inflammation may be present

OTHER HIGH YIELD POINTS
- Mycobacterial organisms can be identified using Ziehl-Neelsen and auramine-rhodamine stains
- Matrix-assisted laser desorption ionization-time of flight (MALDI-TOF) and other polymerase chain reaction-based assays can be used for confirmation and to assist in differentiating tuberculous from non-tuberculous bacterial infections

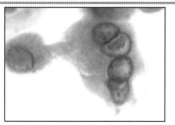

Figure: PAP stain. Cytopathic changes of Herpes, i.e., multinucleation, nuclear molding, and chromatin margination. Courtesy Melissa Hogan, MD

VIRAL INFECTIONS
HERPES SIMPLEX VIRUS (HSV)
CYTOMORPHOLOGY
- Characteristic features of cells infected by HSV are multinucleation, nuclear molding, and margination of chromatin
- Cells show large, eosinophilic intranuclear inclusions (Cowdry type A)

OTHER HIGH YIELD POINTS
- Clinically, can cause necrotizing and ulcerative lesions manifesting as pharyngitis, laryngotracheitis, and pneumonia
- After acute infection, can spread via sensory neurons to establish a latent phase; the virus can then reactivate and affect the mucous membranes or skin, where it undergoes replication

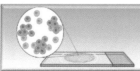
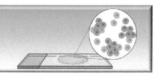

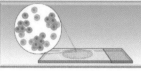

	• Greatest risk of HSV infections is seen in the following groups:
	  ➤ Patients with defective mucosal defense (e.g., burns, trauma)
	  ➤ Newborns
	  ➤ Severely immunocompromised patients

 Figure: PAP stain. Cytopathic changes of CMV from a BAL specimen. Courtesy Syed Ali, MD (Twitter: @sza_jhcyto)	**CYTOMEGALOVIRUS (CMV)** CYTOMORPHOLOGY • Infected cells show nuclear and cytoplasmic enlargement and large, basophilic nuclear inclusions with a halo (inclusions can be highlighted with PAS and GMS) • Smaller basophilic inclusions can also be identified within the cytoplasm of affected cells • These features can be seen in pneumocytes, bronchial lining cells, vascular endothelial cells, or fibroblasts OTHER HIGH YIELD POINTS • Is an important diagnostic consideration in AIDS patients (when CD4+ count <50/cubic mm) and in hematopoietic stem cell transplant recipients • While immunocompetent patients present with a mononucleosis-like illness, immunosuppressed patients with CMV infection present with fever, cough, shortness of breath, night sweats, muscle, and joint pain • Pulmonary imaging shows 2 - 4 cm miliary nodules in the lung periphery combined with diffuse interstitial infiltrates • Histologically, CMV infection is associated with hemorrhagic necrosis and mononuclear infiltrates with pneumocyte hyperplasia
	MEASLES VIRUS CYTOMORPHOLOGY • Infected cells are very large, multinucleated epithelial cells that can display nuclear as well as cytoplasmic inclusions • Nuclear inclusions are large, solitary Cowdry type A inclusions OTHER HIGH YIELD POINTS • Similar cytomorphologic findings can be seen in cases infected by respiratory syncytial virus

	ADENOVIRUS
	CYTOMORPHOLOGY
	• Is characterized by two types of nuclear inclusions in epithelial cells:
	  ➤ A large, brick-like, homogenous basophilic inclusion filling whole nucleus (smudge cell)
	  ➤ Small eosinophilic nuclear inclusions resembling Cowdry A inclusions
	• Prominent ciliocytophthoria can be present (detachment of the apical portion of ciliated columnar cells, thus resulting in terminal bar and cilia devoid of nucleus)
	HISTOLOGIC FEATURES
	• Two patterns can be seen:
	  ➤ Diffuse alveolar damage like pattern with mononuclear inflammation and intra-alveolar exudative fluid accumulation and hyaline membranes
	  ➤ Necrotic pattern showing necrosis of airways, alveoli with neutrophilic and histiocytic infiltrates; interstitial fibrosis and obliterative bronchiolitis can subsequently occur
	OTHER HIGH YIELD POINTS
	• Children and immunocompromised cases (e.g., post solid organ/stem cell transplant) are at risk for Adenovirus pneumonia and severe symptoms
	• Radiology shows bilateral, patchy, ground-glass opacities

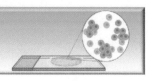

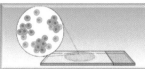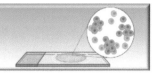
FUNGAL INFECTIONS

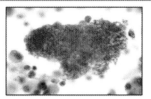

Figure: PAP stain. Frothy cast seen in a BAL specimen positive for *Pneumocystis Jirovecii*. Courtesy Syed Ali, MD (Twitter: sza_jhcyto)

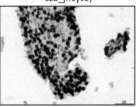

Figure: GMS stain. Pneumocystis Jirovecii - highlighted cup-shaped cysts with a central dark zone. Courtesy Samer Khader (Twitter: @SamKhader)

PNEUMOCYSTIS JIROVECII
- Current morphological evidence favors classification of this organism as a fungus

CYTOMORPHOLOGY
- Organisms may not be directly visible with pap stains, cytology can show green, foamy alveolar casts which are masses of organisms within proteinaceous material and cell debris
- Cysts are cup-shaped or boat-shaped, 5-7 microns in diameter, and often display a central dark zone
- Romanowsky stains show the cysts as negative images but highlights the intracystic bodies or trophozoites
- In some cases, the organisms are present only within the cytoplasm of macrophage – in such cases, they can be distinguished from Histoplasma by their lack of budding
- Gomori Methenamine Silver stain (GMS) highlights cysts with ovoid morphology and prominent central dot

OTHER HIGH YIELD POINTS
- Commonly seen in immunocompromised patients; high risk in AIDS patients especially if CD4 count <200/μL and associated with protein-calorie malnutrition
- Patients present with dry cough, fever, and dyspnea
- Radiology shows bilateral pulmonary infiltrates and ground-glass opacities
- Can be detected in BAL fluid and bronchial washings, but PCR and direct immunofluorescence using induced sputum is recommended for detection

Disease and organism	Morphology and diagnostic clues	Clinical disease	Predominant distribution	Cytology (©CytoAtlas)
Cryptococcus (C. neoformans)	• Narrow budding, thin-walled yeast with mucin capsule and refractile center • 4-15 microns in diameter	• Cough, dyspnea, fever, weight loss • Can cause lung nodules	• Worldwide Figure: Diff-Quik stain.	Figure: GMS Stain.
Histoplasmosis (H. capsulatum)	• Budding intracellular yeasts • 1-15 microns in diameter	• Can cause chronic pneumonia (with predilection for lung apices), peripheral calcified nodular lesions, and mediastinal adenopathy • Necrotizing granulomas may be present	• Mississippi and Ohio river valleys Figure: Diff-Quik stain. ©CytoAtlas	

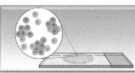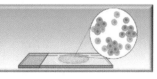

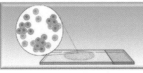

				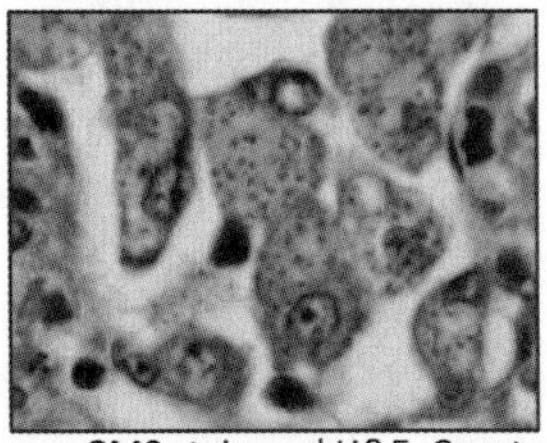 Figure: GMS stain and H&E. Courtesy Sanjay Mukhopadhyay, MD (Twitter: @smlungpathguy)
Blastomycosis (B. dermatitidis)	• Broad-based budding yeast with thick cell wall • 8-20 microns in diameter	• Chronic, progressive infection • Dry hacking cough, dyspnea, chest pain, fever • Also involve skin, bone, CNS, genitourinary	• Mississippi, Missouri and Ohio river valleys, Southern Canada 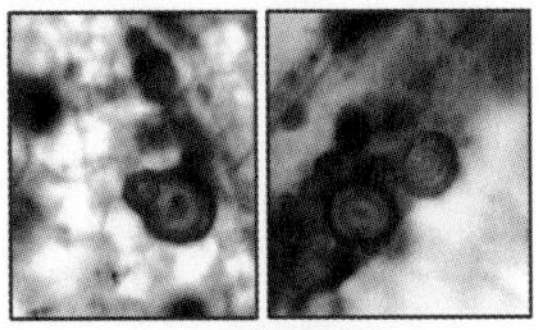 Figure: Diff-Quik stain.	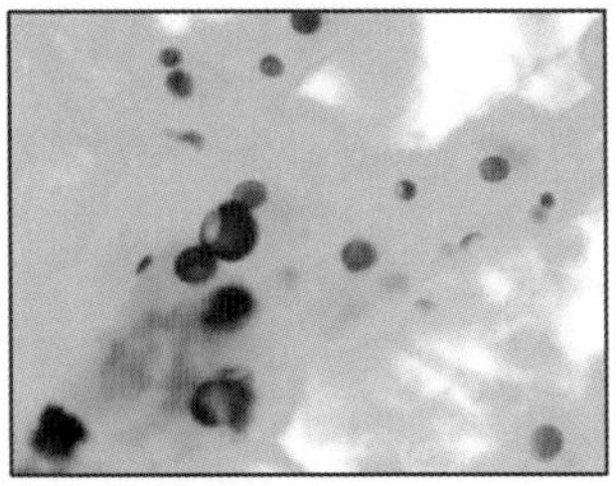 Figure: GMS stain.
Coccidioidomycosis (C. immitis)	• Mature or immature spherules (15-60 microns) with "broken ping-pong ball" appearance • Can also be seen as free endospores (1-2 microns) in a background of granular eosinophilic debris; can occasionally show hyphae	• Spontaneously resolving pulmonary infection, can mimic bacterial pneumonia • Can persist as a mass lesion with cavity formation • Multiorgan infection seen in immunocompromised patients	• Endemic to deserts of west and southwest USA 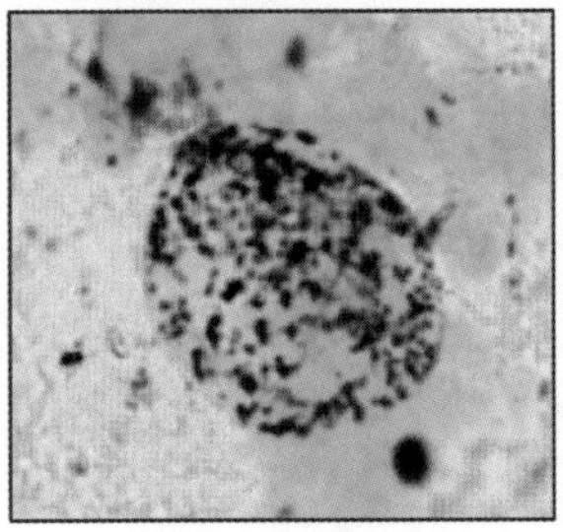 Figure: GMS stain.	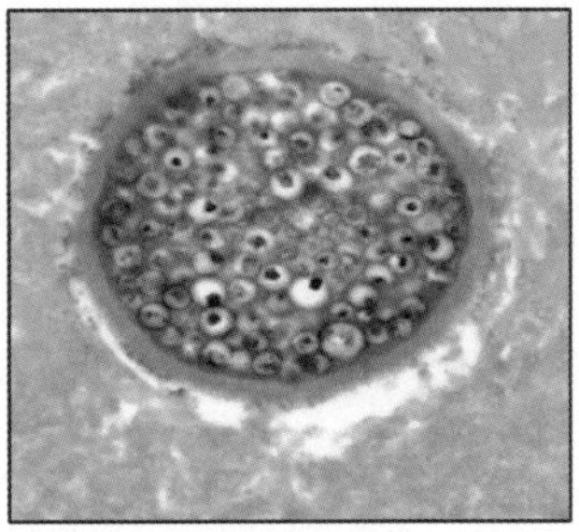 Figure: PAP stain. Courtesy Michael Bayerl, MD (Twitter: @MGBayerl_MD)
Paracoccidioidomycosis (P. braziliensis)	• Yeast with multiple budding (Mariner wheel appearance) • 4-40 microns in diameter • Can induce atypical squamous metaplasia in overlying mucosa	• Mimics tuberculosis clinically	• Central and South America	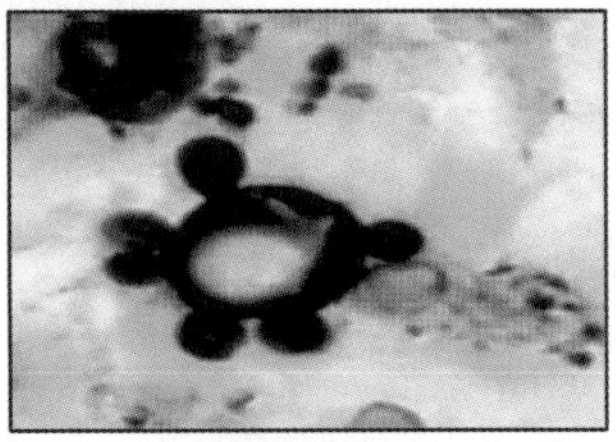 Figure: GMS stain.
Sporotrichosis (S. schenckii)	• Intracellular ovoid yeasts with slight halo • 2-4 microns in diameter • Resembles Cryptococcus, Histoplasma, Candida	• Pulmonary infection usually immunocompromised patients • Chronic infection • Mass lesions with cavitation	• Worldwide	

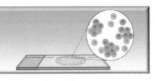

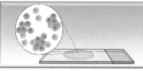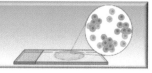
INVASIVE PULMONARY FUNGAL INFECTIONS

- Characterized by invasion of pulmonary tissue and vasculature
- Commonly seen in immunocompromised patients
- These organisms show a worldwide distribution

Organism	Morphology	Clinical features	
Aspergillosis	• Septate hyphae (10-30 micron wide) showing acute angle branching • Characteristic 'Fruiting head' is seen in cavitary lesions; these are associated with polarizable calcium oxalate crystals (crystal may be found in sputum cytology)	• Bronchopulmonary aspergillosis is associated with expectoration of thick mucus plugs, along with Charcot-Leyden crystals and abundant eosinophils • Can invade pulmonary vessels and result in pulmonary hemorrhagic infarction/necrosis • High-risk groups are transplant recipients and patients with prolonged neutropenia or hematologic malignancies	Figure: PAP stain and GMS stain. Courtesy Eduardo Alcaraz, MD, PhD (Twitter: @edusqo) (GMS only)
Zygomycosis (Mucor, Rhizopus, Absidia)	• Variably sized, pauci-septate, ribbon-like hyphae (10-30 micron wide) with right angle branching	• Rapidly progressive, often fatal disease • High risk in neutropenic and diabetic patients • Shows rapid and diffuse growth in culture, hyphal growth can lift the lid off agar culture plates	Figure: Diff-Quik stain.
Candidiasis	• Budding yeast with pseudohyphae (2-10 microns wide)	• Invasive disease associated with Candida sepsis • Can be seen in the setting of aspiration pneumonia, lung abscess	

PARASITIC INFECTIONS

Organism	Morphology	Clinical features	Images
Strongyloidiasis (Strongyloides stercoralis)	• Large roundworms that are characterized by a notched tail and presence of a short buccal cavity	• Primarily affects the GIT • Pulmonary infections present as pneumonitis with hemoptysis after larval migration to lung • More commonly seen in immunosuppressed patients	Figure: H&E stain. Courtesy Joyce Johnson, MD
Dirofilariasis (Dirofilaria immitis)	• These organisms display pointed posterior ends with empty caudal spaces • FNA yields necrotic material with infarcted pulmonary tissue, inflammation, and fragments of the parasite	• Causes lung infarction due to entrapment of microfilaria within pulmonary vessels	

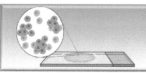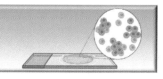

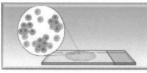

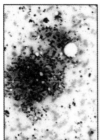

Figure: Diff-Quik and PAP stain. Non-necrotizing granuloma in a background of lymphocytes.
@CytoAtlas

SARCOIDOSIS
CYTOMORPHOLOGY
- Noncaseating, well-formed granulomas comprising of epithelioid histiocytes and lymphocytes, with or without multinucleated giant cells
- The epithelioid histiocytes are arranged in a pseudosyncytial pattern and show round, curved or spindle-shaped nuclei with vacuolated cytoplasm

OTHER HIGH YIELD POINTS
- Diagnosis of exclusion
- Most commonly seen in young adults (20-40 years) with higher incidence amongst females and African Americans
- Angiotensin-converting enzyme levels are increased during active disease phase (not specific)
- Bronchial lavage in cases of sarcoid can show increased CD4+ T-helper cells
- Can be associated with serum polyclonal hypergammaglobulinemia
- Patients with severe end-stage sarcoidosis show susceptibility to superimposed infections such as Aspergillus

AMYLOIDOSIS
CYTOMORPHOLOGY
- Cytology of limited value and cellular yield is usually scant
- FNA shows amorphous, waxy material that appears blue-green on pap stains
- Calcification, ossification, and multinucleated giant cells can be present

OTHER HIGH YIELD POINTS
- Amyloid displays apple-green birefringence under polarized light after staining with Congo Red
- Proteomic analysis based on mass spectrometry can be performed on formalin fixed, paraffin embedded tissue for amyloid subtyping

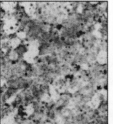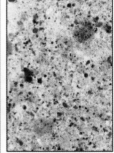

Figure: Diff-Quik and PAP stain. Pulmonary alveolar proteinosis: almost acellular preparations with large eosinophilic blob in Diff-Quik preparation, appear carrot-shaped aggregates in pap preparation.
Courtesy Naomi Hardy, MD (Twitter:@nhardy_path)

PULMONARY ALVEOLAR PROTEINOSIS (PAP)
CYTOMORPHOLOGY
- Specimens are paucicellular or acellular and show large, eosinophilic, blobs of PAS-positive, PAS-D-resistant protein-rich material on pap stain
- Teardrop and carrot-shaped aggregates of eosinophilic material can be seen
- Pulmonary foamy macrophages may be present

OTHER HIGH YIELD POINTS
- Is not a specific disease entity, but rather a reactive pattern to alveolar injury characterized by intra-alveolar accumulation of surfactant-rich material
- Majority of patients are smokers
- Differential diagnoses include other conditions that show the presence of acellular, eosinophilic material such as pulmonary edema, P. jirovecii pneumonia, and alveolar mucinosis

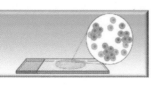

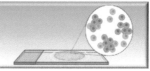

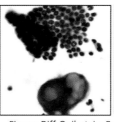

Figure: Diff-Quik stain. Pulmonary Hamartoma: Bronchial epithelial cells with mature cartilage, fibromyxoid matrix. Few macrophages can also be seen.

PULMONARY HAMARTOMA

CYTOMORPHOLOGY
- Specimens show a mixture of epithelial and mesenchymal elements
- Epithelial component shows benign cuboidal, monomorphic glandular cells
- Mesenchymal component is represented by immature fibromyxoid matrix with bland spindle/stellate cells, and chondroid material, which is homogenous, and glassy with or without chondrocytes within lacunae
- Adipocytes can also be seen on cytologic specimens

HISTOLOGIC FEATURES
- Tumor shows mesenchymal elements such as mature, disorganized hyaline cartilage, fat, smooth muscle, and myxomatous tissue as well as entrapped clefts lined by respiratory epithelium (ciliated or non-ciliated)

OTHER HIGH YIELD POINTS
- Neoplasms with recurrent genetic rearrangements involving the HMGA2 and HMGA1, and are the most common benign neoplasm of lung
- Usually found incidentally on radiology as solitary and discrete masses that are <4 cm and commonly seen in the peripheral zones

PAPILLOMA

CYTOMORPHOLOGY
- Cellular specimens with small, dark, pyknotic nuclei showing varying degrees of reactive atypia, with or without mitoses
- Type of epithelial cells seen depends on histology of the papilloma (see histology below)

HISTOLOGIC FEATURES
- Lesion composed of fibrovascular cores lined by layers of epithelial cells. Following types of epithelial cells can be seen:
  - Mature squamous epithelium
  - Mucinous glandular epithelium
  - Ciliated epithelium
  - Mixed epithelium

OTHER HIGH YIELD POINTS
- Associated with cigarette smoking
- These lesions can rarely display malignant transformation to squamous or adenocarcinoma (higher incidence in squamous and mixed type papillomas)
- Due to the presence of reactive epithelial atypia, benign papillomas can falsely be diagnosed as carcinoma

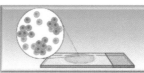
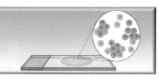

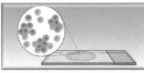

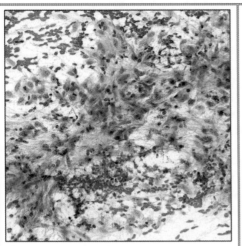

Figure: PAP stain. Inflammatory myofibroblastic tumor of the lung (ALK-positive, Pap): low power view shows bland spindle cells with background inflammation. Courtesy Susan Shyu, MD (Twitter: @susanshyu)

INFLAMMATORY MYOFIBROBLASTIC TUMOR (IMT)

CYTOMORPHOLOGY

- Yield spindle cells admixed with a significant polymorphous inflammatory infiltrate
- The bland-appearing spindle to stellate cells show minimal pleomorphism with rare mitoses
- The inflammatory infiltrate can be marked and can show lymphocytes, plasma cells, histiocytes, and Touton type giant cells
- A minimal amount of necrosis is not incompatible with this diagnosis, but is usually absent

OTHER HIGH YIELD POINTS

- Majority of IMTs show rearrangements of the anaplastic lymphoma kinase (ALK) gene on chromosome 2
- Multiple ALK fusion partners have been identified such as EML4, TPM3, TPM4, CARS, RANBP2, IGFBP5, etc.)
- On FNA, the spindle cell component gives rise to differentials such as organizing pneumonia, and spindle cells tumors such as solitary fibrous tumor and benign fibrous histiocytoma
- In cases wherein the inflammatory component dominates, differentials such as plasmacytoma and lymphoma can be considered

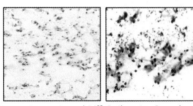

Figure: Pap stain and Diff-Quik stain. Granular Cell Tumor: Monotonous epithelioid cells with granular cytoplasm.

GRANULAR CELL TUMOR

CYTOMORPHOLOGY

- Variably cohesive clusters of monotonous, epithelioid tumor cells
- Tumor cells show characteristic abundant, granular, eosinophilic cytoplasm, and small, round to oval, uniform nuclei

OTHER HIGH YIELD POINTS

- IHC: S-100 positive

LANGERHANS CELL HISTIOCYTOSIS (LCH)

CYTOMORPHOLOGY

- Show a combination of Langerhans cells, pigmented macrophages, and a mixed inflammatory infiltrate
- Lesional cells show histiocytoid morphology characterized by abundant granular, mildly eosinophilic cytoplasm, elongated or convoluted nuclei with prominent nuclear grooves
- The mixed inflammatory infiltrate often shows abundant eosinophils which is an important clue to the diagnosis

OTHER HIGH YIELD POINTS

- Almost exclusively seen in adult smokers
- Radiological examination generally shows multiple nodules with a cystic component, predominantly involving the upper and middle lobes of bilateral lungs
- Nodules and symptoms often resolve upon cessation of smoking
- IHC: S100, CD1a and Langerin positive
- Molecular: Associated with BRAF V600E mutations
- Electron microscopy, Langerhans cells show Birbeck's granules, which are tennis racket-shaped intracytoplasmic structures

Figure: Diff-Quik stain. Langerhans's Cell Histiocytosis – low power image showing Langerhans's cells with an inflammatory background. Insert: PAP stain. Coffee bean grooved nuclei. Courtesy Syed Ali, MD (Twitter: @sza_jhcyto)

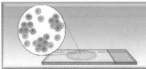
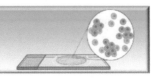

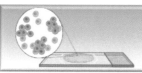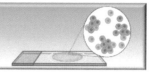
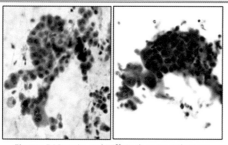

Figure: PAP stain and Diff-Quik stain. Sclerosing pneumocytoma: shows a dual population of monomorphic stromal cells and pneumocyte-like cells. Courtesy Sinchita Roy (Twitter: @Sinchita_Roy)

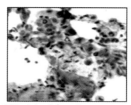

Figure: PAP stain. Sclerosing pneumocytoma. Note visible intranuclear inclusions.

SCLEROSING PNEUMOCYTOMA

CYTOMORPHOLOGY

- Cellular specimen showing two populations of cells:
  - ➢ Monomorphic, ovoid stromal cells (predominant population) that have pale cytoplasm, round nuclei, smooth nuclear borders, finely textured chromatin, and one or more small nucleoli
  - ➢ Cuboidal surface cells (pneumocyte-like cells)
- Both populations of cells are believed to be neoplastic but are mitotically inactive
- Papillary microarchitecture can be seen showing pneumocyte-like cells lining a core of round stromal cells
- Cases can show a degree of pleomorphism, mild nuclear atypia, intranuclear pseudoinclusions, and prominent nucleoli
- Background can show hemorrhage with hemosiderin-laden macrophages

OTHER HIGH YIELD POINTS

- Can be mistaken for lung adenocarcinoma due to the high cellularity yield on FNA, and TTF-1 positivity in the cells
- Factors that favor sclerosing pneumocytoma over adenocarcinoma are cellular monomorphism, lack of mitotic figures, two-cell population and slow growth of the lesion

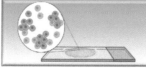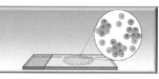

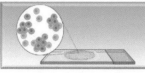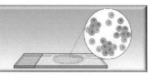
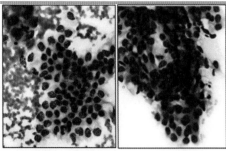

Figure: Diff-Quik stain. Adenocarcinoma: Sheets of tumor cells with wispy, mucin-filled cytoplasm.

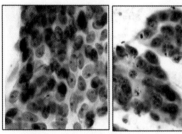

Figure: PAP stain. Adenocarcinoma: On high magnification, cells have large nuclei with fine chromatin and easily identifiable nucleoli.

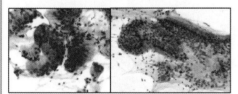

Figure: H&E stain. Mucinous adenocarcinoma showing sheets of low-grade mucinous cells; background mucin can be seen. Courtesy Melissa Hogan, MD

ADENOCARCINOMA
CYTOMORPHOLOGY

- FNA can show heterogeneity that reflects the histologic patterns within the tumor
- Are seen as flat sheets, densely packed solid 3D clusters, true papillary structures, micropapillary balls, acinar formations, or as isolated, discohesive cells
- Display nuclei with smooth to highly irregular nuclear membranes and often prominent, red nucleoli
- Chromatin texture can range from fine and delicate (common) to dense and coarse (seen in less differentiated tumors)
- Malignant cells possess translucent or foamy cytoplasm; cytoplasmic mucin vacuoles can be seen
- Mucinous variants of adenocarcinoma can be missed due to its low-grade cytologic features:
  - ➢ Mitotically inactive malignant cells in a background of mucin
  - ➢ Cells can be scattered or arranged in honeycomb-like sheets
  - ➢ Can resemble papillary thyroid carcinoma due to the presence of optically clear nuclei, inconspicuous nucleoli, grooves, and nuclear pseudoinclusions

OTHER HIGH YIELD POINTS

- IHCS: Most primary lung adenocarcinomas label with CK7, TTF-1, and Napsin A
- Are commonly used to distinguish adenocarcinomas from squamous cell carcinoma - should include TTF-1, p40, Napsin-A, CK7, synaptophysin and INSM-1; cases positive for one or more of these markers: TTF-1, Napsin-A and Ck7 should be classified as non-small cell carcinoma, favor adenocarcinoma; if focal P40 positivity is seen in neoplastic cells, possibility of adenocarcinoma with squamous differentiation or adenosquamous carcinoma should be commented
- Mucinous adenocarcinomas and enteric adenocarcinomas mimic metastatic GI carcinomas due to their immunoprofile (often TTF-1 negative, and CK20, CDX-2 positive)
- Distinction between in-situ and invasive adenocarcinoma cannot be made on cytology alone
- Differential diagnoses for adenocarcinoma on cytology are listed in table1

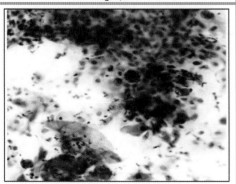

Figure: Pap stain. Squamous carcinoma: Keratinized neoplastic squamous cells, which can be more evident in pap preparation.

SQUAMOUS CELL CARCINOMA (SCC)
CYTOMORPHOLOGY

- Cytomorphologic features vary depending on the degree of squamous differentiation within the tumor (see table 2)
- Squamous cells are characterized by smooth and dense 'squamoid' cytoplasm that is filled with keratin; it stains green or orange with Pap stains and blue with Romanowski stains
- Differential diagnoses for pulmonary squamous carcinomas are listed in table 3

OTHER HIGH YIELD POINTS

- Strongly associated with male gender and smoking history
- Strongly positive for p40, p63, and high molecular weight cytokeratins
- Squamous cell carcinomas are associated with tumor cavitation

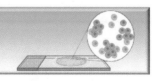

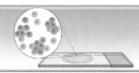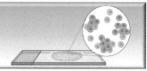
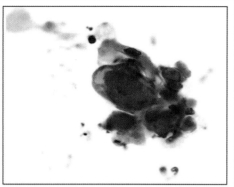
Figure: PAP stain. Squamous cell carcinoma: Cells with dense cytoplasm characteristic of squamous differentiation.

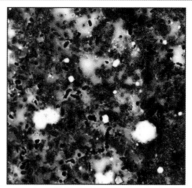
Figure: Diff-Quik stain. Squamous cell carcinoma spindle cell variant: Spindle cells with background debris.

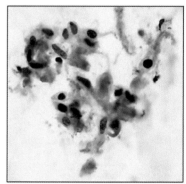
Figure: PAP stain. Squamous carcinoma spindle cell variant with cytoplasmic tails.

Figure: Diff-Quik stain. Squamous cell carcinoma with background inflammation.

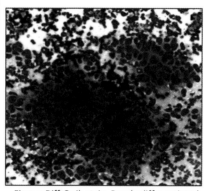
Figure: Diff-Quik stain. Poorly differentiated squamous cell carcinoma cells in a densely packed cluster.

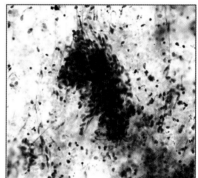
Figure: Diff-Quik stain. Squamous cell carcinoma (basaloid variant) with basaloid cells and necrosis.

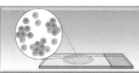
Figure: Diff-Quik. Sarcomatoid carcinoma on low and high magnification displaying large atypical, spindled cells.

SARCOMATOID CARCINOMA

- Generic term for a heterogeneous group of poorly differentiated non-small cell carcinomas that includes spindle cell carcinoma, giant cell carcinoma, pleomorphic carcinoma, carcinosarcoma, and pulmonary blastoma

CYTOMORPHOLOGY

Figure: PAP stain.

OTHER HIGH YIELD POINTS

- Sarcomatoid carcinomas have a worse prognosis than well-differentiated non-small cell carcinomas

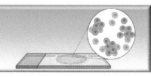

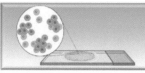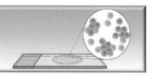
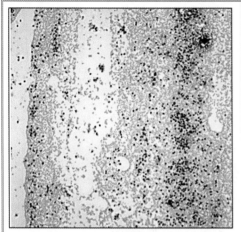

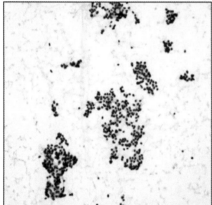

Figure: Diff-Quik and PAP stain. Low magnification view of low-grade NET yielding cellular smears with dispersed cells (above) and cells in loose clusters (below).

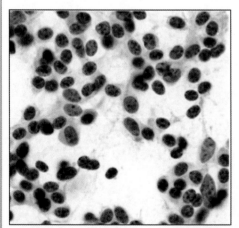

Figure: PAP stain. Low grade NET on high powers shows cells with characteristic speckled 'salt and pepper' chromatin.

NEUROENDOCRINE TUMORS
- Group of neoplasms that display neuroendocrine morphology in addition to neuroendocrine differentiation and immunohistochemical profile
- WHO 2021, classifies neuroendocrine neoplasms into 4 categories based on tumor morphology, presence of necrosis, and mitotic activity within tumor cells:
  - ➢ Typical carcinoid tumor
  - ➢ Atypical carcinoid tumor
  - ➢ Small cell carcinoma
  - ➢ Large cell neuroendocrine carcinoma

TYPICAL AND ATYPICAL CARCINOID- CARCINOID NOT OTHERWISE SPECIFIED (NOS)
CYTOMORPHOLOGY
- Tumor cells are arranged in loose clusters or as isolated cells; rosettes can be appreciated in cytologic material
- Uniform population of round, plasmacytoid, spindle, or elongated cells with moderate to abundant granular cytoplasm
- Nuclei are round to oval with smooth membranes and characteristic speckled (salt and pepper) chromatin, and inconspicuous nucleoli
- Mitoses are rare or absent
- Necrosis is absent
- Due to the vascular nature of the tumor, cytology preparations can show branching capillaries
- Atypical carcinoid may show greater mitotic rate and focal necrosis
- Accurate classification requires resected specimen
OTHER HIGH YIELD POINTS
- Around 15% of patients have regional lymph node involvement at presentation
- Tumor cells are diffusely and strongly positive for neuroendocrine markers chromogranin, synaptophysin, CD56 (not to be used alone) and INSM-1; cytokeratins usually positive
- Around 50% of pulmonary carcinoids are TTF-1 positive
- WHO 2021, recommends using the term carcinoid NOS for typical and atypical carcinoid tumor on cytology and small biopsy specimens and specify the mitotic rate, and Ki-67 proliferation index in comments
- However, elevated mitotic count and presence of punctate necrosis warrants an atypical carcinoid diagnosis even in small specimen

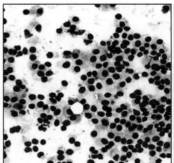
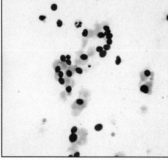

Figure: Diff-Quik stain. Low grade NET – cells are uniform with plasmacytoid morphology and regular round nuclei.

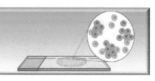

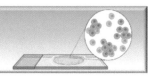
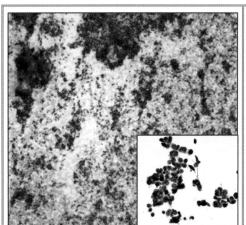

Figure: Diff-Quik and PAP stain. Small cell carcinoma: highly cellular smear with small blue cells.

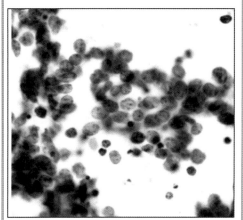

Figure: PAP stain. Small cell carcinoma: small blue cells with high N/C ratio showing single cell apoptosis.

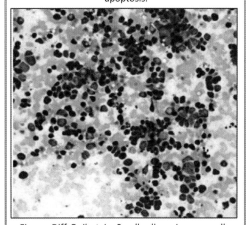

Figure: Diff-Quik stain. Small cell carcinoma – cells have high N/C ratio and prominent cellular molding.

SMALL CELL CARCINOMA

CYTOMORPHOLOGY

- Loose aggregates or dispersed, isolated tumor cells
- Cells are small to intermediate in size and have scant cytoplasm
- Nuclei are round to oval or stretched out and elongated; frequent nuclear molding is characteristic of this tumor
- Chromatin is very finely granular, and nucleoli are absent or inconspicuous
- Crush artifact and stripped "naked" nuclei can be seen due to the delicate nature of the cells
- Cells show high mitotic rate (often >10/10 hpf), abundant apoptotic cells, and single cell necrosis
- Occasionally, cells can show solitary, blue, homogeneous spheres that indent the nucleus (paranuclear blue bodies) - these are seen with Romanowsky stains but not with alcohol or formalin fixed sections
- Small cell carcinomas have several differential diagnoses (table 6)

OTHER HIGH YIELD POINTS

- Majority of tumors are centrally located
- Almost exclusively associated with cigarette smoking/ tobacco exposure
- Tumors often shows advanced disease at presentation and have associated paraneoplastic syndromes with increased levels of ACTH and ADH)
- Tumor cells are usually positive for at least one neuroendocrine marker (Synaptophysin, Chromogranin, CD56 and INSM-1)
- POU2F3 : new marker for neuroendocrine low/negative small cell lung carcinoma; Rb-1 frequently lost in this subset
- TTF-1 positive in cases with high neuroendocrine marker expression

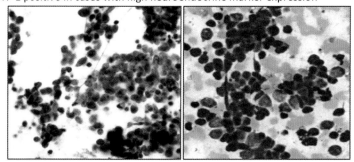

Figure: PAP and Diff-Quik stain. High magnification view of small cell carcinoma – tumor cells are small to intermediate in size with scant cytoplasm; frequent nuclear molding is easily identified; cells show fine granular chromatin with inconspicuous nucleoli.

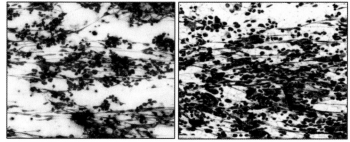

Figure: Small cell carcinoma smear on Diff-Quik (left) and PAP stain (right) – notice prominent crush artifact due to the fragile nature of the cells.

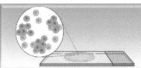
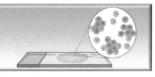

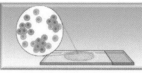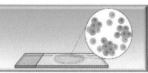
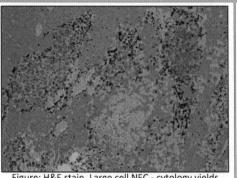

Figure: H&E stain. Large cell NEC - cytology yields large tumor cells with pleomorphic nuclei and a prominent nucleolus with associated necrosis.
Courtesy Terrance Lynn, MD

LARGE CELL NEUROENDOCRINE CARCINOMA

CYTOMORPHOLOGY

- Hypercellular aspirate with tumor cells in rosettes or loose 3D clusters
- Tumor cells are large, with moderate cytoplasm, pleomorphic nuclei, coarsely granular or vesicular chromatin, and a prominent nucleolus
- High mitotic rates (usually >10/ 10hpf) are seen
- Some amount of nuclear molding and crush artifact is permitted
- Necrosis can be marked

OTHER HIGH YIELD POINTS

- Can be seen in combination with other non-small cell carcinomas
- Paraneoplastic syndromes less commonly seen than in small cell carcinoma
- At least one of the three neuroendocrine markers (synaptophysin, chromogranin or CD56) should be positive with no minimal percentage of tumor cells subset positive for one of the markers

RARE TUMORS AND METASTATIC TUMORS

LYMPHOEPITHELIAL LIKE CARCINOMA

CYTOMORPHOLOGY

- Syncytial sheets and clusters of large, atypical cells that display hyperchromatic nuclei with irregular membranes, vesicular chromatin, and prominent nucleoli
- Cells show scant granular cytoplasm; frequent mitosis seen
- The tumor is characteristically associated with infiltrating lymphocytes

OTHER HIGH YIELD POINTS

- Tumor cells are often positive for EBER and squamous markers (p40/p63)

SALIVARY GLAND-TYPE TUMORS OF THE LUNG

- Show similar cytomorphology as their primary salivary gland counterparts
- Most common is mucoepidermoid carcinoma, followed by adenoid cystic carcinoma

CYTOMORPHOLOGY

- Adenoid cystic carcinoma of the lung shows small, bland uniform epithelial cells that surround cylinders of myxochondroid matrix
- FNA of mucoepidermoid carcinoma can be low or high grade and shows varying proportions of squamous, glandular, and intermediate cells

OTHER HIGH YIELD POINTS

- Adenoid cystic carcinomas are usually positive for S100; luminal cells are positive for CD117 while basal cells express p63; tumors can show MYB gene rearrangements
- Mucoepidermoid carcinomas are associated with MAML2 gene rearrangements

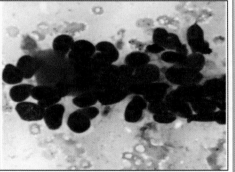

Figure: Diff-Quik stain. Small, bland tumor cells surround cylinders of myxochondroid matrix

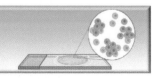

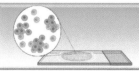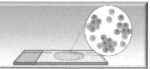
	PECOMA (CLEAR CELL "SUGAR TUMOR") CYTOMORPHOLOGY • FNA yields clusters of bland polygonal and spindle cells with central oval or elongated nuclei • Tumor cells possess clear to slightly eosinophilic glycogen-filled cytoplasm, thus giving rise to differentials such as adenocarcinoma, granular cell tumor, renal cell carcinomas, and adrenocortical carcinomas • Transgressing capillaries can be present OTHER HIGH YIELD POINTS • IHC - PEComas are positive for HMB45 and Melan-A, but negative for cytokeratins

	METASTATIC TUMORS TO THE LUNG
	• Lung is a common site of metastases; features that favor metastasis over common primary lung carcinomas are:
	  ➢ Presence of multiple lesions that are sharply demarcated from surrounding lung parenchyma
	  ➢ Bilateral lesions
	  ➢ Rapidly growth of tumor
	CYTOMORPHOLOGY
	• Refer table 7
	OTHER HIGH YIELD POINTS
	• Most primary lung adenocarcinomas are positive for CK7 and TTF-1 and negative for CK20

MOLECULAR TECHNIQUES IN RESPIRATORY CYTOLOGY • Identification of genetic aberrations within lung carcinomas is necessary for assessment of gene-specific targeted therapy and for accurate molecular classification of tumors (refer to table 8)	

Table 1 - ADENOCARCINOMA VS DIFFERENTIALS

DIFFERENTIAL	CYTOLOGICAL CHALLENGE	DISTINGUISHING FACTORS FROM ADENOCARCINOMA
Benign, atypical, and hyperplastic bronchial cells	• Reactive atypia within bronchial cells can be misdiagnosed as well-differentiated adenocarcinoma	• Presence of cilia favors benign changes • continuous spectrum of changes from obviously benign to atypical, i.e., lack of distinct two cell population
Florid type II pneumocyte hyperplasia	• Hyperplastic type II pneumocytes can yield cellular specimens with worrisome, atypical features and TTF-1 positivity	• Consider pneumocyte hyperplasia if the clinical history and imaging findings are suggestive of lung injury/respiratory distress • Lung injury usually resolves by one month; thus, subsequent specimens show no atypia
Benign mesothelial cells	• Can resemble well-differentiated adenocarcinoma and mucinous adenocarcinoma	• Mesothelial cells are seen as sheets of uniform cells with round nuclei showing characteristic slit-like windows separating the cells • Mesothelial cells are positive for WT1, Calretinin, D2-40, and CK5/6, and are negative for BerEp4 and MOC-31

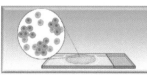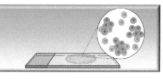

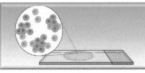

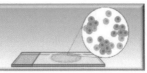

Pulmonary hamartoma	• Prominent glandular component of hamartomas can mimic well/moderately differentiated adenocarcinoma	• Presence of chondromyxoid matrix points towards a diagnosis of hamartoma
Epithelioid vascular tumors of lung, e.g. epithelioid hemangioendothelioma (EHE), epithelioid angiosarcoma (EA)	• These vascular tumors can present as solitary or multiple lung masses +/- pleural involvement, thus mimicking pulmonary adenocarcinoma • Like adenocarcinoma, EHE and EA can display intracytoplasmic vacuoles and intranuclear inclusions	• A diagnosis of a vascular tumor can be established by positivity with vascular markers (e.g., CD31, CD34, ERG) • Note that vascular tumors can also label with keratins (similar to carcinomas)
Squamous Cell Carcinoma	• Both are common primary lung non-small cell carcinomas with morphological overlap that can cause considerable diagnostic difficulty	• Fine texture of chromatin, thin delicate cytoplasm, intracytoplasmic vacuolation, and abundant intracellular mucin favors adenocarcinoma (note that squamous carcinoma can also show cytoplasmic mucin) • Tumor cavitation favors squamous cell carcinoma

TABLE 2 - CYTOLOGY OF SQUAMOUS CELL CARCINOMA

FEATURES	WELL-DIFFERENTIATED SQUAMOUS CELL CARCINOMA	MODERATELY/POORLY DIFFERENTIATED SQUAMOUS CELL CARCINOMA
Cytology	• Cell clusters are discohesive and show polygonal, round, spindle, and tadpole-shaped cells • Frequent anucleate cells are seen	• Larger, denser, and more cohesive clusters of spindle cells that exhibit 'school of fish' appearance, i.e., Tumor cell nuclei streaming in parallel along their long axes
Cytoplasm	• Abundant, smooth, dense 'squamoid' cytoplasm filled with keratin • Stains green, yellow, or densely orange with pap stains and blue with Romanowski stains	• Can range from smooth and dense (similar to well-differentiated squamous cell carcinoma) to granular • Keratinization is much less prominent and can be difficult to appreciate
Nuclei	• Small, hyperchromatic, smudgy pyknotic-looking nuclei	• Larger nuclei with coarsely textured chromatin
Nucleoli	• Inconspicuous	• Prominent

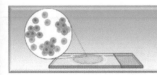

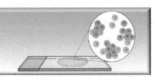

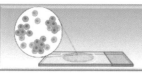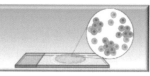
TABLE 3 - SQUAMOUS CELL CARCINOMA (SCC) VS DIFFERENTIALS

DIFFERENTIAL	DISTINGUISHING FEATURES FROM SQUAMOUS CELL CARCINOMA
Squamous metaplasia	• Metaplastic cells have small, round nuclei without hyperchromasia
Degenerative changes	• Even though degenerative cells have dark pyknotic nuclei, they are generally of smaller size and show much less anisonucleosis than SCC
Reactive squamous atypia	• Consider reactive squamous atypia in the differential when sampling is adjacent to a site of lung injury (e.g., stoma, cavitary fungal infection) or in the setting of sepsis, chemo/radiation therapy, alveolar damage, or any lung injury
Adenocarcinoma	• Refer table 1
NUT midline carcinoma	• Cytology of NUT midline carcinoma shows dispersed primitive-appearing, monomorphic, non-cohesive cells with vesicular chromatin, scant cytoplasm +/- prominent nucleoli • Tumor cells can resemble SCC, lymphoma, small cell carcinoma, and germ cell tumors • Diffuse nuclear expression of NUT protein IHC confirms the diagnosis
SMARCA4-deficient thoracic sarcoma	• SMARCA4-deficient thoracic sarcoma morphologically resembles poorly differentiated squamous carcinoma but shows characteristic loss of SMARCA4 IHC, correlating with underlying SMARCA4 mutation

TABLE 4 - SARCOMATOID CARCINOMAS

TYPE	HISTOLOGY	CYTOLOGY
Pleomorphic carcinoma	• Poorly differentiated adenocarcinoma, squamous carcinoma, or large cell carcinoma in which a spindle cell or giant cell component comprises at least 10% of the tumor	• Giant, pleomorphic spindle or giant cells seen along with adenocarcinoma, squamous carcinoma, or large cell carcinoma
Spindle cell carcinoma	• Non-small cell carcinoma that consists only of spindle-shaped malignant cells • No differentiated component is seen	• Large, malignant spindle cells with nuclear hyperchromatic
Giant cell carcinoma	• Tumor composed almost entirely of large, often multinucleated giant cells with syncytial-like appearance (can show beta hCG positivity) • No differentiated component is seen • Inflammatory stroma with emperipolesis	• Loose clusters or scattered, isolated tumor cells that are enormously large, pleomorphic, and often multinucleated • Cells show abundant, thick, well demarcated cytoplasm with round, markedly atypical nuclei and prominent nucleoli • Prominent neutrophils in the background, with possible neutrophil engulfment
Pulmonary blastoma	• Biphasic tumor composed of primitive glandular and stromal elements that resembles fetal lung (hence the name)	• Biphasic histological elements are represented in cytologic samples

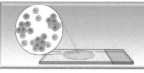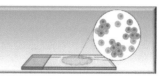

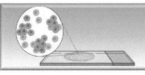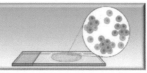
	• Epithelial component (keratin positive) shows tubules of cuboidal to columnar cells with frequent mitoses and sub- or supra-nuclear glycogen-containing vacuoles, thus giving it a piano-key appearance reminiscent of secretory endometrium • Squamoid morules may be seen • Spindle cell stromal component (muscle specific actin positive) can show myxoid, chondroid, osteoid, or rhabdomyoblastic differentiation	• Both elements show nuclear expression of beta-catenin
Carcinosarcoma	• Biphasic tumor composed of malignant epithelial and spindle cell components • Epithelial component composed of malignant adenocarcinoma or squamous carcinoma • Spindle cell component can show malignant cartilage, bone, or skeletal muscle	• Biphasic histological elements are represented in cytologic samples, but sometimes only epithelial elements can be present

TABLE 5 - TYPICAL VS ATYPICAL CARCINOID

Character	Typical carcinoid	Atypical carcinoid
Cell size	• Cell size tends to be smaller	• Medium sized cells
Nucleoli	• Small, inconspicuous nucleoli	• Nucleoli can be prominent
Mitosis	• Mitoses rare (<2/10hpf)	• Mitoses between (2-10/10 hpf)
Pleomorphism	• No/mild nuclear pleomorphism	• Moderate pleomorphism
Necrosis	• Necrosis absent by definition	• Necrosis can be present

TABLE 6 - SMALL CELL CARCINOMA VS DIFFERENTIALS

Differential	Similarities	Differences
Reserve cell hyperplasia	• Small cells that show molding	• RCH cells are smaller and tend to cluster • RCH does not show necrosis or mitoses • RCH cells have smudged, featureless chromatin whereas small cell carcinoma cells have finely textured chromatin
Lymphoid cells	• Discohesive cells with scant cytoplasm	• Lymphoid cells are smaller (one half to one third the size of small cell carcinoma cells) • Lymphoid cells are evenly spaced rather than molded

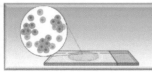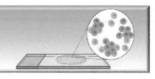

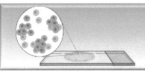
Typical carcinoid tumor	• Some typical carcinoid tumors can bear slight resemblance to small cell carcinoma (e.g., spindle cell variant)	• Typical carcinoids lack molding, necrosis, high mitotic activity • Ki-67 rate tends to be >50% in small cell carcinoma and <20% in typical carcinoids
Atypical carcinoid tumor	• Medium sized cells with scant cytoplasm • Both tumors can display nuclear molding, necrosis and nuclear pleomorphism	• Small cell carcinoma cells tend to be dispersed, with finely granular chromatin unlike atypical carcinoids which form clusters/rosettes and have coarsely granular chromatin • Small cell carcinomas have a greater degree of necrosis, nuclear crush artifact, and nuclear molding • Mitotic rate much higher in small cell carcinoma
NUT midline carcinoma	• Poorly differentiated appearance of tumor • Pulmonary NUT midline carcinomas can express TTF-1	• IHC: Nut carcinomas label with NUT protein IHC and often with p63/p40
Small round cell tumors	• Similar cytologic appearance	• Clinical history, age, IHC marker expression

TABLE 7 - METASTATIC TUMORS TO THE LUNG

PRIMARY SITE	CYTOLOGY	IHC
Colorectal carcinoma	• Tall, columnar glandular cells with picket fence appearance • Dirty necrosis, Tumor cavitation	• CK20, CDX2
Renal cell carcinoma (clear cell)	• Large, polygonal cells with abundant clear or vacuolated cytoplasm • Enmeshed capillaries can be present	• PAX8, CA IX, CD10
Breast carcinoma	• Tends to replicate morphology of the primary tumor • Single file appearance, lumen formation, and intracytoplasmic mucin might be present	• CK7, GATA3, GCDFP-15, hormone receptors
Melanoma	• Highly variable in appearance; classical cytology is of discohesive epithelioid or spindle cells with large, atypical nuclei and characteristically prominent red nucleoli • intracytoplasmic melanin pigment and melanophages might be present	• SOX 10, S100, Melan A, HMB45, Tyrosinase, MiTF, PRAME
Papillary thyroid carcinoma	• Characteristic cytology shows elongated overlapping tumor cells with nuclear grooves, clearing, and intranuclear pseudoinclusions; papillary architecture can occasionally be represented on cytology • Psammoma bodies can be seen	• PAX8, TTF-1, Thyroglobulin

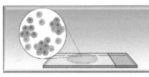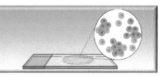

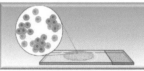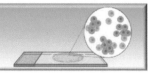
TABLE 8 - MOLECULAR TESTING OF LUNG TUMORS

GENE	SALIENT POINTS
EGFR	• TKI* drugs against EGFR mutant lung carcinomas show good clinical response with favorable toxicity profile • Resistance to TKI therapy can occur with acquisition of T790M amino acid substitution • Osimertinib is a third-generation TKI that can be used in cases with T790M mutation
MET	• C-MET amplification is another possible mechanism of resistance to EGFR inhibitors • Responds to Crizotinib therapy
HER2	• Amplified in a fifth of non-small cell lung carcinomas • Associated with poor prognosis • Non-selective TKI, single anti-Her-2 antibody (Trastuzumab) not found superior to chemotherapy alone; respond well to novel selective HER2 TKI such as Poziotinib and Pyrotinib
ALK	• EMK4-ALK translocation is the most common ALK translocation • Seen in non-smokers, younger male patients, and is associated with solid or signet ring cell histology • ALK translocations are mutually exclusive of EGFR and KRAS mutations • ALK mutated tumors are susceptible to TKIs such as Crizotinib
ROS1	• Clinical and histologic features similar to ALK-translocated tumors and show similar TKI susceptibility
PIK3A pathway	• Not mutually exclusive to EGFR and KRAS mutations • PTEN mutations (negative regulator for PIC3K) more common in squamous carcinomas than adenocarcinomas
KRAS	• KRAS mutations are mutually exclusive of EGFR, ALK, and ROS1 mutations • Associated with resistance to TKI therapeutics and worse prognosis • KRAS mutations are associated with mucinous adenocarcinomas and have a worse prognosis
PD-L1	• PD-1/PD-L1 pathway alterations can be seen in both squamous as well as adenocarcinomas • Inhibitors of the PD-1/PD-L1 pathway have been granted FDA approval for treatment of lung carcinomas and have been shown to improve outcomes

*TKI - tyrosine kinase inhibitor

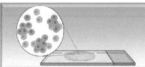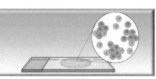

Chapter 4: Mediastinal Cytology

Varun Bhat, MD

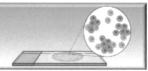
Thymoma

Thymic carcinoma

Lymphoma

Germ cell tumor

Molecular Techniques in
Mediastinal Cytology

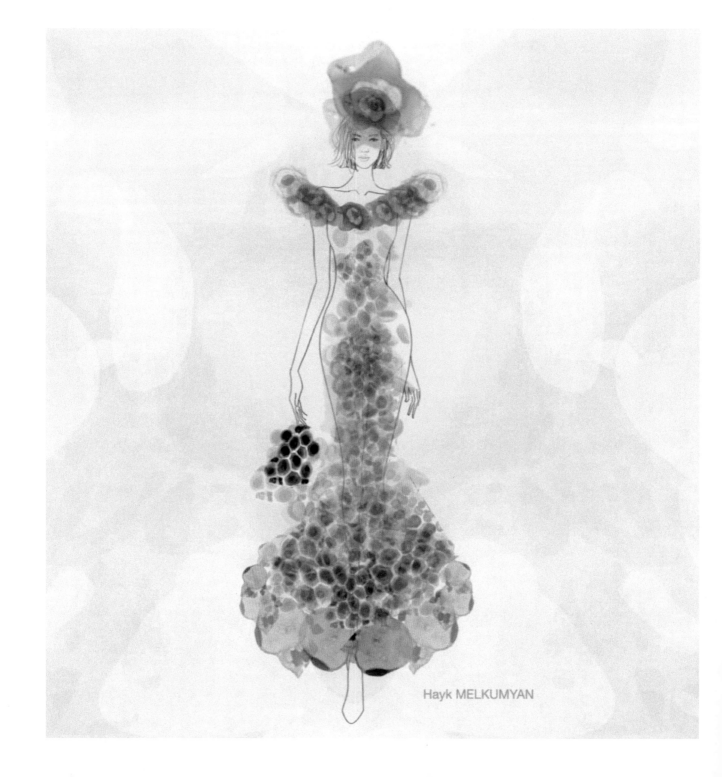

Hayk MELKUMYAN

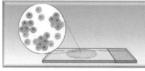
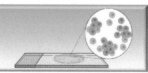

THYMOMA

CYTOMORPHOLOGY
- FNA shows variable proportions of thymic epithelial cells and small lymphocytes
- Type A thymomas:
    - Bland spindled to ovoid epithelial cells with few or no lymphoid cells
    - Mimic spindle cell lesions
- Type B thymoma:
    - Epithelial cells are round or polygonal
    - Type B1: very rich in lymphocytes, can resemble normal thymus
    - B2: features in between types B1 and B3
    - B3: rich in epithelial cells which can show atypia, low proportion of lymphoid cells
- Type AB thymoma: features of both type A and type B thymomas

OTHER HIGH YIELD POINTS
- Most common neoplasm of the anterior mediastinum
- Thymomas can be associated with paraneoplastic syndromes such as myasthenia gravis, hypogammaglobulinemia and pure red blood cell aplasia
- IHC:
    - Thymic epithelial cells are positive for p63, CK5 and PAX8
    - Lymphocytes are positive for TdT, CD3 and CD99

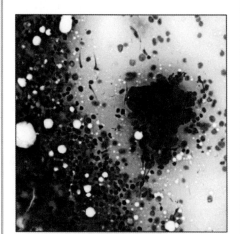

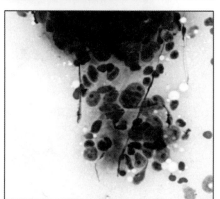

Figure: Diff-Quik stain. Thymoma: Smears featuring clusters of epithelial cells and small lymphocytes. ©CytoAtlas

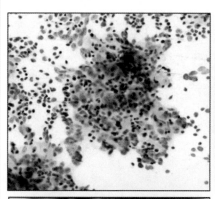

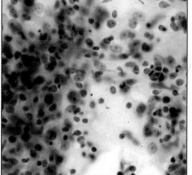

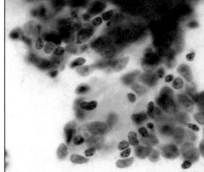

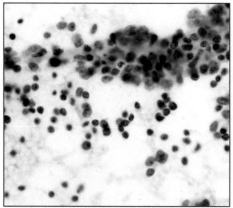

Figure: PAP stain. Thymoma: Clusters of epithelial cells and scattered lymphocytes. ©CytoAtlas

Figure: PAP stain. Thymoma B2: low and high magnification showing clusters of round to oval epithelial cells with large nuclei and prominent nucleoli and scattered background lymphocytes. ©CytoAtlas

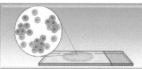
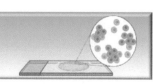

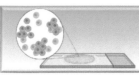

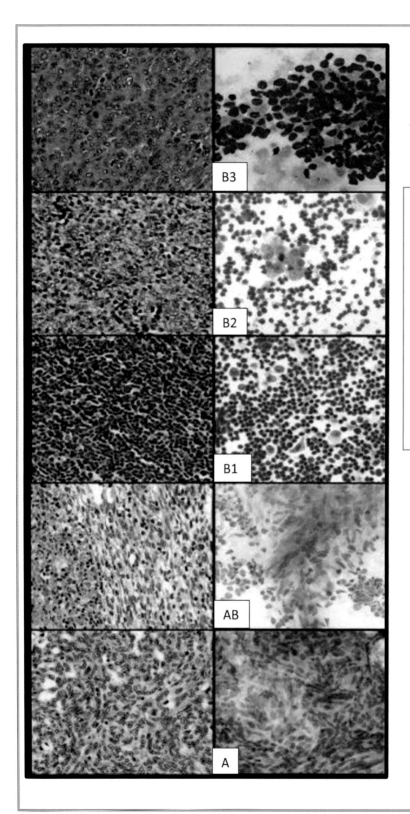

Spectrum of Thymoma cytology of different WHO subtypes A1, AB, B1, B2 and B3: H&E images (left) with corresponding cytology (right). Type A thymoma has predominant cohesive spindle cell component with rare lymphoid cells, AB is mixed with both spindled and round cells, B1- has more lymphocytes, B2 is a mixture of both round cells and lymphocytes, B3 has frankly malignant appearing cells. Courtesy Sanjay Mukhopadhyay (Twitter: @smlungpathguy)

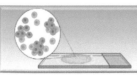

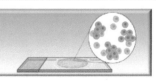

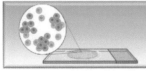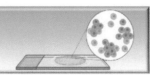
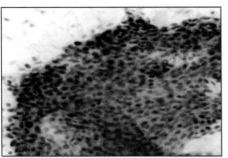

Figure: PAP stain. Thymic carcinoma: Sheets of squamoid appearing atypical cells which can be challenging to distinguish from squamous cell carcinoma based on cytology. ©CytoAtlas

THYMIC CARCINOMA

CYTOMORPHOLOGY

- Thymic carcinomas show unequivocally malignant cells and appears as poorly differentiated large cell carcinomas, and can be of the following subtypes:
  - ➢ Squamous cell carcinoma of thymus
  - ➢ Basaloid carcinoma of thymus
  - ➢ Lymphoepithelial carcinoma of thymus
  - ➢ Mucoepidermoid carcinoma (MAML2 fusion) of thymus
  - ➢ NUT Carcinoma (NUTM1 fusion)
  - ➢ Clear cell carcinoma of thymus including hyalinizing clear cell carcinoma (EWSR1 fusion)
  - ➢ Adenocarcinoma of the thymus

OTHER HIGH YIELD POINTS

- Thymic carcinomas are positive for CD5 and CD117

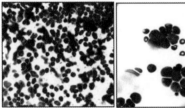

Figure: Diff-Quik. Mediastinal lymphoblastic lymphoma: Cells displaying very scant cytoplasm and finely dispersed chromatin. ©CytoAtlas

LYMPHOMAS OF THE MEDIASTINUM

- Vast majority of lymphomas seen in the mediastinum are due to secondary involvement
- Common primary mediastinal lymphomas are:
  - ➢ Hodgkin's lymphoma (Nodular sclerosis)
  - ➢ Primary mediastinal (thymic) large B-cell lymphoma
  - ➢ T Lymphoblastic lymphoma
  - ➢ Mediastinal gray zone lymphoma

CYTOMORPHOLOGY

- Refer table 2

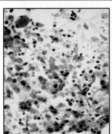 

Figure: PAP stain and Diff-Quik stain. Germ cell tumor of mediastinum: Non-seminomatous germ cell tumor can be pleomorphic, with coarse chromatin and prominent nucleoli with frequent apoptotic bodies. Courtesy Jillian Schook (Twitter: @JS_Cytotech)

GERM CELL TUMORS (GCT)

CYTOMORPHOLOGY

- See table 1

OTHER HIGH YIELD POINTS

- GCTs occur in the mediastinum due to a failure of the germ cell migration during embryonic development
- Commonly seen in young adults and is the second most common tumor of the mediastinum after thymoma.
- Histologically classified as Seminomas, Non-seminomatous (Choriocarcinoma, yock sac tumor, embryonal carcinoma and mixed), Teratomas
- Seminoma associated with any non-seminomatous component is classified as Non-seminomatous GCT
- Malignant GCTs are far more common in men

TABLE 1 - GERM CELL TUMORS OF THE MEDIASTINUM

TYPE	CYTOLOGY	IMPORTANT POINTS
Teratoma	• Epithelial and mesenchymal elements can be present in cytology specimens, along with cyst contents	• Most common mediastinal GCT • Commonly asymptomatic
Seminoma	• Hypercellular specimen showing clusters and isolated tumor cells in a background of small, mature lymphoid cells	• Most common mediastinal malignant GCT • Common in young adult men

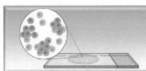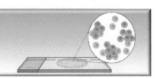

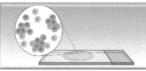
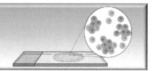

	• Large tumor cells with round/oval nuclei, coarse chromatin, single prominent nucleus, and abundant cytoplasm that is filled with glycogen-containing vacuoles • Tigroid background seen due to disrupted glycogen vacuoles (not specific to seminoma)	• Treatment for seminoma with non-seminomatous component is with intensive chemotherapy alone
Non-seminomatous GCT	• Includes: embryonal carcinoma, yolk sac tumor and choriocarcinoma • Cytology of all non-seminomatous GCTs show large malignant in loose or tight clusters and in papillary or gland like arrangement • Tumor cells show moderate to abundant cytoplasm, prominent large nucleoli, and a background of necrosis	• Given the similar treatment of all non-seminomatous GCTs, distinction between the subtypes may not be necessary on cytology • IHC: Embryonal carcinoma: CD30, SALL4, AE1/AE3, OCT3/4 Yolk-sac tumor: SALL4, AFP, Glypican-3. Choriocarcinoma: Keratins, SALL4, GATA-3, Beta-HCG

TABLE 2 - LYMPHOMAS OF THE MEDIASTINUM

TYPE	CYTOLOGY	DIAGNOSTIC CLUES
Primary mediastinal large B-cell lymphoma	• FNA can show low cellularity admixed with collagen fragments due to the sclerotic nature of the tumor • Cells are intermediate to large lymphoid cells with round, oval or elongated nuclei, and one or more nucleoli	• Female predominance • Localized to the mediastinum • Positive for B cell markers (CD19, CD20, CD79a) • Unlike Hodgkin's lymphoma, cells show CD45 positivity and strong PAX5
Hodgkin's lymphoma	• Characterized by the presence of Reed-Sternberg cells that show bilobed mirror image nuclei with visible nucleoli and abundant cytoplasm	• Most common mediastinal lymphoma, usually nodular sclerosing type • Reed-Sternberg cells label with CD15, CD30 and can be positive for EBV
Lymphoblastic lymphoma	• Blasts are large cells with N/C ratio, delicate chromatin, and small to indistinct nucleoli	• Usually seen in pediatric age group, uncommon in adults • Majority are T cell derived, are label with CD2, cytoplasmic CD3, CD5, CD7, and TdT

4.5 THYMIC NEUROENDOCRINE NEOPLASMS (TNEN)

The histological subtypes of thymic neuroendocrine neoplasms are similar to pulmonary NEN and can be referred in Respiratory Cytology chapter.

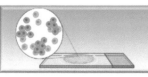
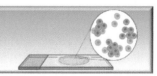

Chapter 5: Urine Cytology

Sakshi Gupta (Sakshi), MD

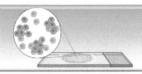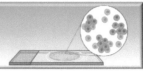
Specimen Types

Paris System Categories and Adequacy Criteria

Normal Urine

Non-Neoplastic

  Stones

  Malakoplakia

  Viruses: Polyoma

  Crystal and Casts

  Radiation and Chemo Effect

AUC

Neoplasms

  Urothelial: HGUC, SHGUC, LGUN

  Squamous

  Small Cell Carcinoma

  Metastatic

Eurovision FISH

Molecular Testing

Hayk MELKUMYAN

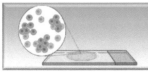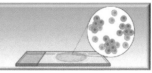

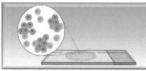
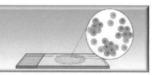
SPECIMEN TYPES

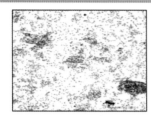

Figure: PAP stain. Benign renal pelvic wash: High cellularity and predominantly flat cohesive sheets of cells.

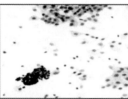

Figure: PAP stain. Benign renal pelvic wash: Large sheet of cells with finely vacuolated cytoplasm, slightly enlarged oval nuclei with no nuclear size variation.

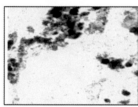

Figure: PAP stain. Ileal conduit: Abundant bacteria in a background of degenerated epithelial cells.

- Different specimen types include: Voided, Catheterized, Bladder washings, Upper tract washings and brushings, Ileal conduits, Neobladders
1. VOIDED URINE
- Avoid morning first urine due to degenerated cells
- 30 mL "clean catch" mid-stream urine preferred
- Advantages
  ➢ Easy to obtain, no instrumentation
- Disadvantages
  ➢ Poor preservation and cellularity
  ➢ Vaginal contamination especially in females
2. CATHETERIZED URINE
- Poor preservation
- Risk of infection
- Benign urothelial cell clusters can be seen – mimic low grade urothelial neoplasm
3. BLADDER WASHINGS AND BRUSHINGS
- Irrigating the bladder with normal saline
- Advantages
  ➢ Well preserved specimen
  ➢ Good cellularity
- Disadvantages
  ➢ Presence of clusters can mimic neoplastic process (false positive)
  ➢ Invasive procedure
  ➢ Instrumentation artifact
4. ILEAL CONDUIT SPECIMEN
  ➢ Screening for recurrent bladder cancer
  ➢ Degenerated poorly preserved intestinal cells
  ➢ Low cellularity
5. NEOBLADDER

PARIS SYSTEM CATEGORIES AND ADEQUACY CRITERIA

Categories (Paris System)
- Negative for high-grade urothelial carcinoma
- Atypical urothelial cells (AUC)
- Suspicious for high-grade urothelial carcinoma
- High-grade urothelial carcinoma (HGUC)
- Low-grade urothelial neoplasia (LGUN)

Adequacy Criteria
Mainly determined by 4 specimen characteristics:
- Collection type
- Cellularity (variable depending on method of collection, higher in instrumented specimen)
- Volume (only in voided specimens, as it is artificially altered in other specimen types)
- Cytomorphological findings
- Of these adequacy criteria, cytomorphological findings are most important - presence of any atypical, suspicious, or malignant findings makes a specimen adequate regardless of the other criteria.

- Volume (voided urines only): Cut-off of 30 mL (appropriate in a laboratory that uses SurePath™ preparation performed on fresh unfixed voided urines).
- Disqualification of a specimen just based on low-volume is not advisable as low-volume specimens can still have diagnostic findings.
- Cellularity: Instrumented specimens – more cellular.
  ➢ >= 20 well-preserved, well-visualized urothelial cells per 10 high-power fields (HPF): "adequate" (cut-off is valid in the absence of obscuring features – lubricant, inflammatory cells, or red blood cells obscuring the urothelial cells)
  ➢ 10–20 well-preserved, well-visualized urothelial cells per 10 high-power fields (HPF): "**satisfactory but limited by low cellularity**"
  ➢ <10 well-preserved, well-visualized urothelial cells per 10 high-power fields (HPF) **OR** lubricant, inflammatory cells, or red blood cells, **obscuring** the urothelial cells **OR marked degenerative** changes: "**unsatisfactory/nondiagnostic**" *
  *Note: Fewer or abnormal degenerated cells, should **not** be interpreted as inadequate

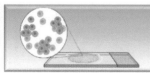
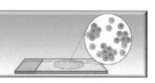

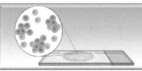
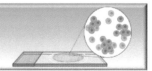

NORMAL URINE

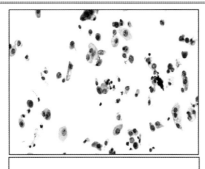

Figure: PAP stain. Normal urine: ThinPrep® showing urothelial cells and umbrella cells with round nuclei, bland chromatin and granular cytoplasm. Courtesy Laila Nomani, MD

CYTOMORPHOLOGY

UROTHELIAL CELLS
- Voided urine
  - ➢ Superficial ("umbrella" cells - large with abundant cytoplasm and large nuclei showing binucleation and multinucleation)
  - ➢ Intermediate cells
  - ➢ Degenerated urothelial cells - contain round, red or green hyaline cytoplasmic inclusions called Melamed–Wolinska (MW) bodies
- Catheterized urine, washings
  - ➢ Superficial
  - ➢ Intermediate, and
  - ➢ Basal cells

SQUAMOUS CELLS
- Common in voided urine samples
- From foci of squamous metaplasia in the trigone of the bladder or from urethra and urethral orifice as the urines passes through them
- Also, can be a vaginal contaminant

SEMINAL VESICLE AND PROSTATIC EPITHELIAL CELLS –
- Very rare

DEGENERATED INTESTINAL EPITHELIAL CELLS –
Only in ileal conduit specimens

NON-NEOPLASTIC URINE CYTOLOGY

Figure: PAP stain. Melamed-Wolinska bodies. Courtesy Laila Nomani, MD

STONES
- Multiple types and shapes based on composition (FIG)
- Urothelium with stones: sheets or clusters of cells that are not true tissue fragments can be seen
- Cells in the fragments or clusters may show:
  - ➢ nuclear enlargement and atypia
  - ➢ slightly increased N/C ratios
  - ➢ nuclear and cytoplasmic degeneration, and/or
  - ➢ squamous metaplasia
- If atypical well-preserved single cells are present, the sample needs to be considered either Atypical (AUC) or Suspicious for HGUC (SHGUC) based upon the criteria for those categories

MALAKOPLAKIA
- Histiocytic inflammatory lesion of the bladder or upper respiratory tract that results from bacterial infection
- Diagnosis by urine cytology is very uncommon
- The cytologic hallmark is the presence of histiocytes whose abundant granular cytoplasm is filled with bacteria and bacterial fragments. The basophilic, round, lamellated bodies known as Michaelis-Gutmann bodies can be seen intracellularly within histiocytes or extracellularly

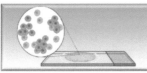
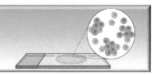

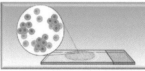
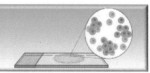

Figure: PAP stain. Polyoma virus: showing glassy inclusions that push the chromatin and give the appearance of thickened membranes.

VIRUSES: POLYOMA
- Human polyomavirus is acquired in childhood and becomes latent in urothelial cells of the kidney and bladder. Immune suppression after transplantation results in BK virus reactivation in transplant recipients and clinical disease in some patients

CYTOMORPHOLOGY
- Sparse to abundant altered cells
- Isolated cells - sometimes binucleated or multinucleated, enlarged, round, eccentrically placed nucleus (teardrop, comet-like cell shapes)
- Basophilic, glassy inclusion fills entire nucleus
- Thick nuclear membrane
- Degenerated nuclei with coarse reticular chromatin pattern
- Polyomavirus-infected cells can be confused with the malignant cells; hence they are called decoy cells

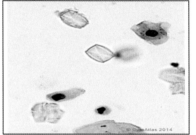

Figure: PAP stain. Oxalate crystals: tetrahedral envelope-shaped oxalate crystals.

CRYSTALS
- Triple phosphate crystals - shaped like prisms and coffin lids
- Ammonium biurate crystals - spheres with protruding spicules ("thorn apples")
- Uric acid crystals - most common, vary markedly in size and shape
- Calcium oxalate crystals - can be oval, dumbbell-shaped, or small and octahedral
- Bilirubin crystals - brown granules and needles
- Cholesterol, Cystine - hexagonal plates
- Leucine - spheres with radiating striations
- Tyrosine - slender needles

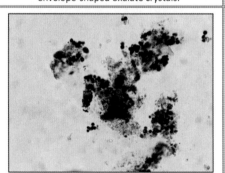

Figure: Geimsa stain. Red blood cell cast. Courtesy Hena Khandakar, MD

RENAL CASTS
- Formed during passage of proteins and other material passing through the renal tubules
- Mostly reflect glomerular or tubular damage
- Hyaline cast can be seen in normal individuals, without significant proteinuria; it is formed due to solidification of Tamm-Horsfall mucoprotein, secreted from tubules
- Red blood cell casts are characteristic of glomerular disease
- White blood cell casts are seen in tubulointerstitial diseases and in association with transplant rejection
- Epithelial casts, composed of degenerated renal tubular cells, can be seen in any disease, including acute tubular necrosis
- Waxy casts are homogeneous and dense, often with sharp edges and fractures
  fatty casts contain lipid vacuoles and are seen in patients with the nephrotic syndrom

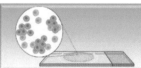
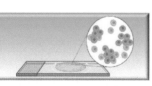

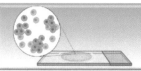
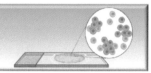

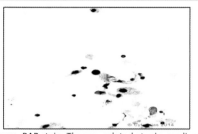

Figure: PAP stain. Therapy related atypia, medium power, showing atypical appearing cells with low N/C ratios, smudgy chromatin, and variable shapes. Unlike HGUC, the nuclear membranes are smooth, and chromatin is not coarse.

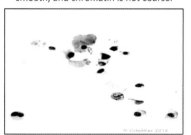

Figure: PAP stain. BCG therapy related atypia, high power (Pap stain), showing singly arranged cells that have smudgy chromatin. Note that cell shapes are polygonal, and, in some cells, the cytoplasmic edges are frayed.

RADIATION, IMMUNOTHERAPY AND CHEMOTHERAPY EFFECT

RADIATION

- Cytomegaly and nucleomegaly, but preserved nuclear: cytoplasmic (N/C) ratio
- Multinucleation, and nuclear and cytoplasmic vacuoles
- Polychromasia

IMMUNOTHERAPY

- Intravesical BCG immunotherapy - granulomatous inflammation

CHEMOTHERAPY

- Intravesical mitomycin and thiotepa - usually affect superficial cells and cause nuclear enlargement, multinucleation and hyperchromasia of those cells
- Systemic cyclophosphamide – nuclear enlargement with increased N/C ratio, urothelial hyperchromasia and degeneration

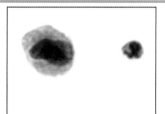

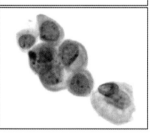

Figure: PAP stain. Atypical urothelial cells with increased nuclear cytoplasmic (N/C) ratio (>0.5) and hyperchromasia. Courtesy Laila Nomani, MD

ATYPICAL UROTHELIAL CELLS (AUC)

DEFINITION:

- Major (required) criterion and only one minor criterion (>=2 minor criteria, including hyperchromasia is diagnostic of suspicious for high grade urothelial carcinoma - SHGUC, unless there are marked degenerative changes)
- Major criterion (required) -
- Non-superficial and non-degenerated urothelial cells with an increased nuclear cytoplasmic (N/C) ratio (>0.5)
- Minor criteria (one required) -
  ➢ Nuclear hyperchromasia
  ➢ Irregular nuclear membranes (chromatinic rim or nuclear contour)
  ➢ Irregular, coarse, clumped chromatin
- To be classified as AUC, the cytologic changes must fall short of a diagnosis of suspicious for high-grade urothelial carcinoma (SHGUC) or high-grade urothelial carcinoma (HGUC)
- Exclude other scenarios that cause "atypia" (polyomavirus and other infections, reactive umbrella cells, seminal vesicle cells, and reactive changes due to stones, instrumentation, and therapy)

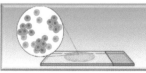
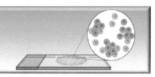

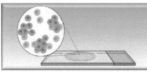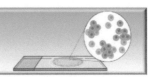
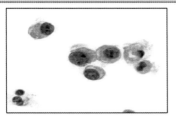

Figure: PAP stain. Suspicious for HGUC.
Courtesy Laila Nomani, MD

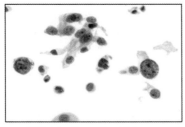

Figure: PAP stain. Two cells with increased N/C ratio, nuclear hyperchromasia and coarse chromatin, suspicious for high grade urothelial carcinoma. Courtesy Laila Nomani, MD

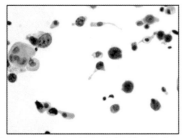

Figure: PAP stain. HGUC: High N:C ratio, irregular nuclear membranes, and coarse clumped chromatin. Courtesy Laila Nomani.

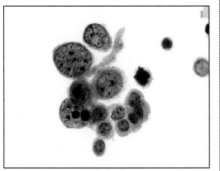

Figure: PAP stain. HGUC: High N:C ratio, irregular nuclear membrane, coarse clumped chromatin. Courtesy Laila Nomani, MD

- Urine cytology is an important test for screening and diagnosis of newly developed urothelial carcinoma (UC) and for surveillance of UC recurrence and new neoplasms
- Urine cytology - gold standard for bladder cancer screening, especially for HGUC

SUSPICIOUS FOR HIGH-GRADE UROTHELIAL (SUSPICIOUS)
- Urothelial cells with severe atypia that is still not qualifying for high-grade urothelial carcinoma (HGUC) but is more than the atypia that is associated with the "atypical urothelial cells" (AUC) category.

Criteria per Paris System
- Increased nuclear to cytoplasmic (N/C) ratio, at least 0.5–0.7 "Required diagnostic criterion"
- Moderate to severe hyperchromasia "Required diagnostic criterion"
- In addition, at least one of the two following features needs to be present:
- Irregular clumpy chromatin
- Marked irregular nuclear membrane
  - Quantitatively <5 atypical/ abnormal cells in a cellular urine cytology specimen (if 5-10 abnormal/ atypical cells with other criteria fulfilling – HGUC)
  - The cells are usually seen as single cells although clusters of atypical cells may also be present. The above diagnostic criteria are most reliably assessed in the single cells

HIGH GRADE UROTHELIAL CARCINOMA (HGUC)
- Cytomorphologic characteristics of HGUC:
- High nuclear to cytoplasmic (N/C) ratio (>=0.7; nucleus occupying more than 70% of the cytoplasm
- Nuclear pleomorphism, nuclear margin irregularity, nuclear overlapping and hyperchromasia
- Chromatin abnormalities such as coarse clumping or homogenous chromatin pattern
- Prominent nucleoli, isolated/single malignant cells and extensive necrosis (indicator for invasive disease)
- Comet, India- ink (single cells with deep black structureless nuclei) and apoptotic cells

Criteria per Paris System
- A cellular cytologic urine specimen with a minimum of 5-10 viable malignant cells will qualify as HGUC.
- The type of specimen contributes to the minimal number of abnormal cells required for a more definitive diagnosis
- Upper urinary tract instrumented specimens require at least 10 abnormal cells
- Voided urine specimens may require a lesser number of cells (at least 5-10)

HGUC WITH SQUAMOUS DIFFERENTIATION
- Presence of keratinization and/or intercellular bridges
- Squamous cells with hyperchromatic, spindle-shaped nuclei and clumped chromatin; dense/ orangeophilic cytoplasm
- Keratin flakes, necrosis
- Diagnosis of squamous cell carcinoma of the urinary tract can only be determined By extensive examination of biopsy or cystectomy tissue

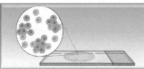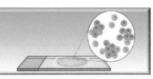

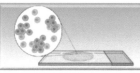
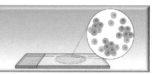

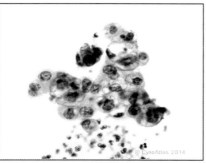

Figure: PAP stain. LGUN: Cluster with irregular outline. Note the cells have homogenous cytoplasm and nuclei and show slight variation in size and slight irregularity in outline. @CytoAtlas

HGUC WITH GLANDULAR DIFFERENTIATION
- Glandular cells with malignant cells showing classic HGUC features
- Diagnosis of adenocarcinoma of the urinary tract can only be determined by extensive examination of biopsy or cystectomy tissue

LGUN
- Combined cytologic term for low-grade papillary urothelial neoplasms (LGPUN) (which includes urothelial papilloma, PUNLMP and LGPUC) and flat, low-grade intraurothelial neoplasia
- Three -dimensional cellular papillary clusters (defined as clusters of cells with nuclear overlapping, forming "papillae") with fibrovascular cores including capillaries – definitive for the diagnosis
- Cytogenetic abnormalities - FGFR3 mutation most often
- The following features with cystoscopic or biopsy findings may suggest the cytologic diagnosis of LGUN; however, these cases should be categorized as "Negative for High-Grade Urothelial Carcinoma (NHGUC)"
- Three-dimensional cellular clusters without fibrovascular cores
- Increased numbers of monotonous single (non-umbrella) cells

The following cytomorphological features in the absence of other HGUC characteristics may suggest a LGUN
- Lesion: However, these cases should be categorized as NHGUC
- Cytoplasmic homogeneity
- Nuclear border irregularity
- Increased nuclear/cytoplasmic (N/C) ratio

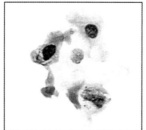

Figure: PAP stain. Squamous cell with marked atypia. Cells have dense orangeophilic cytoplasm. @CytoAtlas

SQUAMOUS CELL CARCINOMA
- Rare in the US, common in Nile River valley
- Strongly associated with Schistosoma hematobium
- A definite diagnosis of squamous cell carcinoma should be deferred to biopsy or resection

SMALL CELL CARCINOMA
- Small cell carcinoma of the bladder is a very rare and highly aggressive
- Cytomorphology - identical to that of small cell carcinoma of other sites
- The differential diagnosis includes metastatic lesions, especially from the lung
- Challenging diagnosis due to:
  - Small, degenerated cells with necrosis
  - Cytoplasm not well preserved (difficult to predict n/c ratio), and the chromatin is finely and evenly distributed (rather than hyperchromatic)
- Cases with poorly preserved and few cells - diagnosed as "atypical

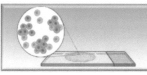

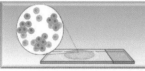
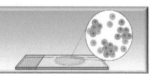

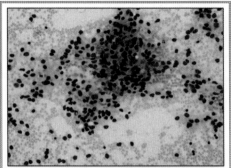

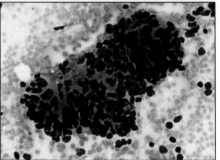

Figure: Diff-Quik stains. Neuroblastoma.

METASTATIC

Renal Cell Carcinoma

- Rare incidence due to imaging techniques
- Renal cell carcinoma cells in urine specimens are:
  - Larger than urothelial cells
  - Relatively low nuclear-to-cytoplasmic ratio, clear to vacuolated cytoplasm, and a relatively large
  - Fluorescence in situ hybridization (FISH) studies may help to diagnose renal cell carcinomas with specific genetic alterations

Colonic Carcinoma

- Difficult to distinguish from urothelial cancer, history is important
- Adenocarcinoma of the bladder is positive for CDX-2; hence, the distinction between urothelial and gastrointestinal origin often requires clinical correlation
- Malignant cells in colonic carcinoma are pleomorphic and degenerated, with hyperchromatic, irregular nuclei

Prostatic Carcinoma

- Clinical history of known malignancy is important.
- Prostatic carcinoma cells in urine specimens almost always occur in patients with poorly differentiated (Gleason score ≥8), unresectable tumors

CYTOMORPHOLOGY

- Cells with prominent nucleolus and relatively abundant cytoplasm and resemble a typical, lower-grade prostatic carcinoma.
- In other cases, the cells have a dark nucleus without a prominent nucleolus and resemble the common type of urothelial carcinoma.
- If no known history of prostatic carcinoma, the possibility of a high-grade urothelial carcinoma should be considered; immunostains for urothelial cells and prostatic markers can be useful.

OTHERS

- Lymphoma/ Leukemia, Neuroblastoma
- Clinical correlation and immunostains can help to make the correct diagnosis

UROVYSION FISH

- The multitarget multicolor U-FISH assay contains four single-stranded DNA probes.
- Three probes are chromosome enumeration probes (CEP) targeting pericentromeric regions of chromosomes 3, 7, and 17. Another probe is a locus-specific identifier (LSI) probe targeting 9p21 locus on gene p16.
- All probes are directly labelled with fluorescent dyes (FIG. / ILLUSTRATION)
  - CEP 3 Spectrum Red
  - CEP 7 Spectrum Green
  - CEP 17 Spectrum Aqua, and
  - LSI 9p21 Spectrum Gold
- The number of signals for all four probes should be counted for each abnormal cell and recorded only when there is a gain (≥2 signals) for two or more chromosomes 3 (red),7 (green), 17 (aqua), or there is a loss of both

copies of 9p21 (gold) as recommended by the manufacturer.
- Total number of abnormal cells analyzed should be recorded. The test is considered positive when ≥4 of the 25 analyzed cells show gains for two or more chromosomes or ≥12 of the 25 cells have zero 9p21 signals.
- If these criteria for test positivity are not met after viewing 25 cells, analysis should be continued until the entire sample is analyzed

MOLECULAR TESTING

IMMUNOCYT/uCYT+ TEST

- FDA cleared in the year 2000 for the diagnosis and monitoring of bladder cancer
- It combines three fluorescent monoclonal antibodies

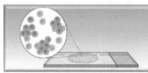

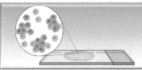
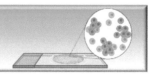
- ➢ Two of them (M344 and LDQ10) - fluorescein (green) - against mucin-like antigens
- ➢ Third (19A211) - Texas red (red) - recognizes a high molecular form of carcinoembryonic antigen
- Simple and less expensive than U-FISH
- Samples are considered positive
  - ➢ At least one green or red fluorescent urothelial cell is observed
- The usefulness of uCyt:
  - ➢ Detect both low-grade and high-grade cancers, including in situ carcinoma
  - ➢ Predict recurrence in patients, all with a negative cystoscopy
  - ➢ Monitoring programs to decrease the frequency of follow-up cystoscopy
- Overall sensitivity is high, ranging from 53 to 100% (average 90%), when combined with cytology (close to 100%)
- Limitation: still needs validation in large-scale prospective and multi-center study

BTA TEST

- The BTA stat and BTA TRAK tests - approved by the FDA to:
  - ➢ Detect bladder cancer in symptomatic patients
  - ➢ Surveillance of patients with bladder cancer
- Measures the presence of human complement factor H and related protein - elevated in urine samples of patients with bladder cancer
- In this test system the signal is decreased by the presence of factor H-like protein-1, an alternatively spliced product of the complement factor H. Thus, outcome of the BTA

immunoassay depends on the combined positive and negative signals of the two proteins in a urine sample

- For the BTA test the urine should be collected without preservatives or fixatives in a clean urine cup and labelled appropriately.
- Limitation:
  - ➢ Any condition causing hematuria may result in a false-positive BTA test, because complement factor H is a normal blood component.
  - ➢ Patients with treatment-related hematuria after intravesical chemo- or immunotherapy without residual or recurrent cancer – false positive.

NMP22 Test

- Immunoassay for the detection of nuclear mitotic apparatus protein - located in the nuclear matrix.
- Level may correspond to the cellularity and cell turnover in the bladder, rather than a tumor-specific protein.
- Its high false-positive rate due to instrumentation, inflammatory, and regenerative urinary bladder processes reduced its application. The urine sample needs to be stabilized immediately after collection and it can then be stored at room temperature for 4 days
- For the point of care NMP22 BladderChek test a median sensitivity of 50% and specificity of 87% was reported
- NMP22 BladderChek point of care test - Increased sensitivity over cytology in the detection of bladder cancer in symptomatic patients, but specificity of cytology was better than the NMP22 test
- Sensitivity (94 %) and specificity (84 %) for high grade UC detection was found for the combination of cytology and NMP22 BladderChek

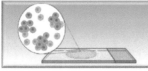
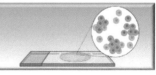

Chapter 6: Fluid Cytology

Sakshi Gupta (Sakshi), MD

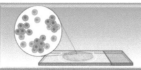

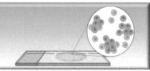

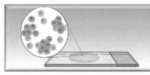

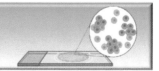

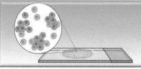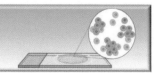

Chapter 6: FLUID CYTOLOGY

PLEURAL AND PERICARDIAL FLUID CYTOLOGY
Specimen collection and types
- Thoracentesis – pleural fluid
- Pericardiocentesis – pericardial fluid
- The ultrasound guided specimen collection – better results
- Fluid can also be collected during surgeries.
- Processing:
  - Unfixed specimen is sent to the lab stat
  - Collection in heparinized tubes prevent clotting
  - Once received the specimen should be refrigerated at 4°C until the time of slide preparation
- Slide preparation types:
  - Cytospin

PLEURAL AND PERICARDIAL FLUID CYTOLOGY
  - Liquid based preparations – ThinPrep® or SurePath™

- Cell blocks preparation – useful for ancillary studies, including immunocytochemistry and molecular studies.

International system for reporting serous fluid cytology
- Non-diagnostic
- Negative for malignancy
- Atypia of undetermined significance- Poorly preserved cells or very few atypical cells
- Suspicious for malignancy - high degree of suspicion but falls short of definitive for malignancy
- Malignant

**Criteria for the adequacy of an effusion specimen have not been established.

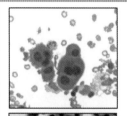 Figure: Diff-Quik stain. Mesothelial cells: round to oval nuclei, smooth to slightly irregular membranes, binucleation, dense cytoplasm and "windows" Figure: PAP stain. Courtesy Aastha Chauhan, MD (Twitter: @ac_pathgal)	**NORMAL ELEMENTS: MESOTHELIAL CELLS AND HISTIOCYTES** **MESOTHELIAL CELLS** **CYTOMORPHOLOGY** • Numerous dispersed isolated cells • Presence of "windows" • Round uniform cells with round nucleus and single nucleolus. Dense cytoplasm with peripheral halo or clear outer rim ("lacy skirt"; due to presence of abundant tonofilaments) • Collagen balls **HISTIOCYTE** **CYTOMORPHOLOGY** • Folded smaller nucleus (compared to the mesothelial cells) • Granular/ vacuolated cytoplasm • Absence of "windows"
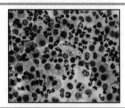 Figure: Diff-Quik stain. Benign effusion with acute inflammation. Smear shows many neutrophils.	**NON-NEOPLASTIC** **ACUTE SEROSITIS** **CYTOMORPHOLOGY** • Bacterial infection usually • Careful screening for metastatic malignant process to rule out acute infection secondary to metastatic malignancy

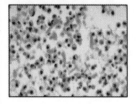 Figure: H&E stain. Eosinophilic pleural effusion with Charcot-Leyden crystals. Courtesy Samer Khader, MD (Twitter: @SamKhader)	**EOSINOPHILIC EFFUSION**
	CYTOMORPHOLOGY
	• Eosinophils comprise 10% or more of the nucleated cells
	OTHER HIGH YIELD POINTS
	• Cause:
	  ➢ Pneumothorax ➢ Drug reactions/ parasitic infections
	  ➢ Hemothorax ➢ Pulmonary infarction
	  ➢ Surgical intervention ➢ Churg-Strauss syndrome
	  ➢ Repeated thoracenteses

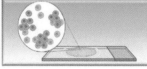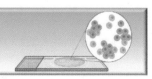

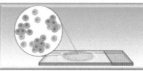
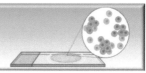

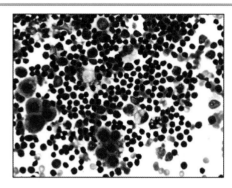

Figure: Diff-Quik stain. Lymphocytic effusion: Abundant small lymphocytes together with mesothelial cells and histiocytes. ©Cytoatlas

LYMPHOCYTIC EFFUSION

CYTOMORPHOLOGY
- Smear shows numerous lymphocytes

OTHER HIGH YIELD POINTS
- Despite the absence of malignant cells, a malignancy is a common cause of a lymphocytic effusion
- However, an effusion is very rarely the initial manifestation of a lymphoid malignancy
- Most common causes of lymphocytic effusions include:
  - Malignancy
  - Tuberculosis
  - Status post CABG

RHEUMATOID PLEURITIS

CYTOMORPHOLOGY
- Moderately cellular specimen with abundant granular material (stain green, pink, red, or orange with the Pap stain), that aggregates into small and large clumps with irregular edges.
- Large, island-like masses can be appreciated in cell block material. Macrophages are predominantly seen, with few lymphocytes and neutrophils.

OTHER HIGH YIELD POINTS
- Usually, unilateral pleural effusion.

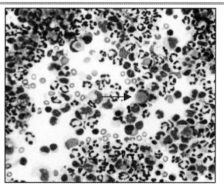

Figure: Diff- Quik stain. L-E cell (arrow).

LUPUS PLEURITIS

CYTOMORPHOLOGY
- The characteristic cell is the lupus erythematosus (LE) cell, a neutrophil or macrophage that contains an ingested cytoplasmic particle called a hematoxylin body (thought to represent degenerated nuclei)
- Hematoxylin body is glassy, homogeneous appearance and often fills the entire cytoplasm of the neutrophil or macrophage, pushing the nucleus to one side
- Pap stain shows green, blue, or purple staining of the hematoxylin body, however, the Romanowsky stain shows magenta color
- Similar cells that contain ingested nuclei with a visible chromatin structure (rather than the glassy, structureless hematoxylin body) are called tart cells

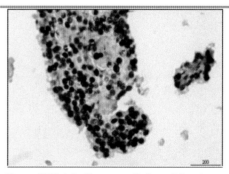

Figure: GMS stain. *Pneumocystis jiroveci.* Courtesy Samer Khader (Twitter: @SamKhader)

INFECTIOUS EFFUSIONS

CYTOMORPHOLOGY
- Organisms identified
- Pneumocystis jirovecii: GMS stain it is visualized as non-budding organisms with thin wall and dark center with not much size variation
- Yeast forms: candida species, Cryptococcus neoformans, Coccidioides immitis, Blastomyces dermatitidis
- Hyphae: Aspergillus niger

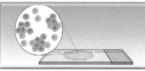
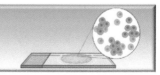

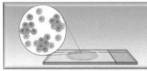
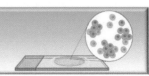
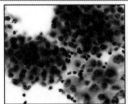
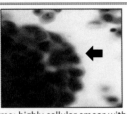

Figure: PAP stain. Mesothelioma: highly cellular smear with large clusters of cells. Knobby contour (right) ©Cytoatlas

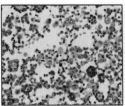
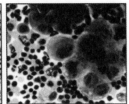

Figure: H&E and Diff-Quik. Mesothelioma: cells arranged in clusters, small balls (left). Cells with large prominent nucleoli and vague peritoneal windows between cells. ©Cytoatlas

MALIGNANT EFFUSIONS
MESOTHELIOMA
CYTOMORPHOLOGY
- Two principal patterns: morular, non-cohesive
- Cytologic Features: cytomegaly with round, centrally placed nucleus, prominent nucleolus, binucleation and multinucleation
- Dense cytoplasm with peripheral "halo"

OTHER HIGH YIELD POINTS
- Most cases associated with asbestos exposure with an average latency time of 30 to 40 years.
- Sensitivity of effusion cytology for the diagnosis of mesothelioma is only 32%.
- Mesothelioma versus reactive mesothelial cells: BRCA-associated protein 1 (BAP1) is expressed in the nuclei of benign mesothelial cells and absent in most mesotheliomas (60% to 79% mesotheliomas have genetic alterations in BAP1)
- FISH: 9p21 (p16) deletion identified in mesothelioma

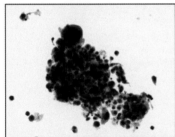

Figure: PAP stain. Cohesive cluster of adenocarcinoma.

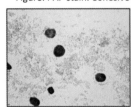
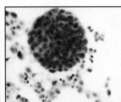

Figure: Diff-Quik stain. Breast carcinoma: large cannon balls (characteristic for breast carcinoma). ©Cytoatlas

ADENOCARCINOMA
CYTOMORPHOLOGY
- Cellular smear with large cohesive clusters or spheres or papilla or single cells
- Tumor cells with a reactive background, mesothelial and inflammatory cell
- Smooth cell borders

HIGH YIELD POINTS
- Almost 30% of all body fluids are malignant
- Carcinomas are most common cause of malignant effusions in adults
- Breast cancer: most common in women (shows cannon ball)
- Lung cancer: most common in males

Mesothelioma versus Adenocarcinoma immunohistochemistry:

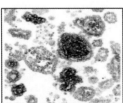
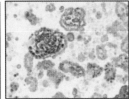

Figure: Mesothelioma left, immunocytochemistry for Calretinin: positive in mesotheliomas with nuclear and cytoplasmic staining. Adenocarcinomas are usually negative; rarely show cytoplasmic staining. ©Cytoatlas. Right, immunocytochemistry for D2-40: mesotheliomas show membranous staining. May be seen in some serous adenocarcinomas. ©Cytoatlas

Stain	Adenocarcinoma	Mesothelioma
MOC-31	+	-
Ber-EP4	+	-
CEA	+	-
Calretinin	-	+ (nuclear and cytoplasmic)
WT-1	-	+ (nuclear)
D2-40	-	+ (membranous)
B72.3	+	-
Leu M-1 (CD 15)	+	-
Claudin-4	+	-
Mucicarmine	+	-
PAS-D	+	-

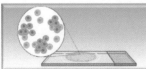
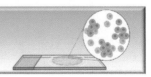

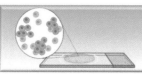
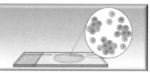

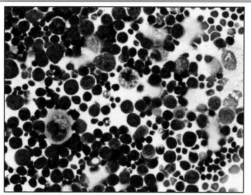

Figure: Diff-Quik stain. PEL: large lymphoid cells with round to irregular nuclei and basophilic vacuolated cytoplasm.
©Cytoatlas

LYMPHOMA
PRIMARY EFFUSION LYMPHOMA (PEL)
CYTOMORPHOLOGY
- Large lymphoid cells with round to irregular nuclei and basophilic vacuolated cytoplasm.

OTHER HIGH YIELD POINTS
- Effusion-based B-cell lymphoma associated with Human Herpes Virus-8 (HHV-8) without an associated mass lesion, lymphadenopathy, or organomegaly
- Can be associated with immunodeficiency
- Frequent co-infection with EBV
- Negative B-cell markers (CD19, CD20, CD79a)
- CD30 and the plasma cell markers CD38 and CD138, are often present
- Poor prognosis with median survival is less than 6 months

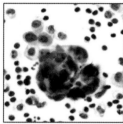
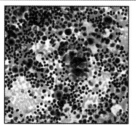

Figure: PAP stain and Diff-Quik stain. Metastatic small cell carcinoma: cluster of malignant cells with scant cytoplasm, nuclear molding. ©Cytoatlas

SMALL CELL CARCINOMA
CYTOMORPHOLOGY
- Small cells with scant cytoplasm, dark nuclei, inconspicuous nucleoli, nuclear molding

OTHER HIGH YIELD POINTS
- Rarely presents as pleural effusion
- Differentials include lymphoma and Merkle cell carcinoma
- Immunostains can be helpful: Chromogranin, Synaptophysin, CD45, Merkel Cell Polyomavirus (MCPyV), dot like CK20

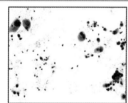
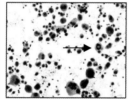

Figure: PAP stain. Metastatic melanoma: singly dispersed cells, intranuclear cytoplasmic inclusion (arrow). ©Cytoatlas

MELANOMA
CYTOMORPHOLOGY
- Single isolated cells with prominent nucleoli, can show binucleation
- Presence of fine brown cytoplasmic pigmentation, intranuclear pseudoinclusions

HIGH YIELD POINTS
- Immunostains: HMB45, Melan A, SOX10, MiTF, PRAME

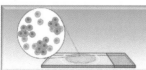
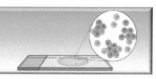

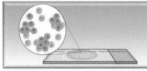

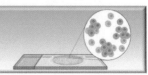

PERITONEAL FLUID CYTOLOGY

COLLECTION AND INDICATIONS

• Types of specimens: peritoneal tap/ascitic fluid tap/peritoneal washing

• Peritoneal washing: 50-200 mL saline is instilled in pelvis, undersurface of diaphragm and paracolic gutters and aspirated

• Cytological examination of peritoneal washings is indicated for the following:

➢ Staging gynecologic malignancies
➢ Rule out occult primary
➢ Assessing response to treatment (the "second-look" procedure)
➢ Staging non-gynecologic malignancies (gastric, pancreatic)

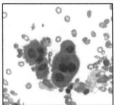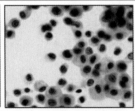

Figure: Diff-Quik and Pap Stain. Smear showing round to oval nuclei, smooth to slightly irregular membranes, binucleation, dense cytoplasm and "windows". Courtesy Aastha Chauhan, MD (Twitter: @ac_pathgal) (left) and ©Cytoatlas (right)

Figure: PAP stain. Collagen ball (left). Peritoneal washing: showing sheets of mesothelial cells. ©Cytoatlas

NORMAL COMPONENTS
CYTOMORPHOLOGY

• **Mesothelial cells**: arranged in sheets in washing
  ➢ On Pap stain - flat sheets of evenly spaced rounds cells with moderate cytoplasm, pale evenly dispersed chromatin and small nucleoli
  ➢ In cell block - long, thin ribbons ("string of pearls" appearance)
  ➢ Sometimes grooved, wrinkled or lobulated nuclei resembling flower ("daisy cells")
• **Histiocytes:**
  ➢ Arranged in groups, mistaken as metastatic cancer
  ➢ Oval, folded, kidney-shaped nuclei; pale chromatin; granular and micro vacuolated cytoplasm
• **Skeletal muscle**
• **Adipose tissue**
• **Collagen balls:**
  ➢ Spherical balls of collagen surrounded by benign, flattened mesothelial cells
  ➢ Normal finding

Figure: PAP stain. Benign glandular elements of Mullerian origin. Sometimes cilia maybe present indicative of tubal elements. ©Cytoatlas

BENIGN PROCESSES
ENDOSALPINGIOSIS/ MULLERIAN INCLUSION CYST
CYTOMORPHOLOGY

• Incidental microscopic findings
• Proliferation of benign glands and cysts lined by ciliated, fallopian tube-like epithelium
• Uniform cells with no atypia and lack mitotic activity
• Psammoma bodies are common

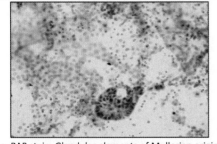

Figure: PAP stain. Glandular elements of Mullerian origin with atypia (serous borderline tumor). ©Cytoatlas

SEROUS ADENOFIBROMAS
CYTOMORPHOLOGY

• Benign glands lined by tubal epithelium and/ or cysts (ovarian surface)
• Presence of broad, fibrous, stromal component
• Psammoma bodies
• Cytomorphology raise suspicion for serous borderline tumor (SBT) or adenocarcinoma

OTHER HIGH YIELD POINTS

• Benign conditions associated with psammoma body formation
  ➢ Pelvic inflammatory disease, ruptured cyst, mesothelial hyperplasia

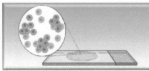

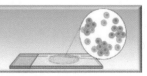

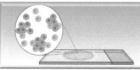

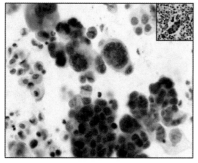

Figure: PAP stain and H&E (inset). High grade serous carcinoma. Inset: Cell block showing clusters of malignant cells in acinar formations and dispersed singly.

MALIGNANT PROCESSES
OVARIAN TUMORS:
HIGH-GRADE SEROUS CARCINOMA
CYTOMORPHOLOGY

- Isolated cells and arranged in clusters
- Enlarged nuclei with nuclear hyperchromasia, coarse chromatin and very prominent nucleoli
- Vacuolated scant cytoplasm
- Psammoma bodies

OTHER HIGH YIELD POINTS

- Most common cause of adnexal pathology with ascites

Figure: PAP stain. Low grade serous carcinoma.

LOW-GRADE SEROUS CARCINOMA
CYTOMORPHOLOGY

- Cohesive three-dimensional clusters
- Low-grade nuclei, inconspicuous nucleoli
- Psammoma bodies can be present

OTHER HIGH YIELD POINTS

- 5% of all serous carcinomas

OTHER RARE OVARIAN TUMORS:

- Mucinous ovarian tumor associated with pseudomyxoma peritonei - likely metastasis (appendiceal primary)
- Ovarian germ cell and sex cord–stromal tumors of the ovaries – rare

ENDOMETRIAL TUMORS
INTRODUCTION

- Important for staging and guiding treatment strategies
- Often associated with lymph node metastases & adnexal involvement
- Types: endometrioid, serous, carcinosarcomas

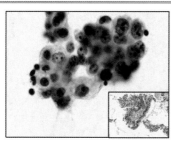

Figure: PAP stain and H&E (inset). 3D clusters of crowded cells with enlarged nuclei, coarse chromatin, prominent nucleoli, and vacuolated cytoplasm. Cell block (inset).

ENDOMETRIOID CARCINOMA
CYTOMORPHOLOGY

- Isolated cells or clusters
- Round and enlarged nuclei, with coarse chromatin and prominent nucleoli
- Scant to moderate cytoplasm with vacuolations
- High-grade tumors show nuclear pleomorphism
- Cell block shows tubular glands and squamous morule formation

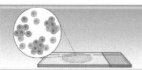

Figure: Diff-Quik stain. Serous carcinoma: 3D clusters of large cells with enlarged nuclei, irregular nuclear membranes and finely vacuolated cytoplasm.

HIGH-GRADE ENDOMETRIAL CANCERS (SEROUS AND CLEAR CELL SUBTYPES)
CYTOMORPHOLOGY

- High-grade cytologic features
- Can show cytoplasmic clearing
- Resemble the ovarian counterpart in morphology
- Strong expression of P53 (serous type)

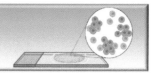

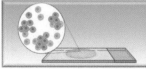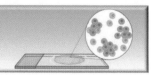
 Figure: Diff-Quik stain. Carcinosarcoma with carcinoma component resembling endometrial carcinoma.	**CARCINOSARCOMA (MALIGNANT MIXED MULLERIAN TUMOR)** CYTOMORPHOLOGY • Usually adenocarcinoma component present (both carcinoma and sarcoma or the sarcomatous component alone however can be rarely present)
 Figure: PAP stain. Clusters of malignant cells.	**PANCREATIC AND GASTROINTESTINAL** **PANCREATIC CANCER** CYTOMORPHOLOGY • Adenocarcinoma with or without mucin OTHER HIGH YIELD POINTS • Seen in patients with increased tumor size (>2 cm), body/tail location, and anterior pancreatic capsule invasion
 Figure: Diff-Quik. Gastric carcinoma: small clusters of atypical cells.	**GASTRIC CANCER** CYTOMORPHOLOGY • Cells can show signet ring cell morphology or small clusters OTHER HIGH YIELD POINTS • Important for staging, T1b or higher tumors • Poor prognostic indicator
	TREATMENT EFFECT • Treated advanced ovarian cancer patients undergo subsequent "second-look" procedures to assess the residual disease • Peritoneal washings are obtained with biopsy specimens from the peritoneum, the omentum, and the retroperitoneal lymph nodes • Low sensitivity as 31% to 86% of patients with negative peritoneal washings show biopsy-proven residual disease • Also, chemotherapy and radiotherapy cause mesothelial cells to look abnormal and hence be misinterpreted as malignant CYTOMORPHOLOGY • Multinucleation and marked variation in nuclear size (anisonucleosis) • Nucleomegaly with abundant cytoplasm, and hence, normal nuclear-to-cytoplasmic ratio (N:C ratio) • Pale and finely granular chromatin • Prominent nucleoli

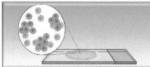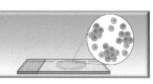

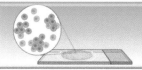
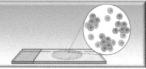

DIFFERENTIAL DIAGNOSIS OF COMMON MALIGNANT EFFUSION

Diagnosis	Morphology	Image (Diff-Quik and Pap Stains)
Gastric adenocarcinoma	• Mainly single cells • Foamy cytoplasm • Nuclear membrane irregularity • Immunocytochemistry: CK7. No specific marker	
Lung adenocarcinoma	• Small clusters • Single cells • Vesicular chromatin with prominent nucleoli • Immunocytochemistry: TTF1, Napsin	
Pancreatobiliary tract adenocarcinoma	• Small clusters with uniform cells • Mucin vacuoles • Fine chromatin • Immunocytochemistry: CK7. No specific marker •	
Mammary carcinoma	• Large clusters/cannon balls • Course chromatin • Immunocytochemistry: GATA3, ER, PR	
Ovarian carcinoma	• Large or small clusters • Open chromatin with • Community borders • Prominent nucleoli • Psammoma bodies (serous carcinoma) • Immunocytochemistry: PAX8, P53 (serous carcinoma)	
Colonic adenocarcinoma	• 3-D clusters • Oval to elongated cells • Lacy cytoplasm • Immunocytochemistry: CK20, CDX2	

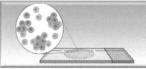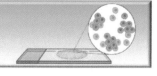

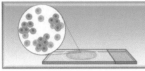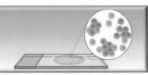
CSF CYTOLOGY
SPECIMEN COLLECTION

- **Specimen types**
  - ➤ Lumbar puncture (L3-4; L4-5)
  - ➤ Cisterna magna, base of brain
  - ➤ Chemoport (Ommaya reservoir)
  - ➤ Lateral ventricle specimen during surgical procedure
- **Quantity of CSF for diagnosis**: Minimum 1 mL (3 mL preferred)

- Delivered to the lab immediately after collection. In case if delayed – refrigerate at 4C, as the cells tend to degenerate rapidly (**DO NOT FREEZE**)
- If delay of >48 hours – add 50% ethanol and RPMI (1:1)

Figure: Diff-Quik stain. Monocyte with kidney bean shaped nucleus in normal CSF specimen.

Figure: Diff-Quik stain. Lymphocyte with round nucleus and scant cytoplasm in normal CSF specimen.

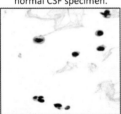

Figure: PAP stain. Numerous polymorphous lymphocytes and few neutrophils from contaminating peripheral blood- favor reactive process.

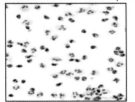

Figure: PAP stain. Abundant neutrophils in the CSF specimen are abnormal.

NORMAL COMPONENTS

- Lymphocytes
- Monocytes
- Brain tissue fragments and components: present in lateral ventricle specimen
- Germinal matrix cells - present in premature neonatal CSF specimen; association with subependymal and intraventricular hemorrhage

Chondrocytes and bone marrow elements can be seen in LP specimen (procedural)

INFLAMMATORY CELLS

- Neutrophils and eosinophils are associated with blood contamination associated with red blood cells on air dried preparations (alcohol fixation - lysis red blood cells).

ABNORMAL INFLAMMATORY CELLS

- **Macrophages in CSF**
  - ➤ Meningitis
  - ➤ Hemorrhage (eg. intraventricular, subarachnoid)
  - ➤ Cerebral infarction
  - ➤ Multiple sclerosis
  - ➤ Different malignancies
- **Plasma cells in CSF**
  - ➤ Viral meningitis (HIV, enterovirus)
  - ➤ Multiple sclerosis
  - ➤ Lyme disease
  - ➤ Tuberculous meningitis
  - ➤ Syphilis
  - ➤ Cysticercosis
  - ➤ Plasma cell neoplasms
- **Eosinophils in CSF**
  - ➤ Parasites
  - ➤ Fungal infections eg. Coccidioides immitis
  - ➤ Ventriculoperitoneal shunts
  - ➤ Malignancies: Hodgkin and non-Hodgkin lymphoma and leukemia
  - ➤ Systemic or intra-thecal medications
- **Neutrophils in CSF**
  - ➤ Traumatic tap leading to peripheral blood contamination
  - ➤ Acute Bacterial meningitis
  - ➤ Viral meningitis (early stage)
  - ➤ CMV radiculopathy
  - ➤ Toxoplasma meningoencephalitis
  - ➤ IVIg therapy

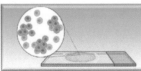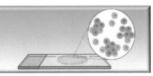

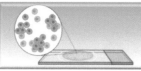

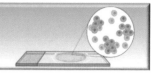

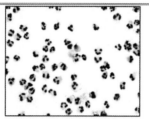

Figure: Diff-Quik stain. Acute inflammation, abundant neutrophils.

NON-NEOPLASTIC: MENINGITIS

BACTERIAL

- Predominantly neutrophils, bacteria +/-
- Differential diagnoses of Acute bacterial meningitis
  - ➤ Traumatic tap leading to peripheral blood contamination
  - ➤ Toxoplasma infection
  - ➤ Cytomegalovirus (CMV) radiculopathy
  - ➤ IVIg therapy
  - ➤ Early aseptic meningitis

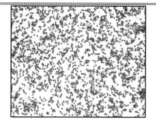

Figure: Diff-Quik stain. Abundant small mature lymphocytes.

ASEPTIC

- Predominantly lymphocytes (small mature) and monocytes. Neutrophils in early phase.
- Mollaret meningitis: idiopathic recurrent aseptic meningitis associated with HSV1 and HSV2 in some cases. "Mollaret cells" – monocytes with deep nuclear clefts – non-specific, can be seen in sarcoidosis and Behcet disease.
- "Cloverleaf (Floret) cells": Human Immunodeficiency Virus-1 (HIV-1) – non-specific finding
- Differential diagnosis of aseptic meningitis
  - ➤ Lymphoma (primary CNS or secondary)
  - ➤ Leukemia

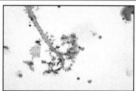

Figure: PAP stain. Cryptococcus.

CRYPTOCOCCAL

- Caused by Cryptococcus neoformans – Yeasts with mucopolysaccharide capsule and thin-neck teardrop budding
- Can be associated with "Refractile cover slipping artifact" due to indented surface and air trapping under the coverslip

TOXOPLASMA MENINGOENCEPHALITIS

- Protozoan – CSF shows neutrophils, monocytes and tachyzoites (crescent-shaped)

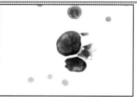

Figure: Diff-Quik stain. Malignant lymphoid cells of large B-cell lymphoma.

NEOPLASTIC

PRIMARY CNS TUMORS

PRIMARY CNS LYMPHOMA

- Diffuse large B-cell lymphoma: most common (>90%). Epstein-Barr virus (EBV) in immunocompromised only. Cranial nerve palsies commonly associated

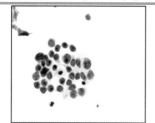

Figure: PAP stain. Medulloblastoma-cluster of cells with high N:C ratio, dense chromatin and scant cytoplasm.

MEDULLOBLASTOMA

- Small, medium-sized cells with scant cytoplasm, prominent nucleoli and nuclear molding Age: predominantly in children; Location: adjacent to 4th ventricle with associated meningeal involvement +/-
- Differential diagnoses of Medulloblastoma:
  - ➤ Germinal matrix (in premature neonates associated with subependymal/ intraventricular hemorrhage)
  - ➤ Neuroblastoma (SRBCT)
  - ➤ Retinoblastoma (SRBCT)
  - ➤ Pineoblastoma
  - ➤ Anaplastic ependymoma
  - ➤ Small-cell carcinoma
  - ➤ Smudged lymphocytes due to preservation artifact

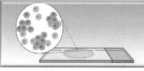

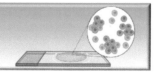

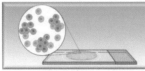

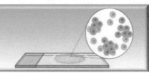

Figures: PAP stain and GFAP IHC. Glioblastoma: Cells with large nuclei, prominent nucleoli and granular, wispy cytoplasm. GFAP immunostain is positive.

ASTROCYTOMAS AND OLIGODENDROGLIAL TUMORS

- Pilocytic astrocytoma (WHO Grade I) – isolated cells/ clusters: isolated cells with long, hair-like processes; clustered epithelioid cells with fine chromatin and cobweb-like cytoplasm

- Diffuse astrocytoma, IDH-mutant (WHO Grade II)
- Anaplastic astrocytoma, IDH-mutant (WHO Grade III)
- Glioblastoma (WHO Grade IV)

Isolated cells/ small clusters hyperchromatic, highly pleomorphic nuclei, coarse chromatin, irregular nuclear contour and prominent nucleoli

ATYPICAL TERATOID/ RHABDOID TUMOR

- Rhabdoid cells with large, round, eccentric nucleus, prominent nucleoli, homogenous cytoplasm with large, dense, inclusion-like structure pushing nucleus to the side. Positive immunostaining with EMA, vimentin, SMA, GFAP, NF protein and keratin. Loss of SMARCB1 (INI1) – highly sensitive and specific for AT/RT.

CHOROID PLEXUS TUMORS

- Predominantly (80%) in children
- Choroid plexus papilloma (WHO Grade I) large, three-dimensional clusters of uniform cuboidal cells with round oval nucleus
- Atypical choroid plexus papilloma (WHO Grade II)
- Choroid plexus carcinoma (WHO Grade III): 80% arise in infants and children. Isolated cells or clusters, pleomorphic nuclei, prominent nucleoli, mimics adenocarcinoma
- Differential diagnosis: In adults, occult lung adenocarcinoma

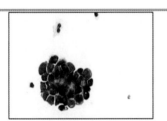

Figure: PAP stain. Pineoblastoma: Cluster of tumor cells with high N:C ratio and scant cytoplasm.

PINEAL GLAND TUMORS

- Affect children more than adults
- Pineocytoma (WHO Grade I): localized neoplasms, do not metastasize
- Pineal parenchymal tumor of intermediate differentiation (WHO Grade II or III): Leptomeningeal dissemination can be seen in minority
- Pineoblastoma (WHO Grade IV): commonly spread via CSF pathways. Indistinguishable from Medulloblastoma

PAP stains. Cluster of ependymal cells with eccentric nuclei (left). Single ependymal cell showing binucleation (right).

EPENDYMOMA

- Monomorphic cells (isolated cells/ small clusters) forming perivascular pseudorosettes: cells with round, eccentric nuclei.
- Myxopapillary ependymoma: WHO grade I; young adults, terminal end of the spinal cord
- Anaplastic ependymoma: poorly differentiated, mimic medulloblastoma
- Tanycytic ependymomas: bipolar cells with long, hair-like glial processes

GERM CELL TUMORS

- Midline, pineal and suprasellar areas. Most common – germinoma
- Common in children/ young adults. Males > females
- Isolated cells with large, round nucleus, prominent nucleoli and moderate amount of cytoplasm
- Elevated serum tumor markers like Alpha fetoprotein (AFP), Beta-human chorionic gonadotropin (B-HCG), placental alkaline phosphatase (PLAP
- IHC – OCT 3/4

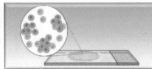

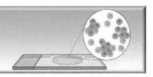

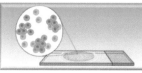

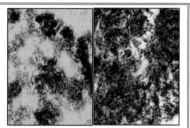

Figure: PAP stain and Diff-Quik stain. Meningioma in CSF (left) and meningotheliomatous type (right). Courtesy Terrance Lynn, MD

OTHERS:

- Meningiomas – rarely spread via CSF, mostly benign
- Pituitary tumors – mostly adenomas, rarely carcinomas. Pituitary carcinomas show cells in clusters and mimic adenocarcinoma

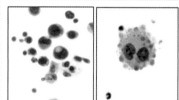

Figure: PAP stain. CSF: Metastatic lung adenocarcinoma (left).CSF: Metastatic Melanoma (right).

METASTATIC

- Solid tumors: Lung, Breast, Stomach
- Hematologic: Lymphomas and Leukemias
- Others: Melanoma

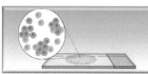
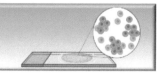

Hayk MELKUMYAN

Chapter 7 : Gastrointestinal Cytology

Laila Nomani, MD

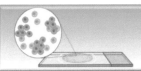
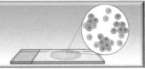

Hayk MELKUMYAN

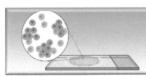
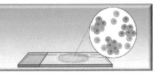

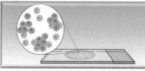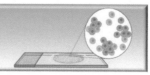
INTRODUCTION

TYPES OF SPECIMENS

- Brushings
  - ➢ Used for areas that are difficult to biopsy
  - ➢ Good sensitivity for detecting infectious organisms
- Washings
  - ➢ Can sample large areas
  - ➢ Can be done at the time of endoscopy
  - ➢ Lower incidence of side effects like bleeding as compared to biopsy

- Endoscopic Ultrasound-Guided Fine Needle Aspiration
  - ➢ Minimally invasive and low risk of complications
  - ➢ Uses ultrasound probes to visualize gastrointestinal wall and adjacent structures
  - ➢ Used for sampling lymph nodes, pancreatic lesions and lesions of the gastrointestinal tract
  - ➢ On site adequacy and diagnosis helps guide management, avoiding another subsequent procedure

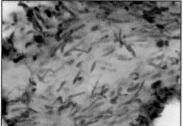

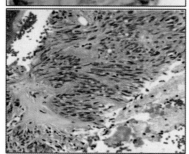

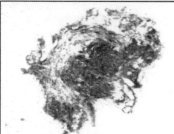

Figures: Diff-Quik, PAP, H&E and IHC stains. Spindle cells with elongated nuclei. Cell block showing similar cells staining positive for DOG-1. @CytoAtlas

SPINDLE CELL NEOPLASMS OF GASTROINTESTINAL TRACT

- Sampled by EUS FNA
- Can arise from the lamina propria, muscularis mucosae, submucosa or muscularis propria
- A panel of IHC with DOG-1, SMA, Desmin, S100 and CD117 is helpful in differentiating spindle cell neoplasms

GASTROINTESTINAL STROMAL TUMOR (GIST)

ETIOLOGY

- KIT/PDGFR alpha mutations
- SDH (succinate dehydrogenase) deficient GIST found only in stomach, with multinodular/plexiform growth pattern, propensity for lymph node and distant metastasis
- Arise from the interstitial cells of Cajal
- Most common site: Stomach followed by small intestine and extraintestinal
- EUS FNA used for sampling, lesions are hypoechoic
- Treatment: Imatinib and Sunitinib

CYTOMORPHOLOGY

- Variably cellular smears
- Fascicles of long bland appearing spindle cells with elongated nuclei
- Rare nuclear pleomorphism
- Epithelioid GIST: Epithelioid cells arranged in nests or sheets, may have cytoplasmic vacuoles, nuclei are round or oval
- Mitoses, necrosis and cellular pleomorphism indicate worse prognosis
- Cell block used for immunostains
  - ➢ IHC Positive: DOG-1, CD117, CD34
  - ➢ IHC Negative: S100, SMA (maybe focal rarely)

DIFFERENTIAL DIAGNOSIS

- Leiomyoma
  - ➢ Bland spindle cells
  - ➢ IHC Positive: SMA, Desmin, H-caldesmon
  - ➢ IHC Negative: DOG-1, S-100 and CD117
- Schwannoma
  - ➢ Tight clusters of spindle cells with fibrillary cytoplasm
  - ➢ Clean background, no necrosis
  - ➢ IHC Positive: S100, SOX-10
  - ➢ IHC negative: DOG-1, CD117, SMA, desmin

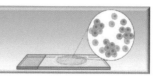

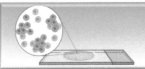
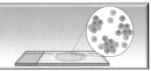

MALIGNANT LESIONS OF THE GASTROINTESTINAL TRACT

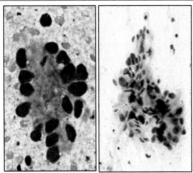

Figure: Diff-Quik and PAP stain. Cluster of malignant adenocarcinoma cells making a gland. Background shows necrosis. @CytoAtlas

ESOPHAGEAL ADENOCARCINOMA
ETIOLOGY
- Males> females, increased risk in patients with h/o Barretts esophagus, obesity, alcohol, smoking and reflux disease

CYTOMORPHOLOGY
- Cellular aspirate with 3-D crowded clusters of malignant cells in a necrotic background
- High N:C ratio, irregular nuclear membranes, coarse chromatin, hyperchromatic and pleomorphic
- Single malignant cells with intracytoplasmic mucin can be seen
- Cell block for immunostains. CK7, CDX-2 are positive but non-specific.

DIFFERENTIAL DIAGNOSIS
- Metastatic adenocarcinoma
- Reactive changes
- Poorly differentiated squamous cell carcinoma

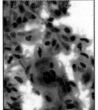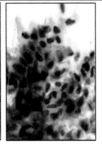

Figures: Diff-Quik stain and PAP stain. Clusters of malignant squamous cells. @CytoAtlas

ESOPHAGEAL SQUAMOUS CELL CARCINOMA
CYTOMORPHOLOGY
- Cellular smears with keratinized squamous cells and non-keratinizing cells
- Flatter sheets of malignant cells
- High N:C ratio, irregular nuclear contours, coarse chromatin, variably prominent nucleoli and dense well-defined cytoplasm (robin's egg blue)
- Tadpole cells, orangeophilic cytoplasm and keratin pearls
- Background is dirty with necrosis

DIFFERENTIAL DIAGNOSIS
- Reactive changes associated with ulcer, radiation esophagitis
- Poorly differentiated adenocarcinoma and sarcomatoid carcinoma

Figure: PAP stain. Gastric adenocarcinoma: Signet ring cells. Left: @CytoAtlas.
Right: Courtesy Abby Salama, MD

GASTRIC ADENOCARCINOMA
ETIOLOGY
- Intestinal and diffuse type
- Associated with *H. pylori* infection, smoked food, smoking

CYTOMORPHOLOGY
- Cellular smears with crowded, overlapping 3D groups of malignant cells
- Single malignant cells with signet ring morphology, abundant foamy cytoplasm
- Targetoid mucin
- Background may show necrosis

DIFFERENTIAL DIAGNOSIS
- Reactive changes associated with ulcer
- Gastric lymphoma

Figure1: Diff-Quik and PAP stain. Ampullary adenoma with columnar cells (left). Ampullary adenocarcinoma with clusters of malignant cells (right).

AMPULLARY CARCINOMA:
- Malignant tumor arising at the ampulla of Vater, causes obstructive jaundice
- Primary ampullary cancers: Adenocarcinoma with intestinal origin
- Ampullary adenomas →ampullary carcinoma
- Periampullary carcinomas include carcinomas arising from pancreatobiliary tract and have a worse prognosis
- EUS and ERCP used for diagnosis

CYTOMORPHOLOGY
- Cellular smears, crowded 3D groups of malignant cells, single malignant cells
- Marked pleomorphism, nuclear atypia, hyperchromasia, prominent nucleoli

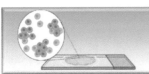
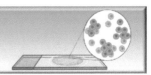

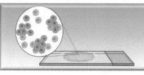
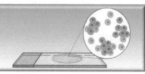
	• Background necrosis
	• Adenoma with high grade dysplasia may be seen in the background
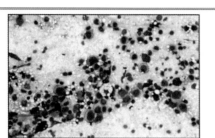 Figure: Diff-Quik stain. Monomorphic large cells.	**GASTRIC LYMPHOMA** ETIOLOGY • *H. pylori* infection, MALT lymphoma/ MALToma, DLBCL CYTOMORPHOLOGY: • MALT lymphoma: polymorphous population of lymphocytes, admixed plasma cells; DLBCL: Monomorphic large cells, scant cytoplasm, vesicular nuclei, variably prominent nucleoli. Necrosis may be seen in the background ANCILLARY TESTS: • Flow cytometry: Positive: CD20, CD43, CD19, Negative: CD5, CD10 • Molecular: *API1-MALT1* (11;18) resistance to *H. pylori* therapy
ANAL CANCER AND SAMPLING: • Predominantly squamous cell carcinoma • HPV related in >90%; HPV 16 and 18 • High-risk groups: men who have sex with men (MSM), HIV positive status, immunocompromised, previous history of lower genital tract neoplasia	• Anal cytology and digital anorectal examination used for screening, recommended annually in HIV positive patients • Anal canal comprises colorectal zone, anal transformation zone and squamous zone • Sample entire anal canal using Dacron swab and include keratinized and nonkeratinized squamous epithelium and transformation zone. • Both conventional and liquid-based cytology is used
CLASSIFICATION • The Bethesda system and LAST guidelines are used for reporting anal cytology. • They are similar to the ones used for gynecologic cytology	
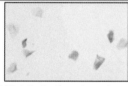 Figure: PAP stain. Inadequate anal pap showing anucleate squamous cells.	**ADEQUACY:** • No definite lower limits established. • 2000-3000 nucleated squamous cells for conventional smears • 1-2 nucleated squamous cells per hpf for ThinPrep® and 3-6/ hpf for SurePath™. • Unsatisfactory: low cellularity, obscuring inflammation and anucleate squames. • Presence of transformation zone: Quality metric. • Atypical cells→ Adequate
 Figure: PAP stain. Mature squamous cells from anal pap without dysplasia.	**NEGATIVE FOR INTRAEPITHELIAL LESION OR MALIGNANCY** • Tight perinuclear halos and small nucleoli: reactive • Parakeratosis and keratotic changes common • Organisms: Pin worm, amoebic cysts, candida, HSV
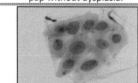 Figure: PAP stain. Exhibiting nuclear enlargement	**ASCUS AND ASC-H** • Similar to gynecologic cytology • Nuclear hyperchromasia and enlargement • ASC-H shows high nuclear to cytoplasmic ratio, nuclear irregularity and hyperchromasia
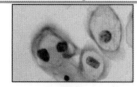	**LSIL** • Nuclei 2.5- 3 times the nucleus of an intermediate squamous cell • Nuclear membrane irregularity and hyperchromasia • Perinuclear clearing / halos with peripheral cytoplasmic condensation • Reactive changes can also have perinuclear halos without the nuclear changes of LSIL

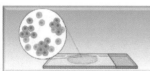

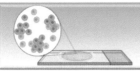
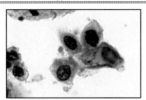
Figure: PAP stain. Atypical squamous cells with halo, nuclear enlargement, irregularity and hyperchromasia.

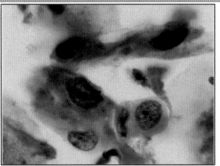
Figure: PAP stain. HSIL cells with high nuclear to cytoplasmic ratio, hyperchromasia and coarse chromatin.

HSIL
- Cellular smears with small groups of dysplastic cells or singly scattered cells
- High nuclear to cytoplasmic ratio, nuclear membrane irregularity, hyperchromasia and coarse chromatin
- Cells can be small or large
- Keratinizing cells also seen

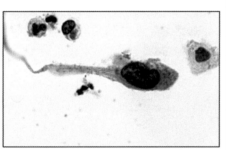
Figure: PAP stain. Keratinizing HSIL with high nuclear to cytoplasmic ratio and dark irregular nuclei.

SQUAMOUS CELL CARCINOMA
- Rare
- HPV mediated, mostly HPV 16 subtype
- Clinical presentation is of pain, bleeding or a perianal mass

CYTOMORPHOLOGY:
- Cellular smears with dirty background
- Highly atypical, pleomorphic, bizarre cells
- Tadpole cells
- Clinging diatheses is characteristic

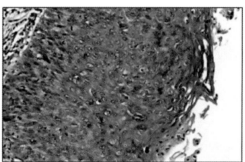
Figure: H&E. CIN 3 biopsy with full thickness dysplasia.

Figure: PAP stain. HSIL cell with tadpole features suspicious for invasive squamous cell carcinoma.

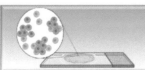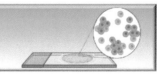

Chapter 8: Liver Cytology

Binny Khandakar, MD

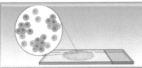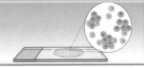

CHAPTER 8: OUTLINE

Introduction

Liver cytology

Normal cytology liver

Infections

    Hepatic Abscess

    Echinococcal Cyst (Hydatid Cyst)

    Other Infections

Benign lesions

    Hemangioma

    Cirrhosis

    Focal Nodular Hyperplasia

    Hepatic Adenoma

    Bile Duct Hamartoma and Adenoma

Malignant Lesions

    Hepatocellular Carcinoma

    Fibrolamellar Variant of Hepatocellular Carcinoma

    Cholangiocarcinoma

    Hepatoblastoma

    Angiosarcoma

    Metastatic Tumors

    Lymphoma

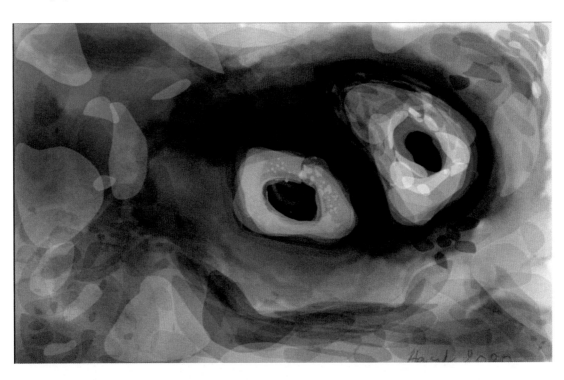

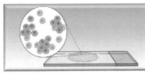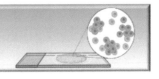

ACE THE BOARDS: CYTOPATHOLOGY ~ 100 ~

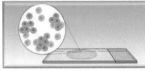
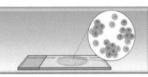
INRODUCTION:

- Cytology is valuable method for initial and rapid diagnosis
- Ultrasound guided procedure
- Complications: pain, bleeding, infections
- Contraindications: coagulopathy, massive ascites, local skin infection

- Diagnostic accuracy:
  - ➢ Liver lesions:
    - Sensitivity: 80%
    - Specificity: about >90%
  - ➢ Biliary tree:
    - Sensitivity: >90%
    - Specificity: about 50

LIVER CYTOLOGY

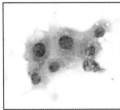
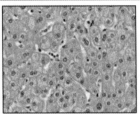

Figure: PAP stain and H&E stain. Benign hepatocytes: aspirate showing benign hepatocytes, large polygonal cells with abundant finely granular cytoplasm. PAP Courtesy Syed Z. Ali, MD (Twitter: @sza_jhcyto). H&E cell block ©CytoAtlas

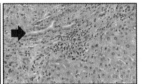

Figure: PAP stain and H&E stain. Benign biliary epithelium showing bland cuboidal epithelial cells (left) ©CytoAtlas. Cell block aspirate with bile duct epithelium in the portal tract (right with arrow).

NORMAL CYTOLOGY OF LIVER

CYTOMORPHOLOGY

Hepatocytes:
- Isolated cells/trabeculae
- Large polygonal cells with central round to oval nuclei, prominent nucleoli, abundant granular cytoplasm and
- occasional binucleation
- Intranuclear cytoplasmic inclusion/pseudoinclusions
- Intracytoplasmic pigments: bile/lipofuscin/hemosiderin

Bile duct epithelium
- Flat monolayer sheets with maintained polarity
- Epithelial cells have a centrally located nucleus, dense cytoplasm and well-defined cell borders
- Chromatin is finely granular and pale
- Nucleoli are inconspicuous
- Bile may be seen in the background as amorphous material that sometimes appears yellow

OTHER HIGH YIELD POINTS
- Biliary duct epithelium is absent in hepatic adenoma and hepatocellular carcinoma
- Bile duct epithelium can be seen in increased in bile duct adenoma/hamartoma, cirrhosis, and focal nodular hyperplasia

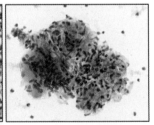

Figure: H&E stain and PAP stain. Hepatic amebic abscess. H&E, left, Courtesy Nishat Afro, MD (Twitter: @DrNishatAfroz2). PAP stain, right, Granulomatous reaction with epithelioid cells. Courtesy Ed Euthman, MD (Twitter: @euthman)

INFECTIONS
HEPATIC ABSCESS
CYTOMORPHOLOGY
- Neutrophils/polymorphonuclear leukocytes
- Macrophages
- Minimal number of hepatocytes on aspirate

OTHER HIGH YIELD POINTS
- Organisms (bacteria/fungus/parasite/virus) may not be apparent
- GMS/AFB/FITE/PAS/Gram/immunocytochemistry can be done for CMV, HSV on cell block
- Minimal inflammation with E. histolytica infection
- Parasitic infection may be rich in Charcot-Leyden crystals
- Granulomas can be seen with fungal or mycobacterial infection

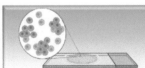
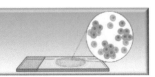

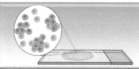
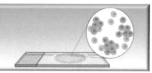
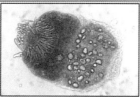
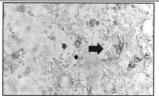

Figure: Hydatid Cyst scloex and hooklets. Courtesy Reenal Patel, MD (Twitter: @reenal_). Right, Diff-Quik stain. Hooklets. Courtesy B. Gizem Özamrak, MD (Twitter: @bgizem_oz)

ECHINOCOCCAL CYST (HYDATID CYST)

CYTOMORPHOLOGY
- Hooklets/protoscolices
- Acellular laminated membrane can be present

HISTOLOGIC FEATURES
- Laminated membrane
- Hooklets
  - ➤ Birefringent
  - ➤ Partially acid-fast on Ziehl-Neelsen stain
  - ➤ Stain with GMS

OTHER HIGH YIELD POINTS
- Right lobe of liver is most common site of involvement
- E. granulosus/E. multilocularis
- Mode of transmission: fecal-oral route

BENIGN LESIONS

HEMANGIOMA

CYTOMORPHOLOGY
- Cellularity: Paucicellular with background hemorrhagic
- Architecture: Small cluster/single cells
- Tumor cell are bland oval- to spindle-shaped cells
- Nucleus with fine vesicular chromatin and occasional nuclear grooves
- Absence of atypia

HISTOLOGIC FEATURES
- Well demarcated lesion from the surrounding liver
- Thin well-formed thin-walled dilated vascular channels lined by bland endothelial cells without nuclear cytologic atypia

OTHER HIGH YIELD POINTS
- Up to 20% in autopsy series
- More common in women
- Can rarely rupture
- Can cause consumptive coagulopathy

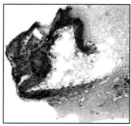
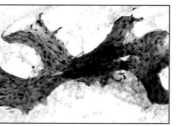

Figure: Diff-Quik stain and PAP stain. Hemangioma smears showing capillaries and red blood cells. Courtesy Syed Z. Ali, MD, (Twitter: @sza_jhcyto)

Figure: H&E stain. Hemangioma of liver with dilated vascular channels containing red blood cells.

CIRRHOSIS

CYTOMORPHOLOGY
- Mixture of normal benign hepatocytes with hepatocytes showing marked atypia

HISTOLOGIC FEATURES
- Regenerative hyperplasia with bridging fibrosis

Figure: PAP stain. Cirrhosis: Liver with hepatocyes showing atypia. Courtesy Terrance Lynn, MD

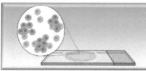
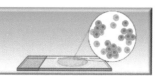

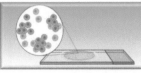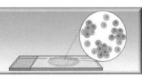

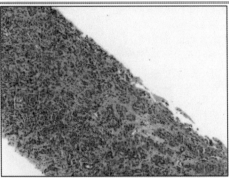
Figure: H&E stain. Focal nodular hyperplasia histology.

FOCAL NODULAR HYPERPLASIA
CYTOMORPHOLOGY
- Two cell thick trabeculae, bile ductular epithelium
- Occasional fibrous stromal fragment
- Benign and bland looking hepatocytes
HISTOLOGIC FEATURES
- Central stellate scar
- Nodules, separated by fibrous septa
- Thick-walled arteries at periphery
OTHER HIGH YIELD POINTS
- Glutamine synthetase: map-like pattern

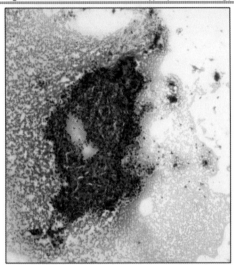
Figure: Diff-Quik stain. Hepatic adenoma. ©CytoAtlas

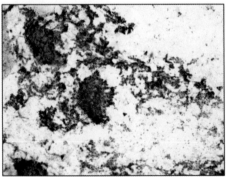
Figure: PAP stain. Hepatic adenoma: trabeculae of benign looking hepatocytes. ©CytoAtlas

HEPATIC ADENOMA
- Architecture:
  - Two cell thick trabeculae
  - No/minimal endothelial wrapping of hepatocytic cords
  - Rare traversing capillaries
- Normal-looking benign hepatocytes with low/normal nuclear: cytoplasmic (n/c) ratio
- Minimal/no cytologic atypia
- Absence of macronucleoli
- Occasional presence of intracytoplasmic glycogen/fat/bile/Mallory-Denk bodies
- Lack of biliary tract epithelium
HISTOLOGIC FEATURES
- Cords of benign hepatocytes with low n/c ratio
- Unpaired arteries with absence of portal structures and bile ducts
- Fat/glycogen in the cytoplasm
- Noncirrhotic liver in background
- Intact reticulin pattern
OTHER HIGH YIELD POINTS
Subtypes of Hepatic Adenoma
- HNF1A inactivated:
  - Associated with MODY3
  - Fat rich
  - Low association with HCC
- Inflammatory:
  - Associated with mutation of IL6ST (up to 60%) STAT3 or GNAS
  - Positive with serum amyloid A & CRP
- β-catenin activated
  - Activation of β-catenin with diffuse nuclear β-catenin staining and Glutamine synthetase staining
  - High risk for HCC

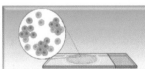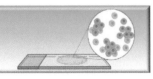

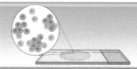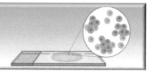

BILE DUCT HAMARTOMA AND ADENOMA

CYTOMORPHOLOGY

- Hypocellular smears
- Benign uniform biliary ductal cells in small tubules or cohesive sheets
- Background benign hepatocytes

HISTOLOGIC FEATURES

- Bile duct hamartoma, also known as Von Meyenberg complex, typically shows haphazardly arranged bile ductules in a fibrous stroma.
- Bile duct adenoma is commonly a subcapsular nodule of <1cm, morphologically similar to bile duct hamartoma

MALIGNANT LESIONS

HEPATOCELLULAR CARCINOMA (HCC)

CYTOMORPHOLOGY

- Cellular aspirate
- Architecture: single cells/acini
- Transgressing vessels with endothelial wrapping
- Well differentiated HCC morphologically resemble hepatocytes with larger nuclei with macronucleoli:
  - ➤ Polygonal tumor cells with increased nuclear cytoplasmic ratio
  - ➤ Intracytoplasmic bile production/hyaline inclusions/Mallory-Denk bodies/fat/clear cell features
  - ➤ Intranuclear cytoplasmic inclusion/pseudo-inclusions
- Poorly Differentiated HCC
  - ➤ Highly cellular smear with mainly single isolated tumor
  - ➤ Tumor cells with marked anisonucleiosis, tumor giant cells/spindle cells with frequent mitotic figures
- Immunocytochemistry
  - ➤ Hepatocytic marker:
    - HepPar 1
    - TTF-1 (cytoplasmic staining, some clones)
    - Glypican 3
    - Arginase-1
    - CAM5.2
  - ➤ Canalicular staining:
    - Polyclonal CEA
    - CD10
  - ➤ Endothelial wrapping:
    - CD34

OTHER HIGH YIELD POINTS

- More common in men
- Causative agents: Hepatitis virus (HBV, HCV)/aflatoxin/ alcohol/ hemochromatosis, tyrosinemia, smoking, anabolic steroid
- FNA diagnostic sensitivity and specificity: 87-100% and 90-94%, respectively

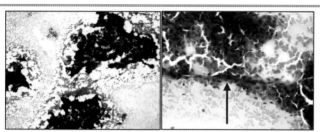

Figure: Diff-Quik. Hepatocellular carcinoma cellular smear showing clusters of cohesive and trabeculae of hepatocyte with traversing capillaries and endothelial wrapping.©CytoAtlas (left) and Courtesy Irem Onur, MD (Twitter: @iremonur8) (right)

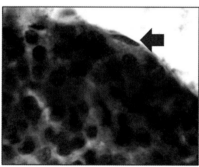

Figure: PAP stain. Hepatocellular carcinoma: smear exhibiting hepatocytes with expanded plates with endothelial wrapping (arrow).

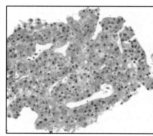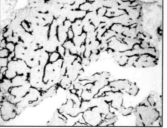

Figure: H&E and IHC (CD34). Hepatocellular carcinoma: cell block showing thickened hepatocytic plates with endothelial wrapping. CD34 highlights the endothelial wrapping.

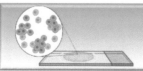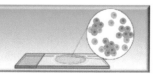

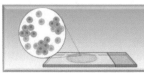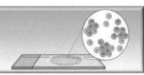
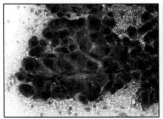
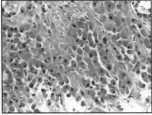

Figure: Diff-Quik and H&E. Fibrolamellar variant of hepatocellular

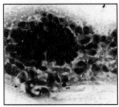

carcinoma. Courtesy Syed Z. Ali, MD, (Twitter: @sza_jhcyto) (above).
Courtesy: Swikrity U Baskota, MD

FIBROLAMELLAR VARIANT OF HCC
CYTOMORPHOLOGY
- Architecture: loose clusters/isolated single cells
- Fibrous bands between tumor cells can be seen
- Tumor cell are large containing abundant cytoplasm
- Gigantic nucleus with prominent nucleolus
- Cytoplasmic hyaline globules can be seen

HISTOLOGIC FEATURES
- Sheets and nests of large polygonal neoplastic cells with vesicular chromatin and prominent nucleoli
- Ample granular oncocytic cytoplasm

OTHER HIGH YIELD POINTS
- Young age (20-30s) women
- DNAJB1-PRKACA fusion
- Better prognosis than the classic HCC

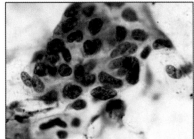

Figure: PAP stain. Cholangiocarcinoma. ©CytoAtlas

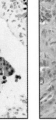
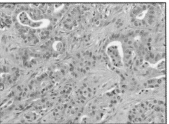

Figure: H&E stains. Intrahepatic cholangiocarcinoma: smear showing small malignant glands (left). Section showing infiltrating glands with a dense desmoplastic stromal reaction (right).

CHOLANGIOCARCINOMA
CYTOMORPHOLOGY
- Architecture: isolated tumor cells/crowded sheet/clusters/glands/acini
  - Tumor cell features:
  - marked anisonucleosis
  - Intracytoplasmic mucin vacuoles
- Immunocytochemistry
  - Diffuse cytoplasmic staining for polyclonal CEA
  - CK7, CK17, and CK19 positivity

HISTOLOGIC FEATURES
- Well to moderately differentiated adenocarcinoma forming gland, nests, cords, and papillae
- Characteristic desmoplastic stroma
- Usually, mucin producing
- Double positivity for CK19 and CK7

OTHER HIGH YIELD POINTS
- 2nd most common primary hepatic malignancy
- Risk factors: primary sclerosing cholangitis/hepatolithiasis/Clonorchis sinensis/nonbiliary cirrhosis
- Hilar cholangiocarcinoma known as Klatskin tumor
- Sensitivity of biliary brush cytology/FNA is 60% to 70%; proliferating ductules with more than 10 ductular clusters favor cholangiocarcinoma
- P53 overexpression with loss of SMAD4 by immunohistochemistry can be seen

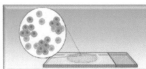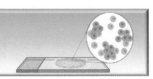

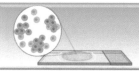
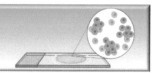
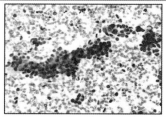
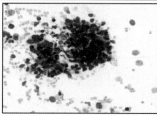

Figure: Diff-Quik stains. Hepatoblastoma. Courtesy Ami Patel, MD (Twitter:@cytologyrocks)

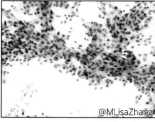
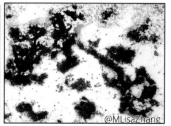

Figure: PAP stain and Diff-Quik Stain. Hepatoblastoma: Aspirate showing mixed epithelial and mesenchymal type hepatoblastoma. The epithelial component resembles immature hepatocytes (right) and the spindled component represent the mesenchymal component (left). Courtesy Lisa Mingjuan Zhang, MD, (Twitter: @MLisaZhang)

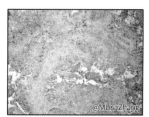

Figure: H&E stain. Hepatoblastoma. Courtesy Lisa Mingjuan Zhang, MD (Twitter: @MLisaZhang)

HEPATOBLASTOMA
CYTOMORPHOLOGY
- Aspirate may show a single pattern or a combination of different components:
- Epithelial component: fetal/embryonal/small undifferentiated
- Fetal cell type:
  - Polygonal or round to oval cell with central round to oval nuclei, inconspicuous nucleoli and voluminous clear to eosinophilic cytoplasm
- Embryonal cell type:
  - Primitive looking small cells, some with round to angulated nuclei with coarse nuclear chromatin, conspicuous to prominent nucleoli
- Small undifferentiated cell type:
  - Very primitive looking cells, resembling neuroblast/blastemal cells/small blue round cells
  - Very high nuclear: cytoplasmic ratio
  - Hyperchromatic nuclei with inconspicuous nucleoli
- Mesenchymal component:
  - Immature spindle cells
- Immunocytochemistry:
  - Nuclear β-catenin staining - epithelial and mesenchymal components and small undifferentiated cells
  - Glypican-3 and Hep-Par1 - fetal and embryonal epithelial cells
  - Loss of INI1/BAF47 – in rhabdoid phenotypes

OTHER HIGH YIELD POINTS
- Most common malignant liver tumor in the pediatric age group
- Most common patterns are the fetal (80-90%) or embryonal (30%).

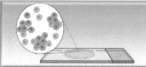
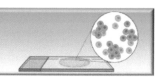

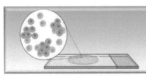
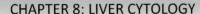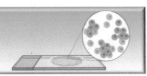
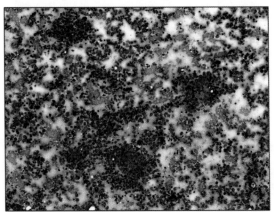

Figure: Diff-Quik. Angiosarcoma.

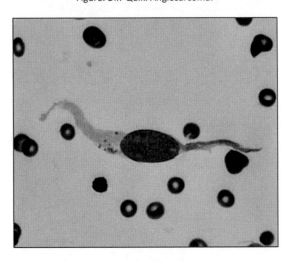

Figure: Diff-Quik stain. Angiosarcoma: aspirate showing single atypical tumor cell with cytoplastic elongation. Courtesy Samer Khader, MD (Twitter:@SamKhader)

ANGIOSARCOMA
CYTOMORPHOLOGY
- Cellularity: Variable, dependent on tumor differentiation; hypo in well differentiated to markedly cellular in poorly differentiated tumors
- Background may be hemorrhagic or with evidence of old hemorrhage (hemosiderin)
- Architecture: isolated cells/ cluster/ syncytia/ whorls/ papilla
- Tumor cells are range from bland to highly atypical with pleomorphism
  - Spindle to epithelioid, with cytoplasmic elongation
  - Signet ring cell-like/rhabdoid
  - Vesicular to hyperchromatic nuclei with marked anisonucleosis in poorly differentiated tumor
  - Delicate cytoplasm with vacuolation
  - Occasional intracytoplasmic lumina containing red blood cell
  - Bar/bullet-shaped nucleoli and chromatin stranding
- Immunocytochemistry
  - CD31, FLI-1, ERG
  - Epithelioid variants can express variable pancytokeratin & EMA
  - Variable: factor VIII, CD34, D2-40, c-MYC
HISTOLOGIC FEATURES
- Anastomosing vessels invading in to pre-existing vascular channels with progressive atrophy of hepatic parenchyma
- Malignant endothelial cells displaying epithelioid to spindled morphology, forming focal papillary structures
- Mitosis is variable
- Background hemorrhage and necrosis
OTHER HIGH YIELD POINTS
- Commonest primary hepatic sarcoma
- Strong male preponderance
- Risk factors: exposure to arsenic, vinyl chloride, Thorotrast, and steroids
- MYC amplifications in radiation associated angiosarcoma

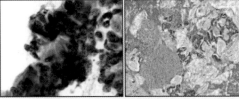

Figure: PAP stain (left) and H&E stain (right). Metastatic colonic adenocarcinoma: aspirate showing elongated cells (left). Cell block showig atypical glands (right).

METASTATIC TUMORS
METASTATIC COLON CARCINOMA
CYTOMORPHOLOGY
- Tall columnar cells with hyperchromatic elongated nuclei and background with 'dirty necrosis'
- Immunocytochemistry
- CK20, CDX2, and SATB2

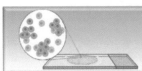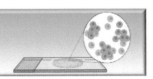

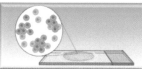
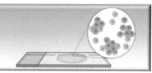

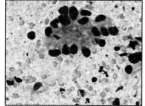
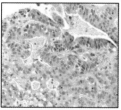

Figure: Diff-Quik stain and H&E stain. Gastroesophageal junction adenocarcinoma. ©CytoAtlas

METASTATIC GASTRO-ESOPHAGEAL CARCINOMA
CYTOMORPHOLOGY
- Adenocarcinoma with cuboidal to columnar cells
- Can resemble colorectal tumors
- Signet ring cell
- Immunocytochemistry
  - CK7, CK20, Variable CDX2 (weak)

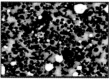

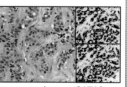

Figure: Diff-Quik stain, H&E stain and IHC. Mammary carcinoma. GATA3 (inset top right), ER (inset bottom right).

METASTATIC MAMMARY CARCINOMA
CYTOMORPHOLOGY
- Ductal/lobular with variable differentiation; occasional signet-ring cell-like morphology (lobular carcinoma)
- Immunocytochemistry
  - GATA-3, mammaglobin, GCDFP-15, SOX10+
  - Hormone receptors: ER/PR/Her2neu

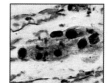

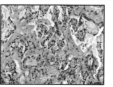

Figure: PAP stain and H&E stains. Pancreatic adenocarcinoma with malignant glands.

METASTATIC PANCREATOBILIARY CARCINOMA
CYTOMORPHOLOGY
  Cohesive clusters tumor cells frequently display intracytomasplmic mucin

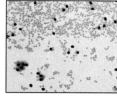
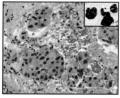

Figure: Diff-Quik and H&E. Neuroendocrine tumor: smear showing singly lying monomorphic plasmacytoid cells with granular cytoplasm. (inset, immunohistochemistry, Synaptophysin)

METASTATIC NEUROENDOCRINE TUMORS
CYTOMORPHOLOGY
- The tumor cells are usually plasmacytoid cells with typical 'salt-and-pepper' type chromatin and abundant finely granular cytoplasm, forming small acini/rosettes. Many dispersed isolated single cells can be seen in the background
- Immunocytochemistry
  - For all NET - NSE, Synaptophysin, Chromogranin, CD56, INSM-1
  - Islet-1/PAX-8 – pancreatic NET
  - Ki-67 varies with grade of NET

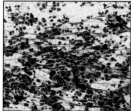
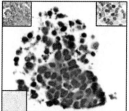

Figure: PAP stain, H&E stain and IHC stains. Insets: top left, Chromogranin; top right, MIB1; bottom left, RB): aspirate showing small cell carcinoma, with background crush artifact and nuclear molding.

METASTATIC SMALL CELL CARCINOMA
CYTOMORPHOLOGY
- Aspirate is usually cellular containing isolated and loosely cohesive clusters of tumor cells, with very hyperchromatic nuclei showing occasional nuclear molding
- Rarely, paranuclear blue bodies can be seen
- Immunocytochemistry
  - Variable expression of NSE, Synaptophysin, Chromogranin, CD56
  - Very high Ki-67, usually >90%

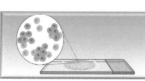
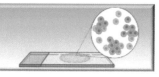

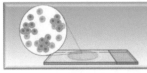

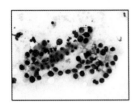
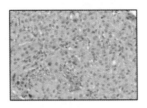

Figure: Diff-Quik stain and H&E stain. Urothelial carcinoma. Courtesy Susan Shyu, MD (Twitter: @susanshyu)

METASTATIC UROTHELIAL CARCINOMA

CYTOMORPHOLOGY

- Cellular aspirate composed of cohesive clusters or isolated tumor cells with moderate to marked nuclear cytologic atypia, nuclear enlargement, nuclear membrane irregularity and pleomorphism, with conspicuous nucleoli
- Many isolated tumor cells and cercariform cells can be seen

Immunocytochemistry
  ➤ GATA3, uroplakin, CK7, CK20

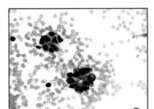
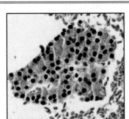

Figure: PAP stin and H&E stain. Clear cell renal cell caricnoma. Courtesy Syed Z. Ali, MD, (Twitter: @sza_jhcyto)

METASTATIC RENAL CELL CARCINOMA (CLEAR CELL TYPE)

CYTOMORPHOLOGY

- Cellular aspirates hemorrhagic background
- Branching blood vessels
- Ample finely vacuolated cytoplasm
- Eccentric nuclei with nucleoli (inconspicuous to prominent, depending on grade)
- Immunocytochemistry
  ➤ AE1/AE3, pax-2, PAX8, RCC, CD10
- Note:
  ➤ For other variant of renal cell carcinoma, refer to kidney chapter of this book

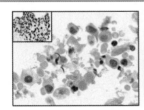
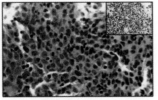

Figure: Diff-Quik stain (left) and H&E stain (right, cell block). Prostatic adenocarcinoma.

METASTATIC PROSTATIC ADENOCARCINOMA

CYTOMORPHOLOGY

- Cellular aspirate with cells forming small acini with prominent nucleoli
- Immunocytochemistry
  ➤ NKX3.1, PSA, PSAP
  ➤ Negative:CK7, CK20

METASTATIC SQUAMOUS CELL CARCINOMA

CYTOMORPHOLOGY

- Well to moderately differentiated tumors shows polygonal to ovoid tumor cell with abundant glassy cytoplasmic, stains Robin blue on Romanowsky-type stain. Nuclei are dark, small pyknotic
- Poorly differentiated carcinomas often resemble other poorly differentiated carcinomas, with limited hint of squamous differentiation
- Immunocytochemistry
  ➤ P63, P40, CK5/6

Figure: H&E stains and IHC. Squamous cell carcinoma (inset left panel, P40, immunohistochemistry; inset, right panel, immunohistochemistry P63).

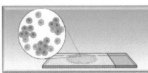
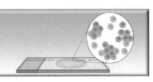

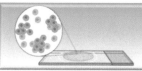

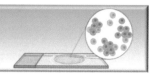

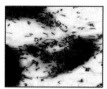 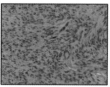

Figure: Diff-Quik and H&E stain. Gastrointestinal stromal tumor showing spindled tumor cells embedded in a myxoid stroma.

METASTATIC GIST

CYTOMORPHOLOGY

- Cohesive clusters of spindle cells with vesicular to hyperchromatic nuclei and minimal nuclear atypia
- Background myxoid
- Immunocytochemistry
  ➢ CD117, DOG1
- Note: Refer to soft tissue chapter for other sarcoma details

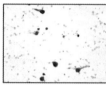 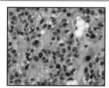 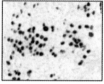

Figure: PAP stain, H&E stain and IHC Sox10. Melanoma. Courtesy Syed Z. Ali, MD (Twitter: @sza_jhcyto) (left). Courtesy Binny Khandakar, MD (middle and right)

METASTATIC MELANOMA

CYTOMORPHOLOGY

- Cellular aspirate with cohesive clusters and singly lying tumor cells with a range of tumor cell morphology –
- Plasmacytoid/spindle/polygonal/round/oval
- Prominent nucleoli
- Immunocytochemistry
  ➢ S-100, HMB-45, Mart-1, SOX-10

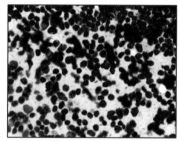

Figure: Diff-Quik stain. Lymphoma: monomorphic lymphoid cells.
©CytoAtlas

LYMPHOMA

CYTOMORPHOLOGY

- Cellular aspirate with mainly isolated atypical lymphoid cells.
- Lymphoid cell morphology and immunohistochemistry is lineage and lymphoma type dependent
- Note: refer to Lymph node chapter of this book for further reading

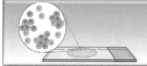

Chapter 9: Pancreas and Biliary Tract Cytology

Binny Khandakar, MD

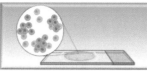

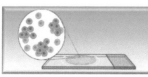
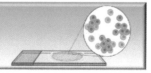

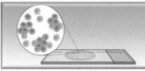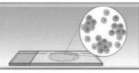
PAPANICOLAOU SOCIETY CYTOPATHOLOGY GUIDELINES FOR REPORTING PANCREATIC AND BILIARY CYTOLOGY

INTRODUCTION
- Proposed scheme of diagnosis with a six-tiered system

CATEGORIES
- I. Nondiagnostic
- II. Negative (for malignancy)
  - Pancreatitis: Acute and chronic
  - Autoimmune pancreatitis
  - Lymphoepithelial cyst
  - Splenule
  - Pseudocyst
- III. Atypical
- IV. Neoplastic
  - Benign
    - Serous cystadenoma
    - Lymphangioma
  - Other:
    - Mucinous cystic lesions (low- and high-grade dysplasia)
    - Well-differentiated neuroendocrine tumors
    - Solid-pseudopapillary neoplasm
- V. Suspicious (for malignancy)
- VI. Positive/malignant
  - Ductal carcinoma and its variants
  - Acinar cell carcinoma
  - Neuroendocrine carcinoma
  - Lymphoma
  - Metastatic malignancy

RISK OF MALIGNANCY:
- It is difficult to directly associate a definitive cancer risk to each category (see table 1)

Table 1: RISK OF MALIGNANCY *	
CATEGORY	**RISK OF MALIGNANCY (%)**
Non-diagnostic	21.4
Benign (negative)	12.6
Atypical	73.9
Neoplastic	14.2
Suspicious	81.8
Malignant	97.2

Laffan TA, Horton KM, Klein AP, et al. Prevalence of unsuspected pancreatic cysts on MDCT. AJR Am J Roentgenol. 2008;191: 802-807. *

DIAGNOSTIC CRITERIA

CATEGORY I. NONDIAGNOSTIC

DEFINITION
- No useful or diagnostic information regarding sampled lesion
- No cytologic atypia i.e., any cellular atypia precludes a non-diagnostic category

CRITERIA FOR DIAGNOSIS
- Preparation/obscuring artifact precluding sample evaluation
- Gastrointestinal contaminant only
- Acellular aspirates of pancreatic mass or pancreatic brushing
- Aspirate showing only benign acinar and/or ductal epithelium, derived from a clearly defined solid or cystic mass lesion on imaging
- Acellular aspirate of a cyst without mucinous etiology, evidenced by:
  - Absence of thick background mucin and/or oncotic cells
  - Absence of elevated CEA in the cyst fluid
  - Lack of KRAS or GNAS mutations

LIMITATION
  - No established criteria for adequacy

MANAGEMENT
- If imaging is highly suspicious for a high-risk lesion, surgery
- Unresectable lesion on imaging – Repeat FNA/tissue biopsy
- Nondiagnostic bile duct brushing – repeat brushing or aspiration

DIAGNOSTIC ACCURACY
  - EUS-FNA of pancreas
    - Sensitivity: approximately 80%
    - Specificity: 60-100%
  - Solid pancreatic mass
    - Diagnostic accuracy: >90

CATEGORY II. NEGATIVE (FOR MALIGNANCY):

DEFINITION
- Adequate cellular and/or extracellular material for evaluation
- Definite nonneoplastic lesion on imaging PLUS identification of the following:
  - Normal pancreatic parenchyma, in the clinical setting of vague fullness of the pancreas
  - No distinct pancreatic mass

CRITERIA FOR DIAGNOSIS
- Benign epithelium:
  - Pancreatic ductal type
  - Pancreatic acinar type
  - Biliary type
  - Gastric type
  - Duodenal type

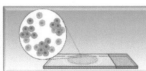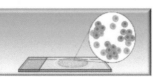

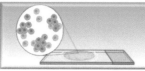
- Aspiration with diagnosis of:
  - Pancreatitis: acute/chronic/autoimmune
  - Cyst: Pseudocyst/lymphoepithelial cyst
  - Spleen: Splenule/Ectopic spleen/Accessory spleen

CATEGORY III. ATYPICAL
DEFINITION
- Aspirate composed of cells with architectural and nuclear and cytoplasmic features that are not consistent with normal or reactive cellular components of the pancreas or bile ducts, and falling short of classifying as a neoplasm or suspicious for a high-grade malignancy
- In addition, the microscopic findings do not explain the lesion identified on imaging.
CRITERIA FOR DIAGNOSIS
- Loss of architectural polarity
- Minimal to mild loss of honeycombing
- Basally located cells at the base
- Absent crowded 3-dimenional groups
- Near normal N/C ratio
- Mild nuclear membrane irregularities
- Mild parachromatin clearing
- Small nucleoli
- Minimal anisonucleosis (2:1)
- Clean or hemorrhagic background
DIFFERENTIAL DIAGNOSIS
- Atypical mucinous epithelium in a pancreatic aspirate in the context of
  - ❖ PanIN
  - ❖ Gastric contaminant
  - ❖ IPMN
- Biliary brush specimens with mucinous epithelium and other atypical findings
  - ❖ BilIN
  - ❖ IPMN-B
- Cellular features suggestive of a PanNET/SPN, however the sample is insufficient in quantity or quality for a definitive diagnosis
MANAGEMENT
- Follow-up evaluation
  - Repeat cytologic examination
  - Biopsy
- Additional imaging studies
- Continued clinical follow up
OTHER HIGH YIELD PEARLS
- In association with chronic pancreatitis and other conditions, can cause false positive diagnostic error

CATEGORY IV. NEOPLASTIC
DEFINITION
Neoplastic

- Cellular aspirate showing sufficient representative material to be diagnostic of a benign neoplasm, with or without clinical, imaging, or ancillary studies.
Differential Diagnosis:
- Serous cystadenoma
- Lymphangioma
- Schwannoma (rare in pancreas
- Cystic teratoma (rare in pancreas)
Neoplastic: Other
  - ❖ Neoplasm, which is either premalignant, or represents a low-grade malignant neoplasm.
Differential diagnosis:
- IPMN or MCN with LGD/MGD/HGD
- Pancreatic neuroendocrine tumor
- Solid pseudopapillary neoplasm
- Extra-adrenal paraganglioma
- Gastrointestinal stromal tumor

CATEGORY V. SUSPICIOUS
DEFINITION
- Specimen with some, but not all features of a specific malignant neoplasm are present, mainly for pancreatic adenocarcinoma
- Features lack either qualitatively or quantitatively for a definitive diagnosis
CRITERIA FOR DIAGNOSIS:
- Sufficient cellular or architectural atypia to be derived from a malignancy, such as:
  - Suspicious for ductal adenocarcinoma
- Significant loss of group and cell polarity, significant anisonucleosis, increased N-C ratio, nuclear membrane irregularities, moderate to markedly coarse chromatin
- Suspicious for acinar cell carcinoma
  - ❖ Cytological features of acinar cell carcinoma, cannot confirm with ancillary studies
- Cyst aspirates with a solid mural nodule and cytological features suspicious for invasive carcinoma
- Others:
  - Lymphoma
  - Metastases
OTHER HIGH YIELD POINTS
- Immunohistochemistry:
  - DPC4/SMAD4, S100P, mesothelin
  - FISH: 3, 7, 17, 9p21
  - miRNA
MANAGEMENT
- Cannot be used as a basis for surgical intervention/adjuvant therapy
- Correlation with other clinical and imaging findings needed
- Additional ancillary testing, external expert consultation, repeat sampling needed

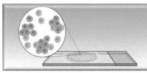
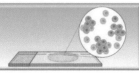
- Treatment-planning conference is essential and discussion of clinical/endoscopic, imaging, and cytologic findings

CATEGORY VI. POSITIVE:
DEFINITION
- Unequivocal feature of malignant cytology

DIFFERENTIAL DIAGNOSIS:
- Ductal adenocarcinoma and its variant
- Neuroendocrine carcinoma, small and large cell type
- Pancreatoblastoma
- Acinar cell carcinoma
- Lymphoma
- Metastases
- Sarcomas

PANCREAS CYTOLOGY

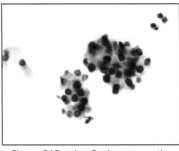
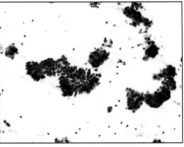

Figure: PAP stains. Benign pancreatic acinar: smear showing grape like clusters of benign pancreatic acinar cells containing abundant granular cytoplasm. ©CytoAtlas

NORMAL PANCREAS CYTOLOGY
BENIGN ACINAR CELLS
CYTOMORPHOLOGY
- Cohesive, grape-like clusters in isolation or with an attached fibrovascular stroma
- Stripped naked nuclei
- Isolated cells
- Individual cells have eccentrically placed round bland nucleus with evenly distributed fine granular chromatin with a small nucleolus
- Cells have abundant granular cytoplasm

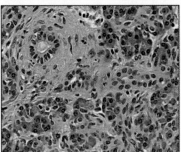

Figure: PAP stain and H&E stain. Benign pancreatic ductal cells Smear (left) showing benign ductal cells, cohesive sheets of small bland cells; typically described as 'honey-combing'. Histology section (right) showing normal pancreas. PAP stain ©CytoAtlas

BENIGN DUCTAL CELLS
CYTOMORPHOLOGY
- Cohesive flat sheets
- Rare, isolated cells
- Even nuclear spacing within a single sheet ('honey-combing')
- Cells usually have a well-defined cytoplasmic border
- Bland nuclear features, round to oval nucleus with evenly distributed fine granular chromatin with a small indistinct nucleolus

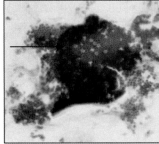
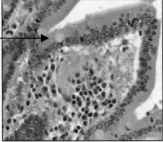

Figure: PAP stain and H&E stain. Benign duodenal epithelium: Flat cohesive monolayered sheet of duodenal mucosa with rare goblet cell, 'fried egg' (arrow). Duodenal mucosa showing goblet cells on histology section. Smear courtesy (left) Terrance Lynn, MD. Histology image courtesy Binny Khandakar, MD

BENIGN CONTAMINANT
DUODENAL MUCOSA
CYTOMORPHOLOGY
- Cohesive flat monolayered sheet
- Intact villi can show papillary configuration
- Smaller groups, isolated cells
- Cells with brush border
- Rare goblet cells with 'fried egg' morphology
- Rare lymphocytes within epithelium

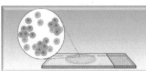
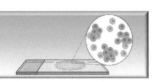

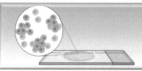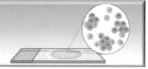
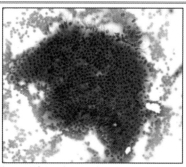
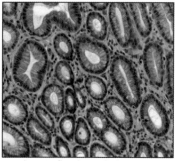

Figure: H&E stains. Benign gastric mucosa: Smear showing flat sheet of cohesive gastric mucosal cells. Histology image showing benign gastric mucosa. Smear Courtesy Melissa Hogan, MD. Histology image courtesy Binny Khandakar, MD

BENIGN GASTRIC MUCOSA
CYTOMORPHOLOGY
- Cohesive flat sheets and strips
- Rare, isolated cells
- Rare gastric pits
- Foveolar cells with visible mucin
- Naked nuclei with grooves

OTHER HIGH YIELD PEARLS
- Normal gastrointestinal tract contaminants only, are categorized as nondiagnostic rather than negative

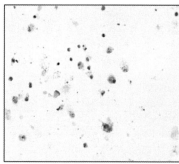
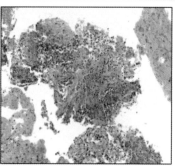

Figure: PAP stain and H&E stain. Acute pancreatitis with pseudocyst formation, smear showing yellow pigments (hematoidin-like pigments), debris, acute and chronic inflammatory cells and macrophages. PAP stain Courtesy Naomi Hardy, MD (Twitter: @NHardy_path)

BENIGN LESIONS
PANCREATITIS
ACUTE PANCREATITIS
CYTOMORPHOLOGY
- Necrotic debris with degenerating cells
- Foamy histiocytes
- Fat necrosis
- Calcifications
- Neutrophilic infiltrate

OTHER HIGH YIELD PEARLS
- Rarely aspirated
- Most common cause in the US is alcohol abuse
- Diagnosis is mainly clinical: raised amylase/lipase level and Ranson's criteria

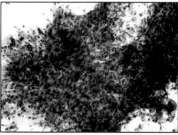

Figure: PAP stain. Chronic pancreatitis: smear showing ill-defined granulomatous reaction and fibrosis. Courtesy Syed Z. Ali, MD @sza_jhcyto

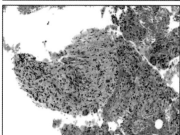

Figure: H&E stain. Chronic pancreatitis: Cell block showing fibrosis, loss of pancreatic parenchyma. Histology section showing loss of pancreatic acini and chronic inflammation. Histology image courtesy Binny Khandakar, MD.

CHRONIC PANCREATITIS
CYTOMORPHOLOGY
- Background shows inflammation, fat necrosis, calcific debris
- Cells are arranged in flat sheets with evenly spaced or minimally crowded nuclei
- Bland nuclear features, with low N-C ratio, round to oval nuclei and smooth nuclear membrane
- Minimal nuclear enlargement and variation (variation with <less than 4:1 diameter ratio in the same sheet)
- Rare, isolated cells with atypia
- Rare mitoses

AUTOIMMUNE PANCREATITIS
- Low cellularity
- Lymphoplasmacytic inflammation and cellular stromal fragments
- Increased IgG4 positive plasma cells

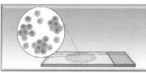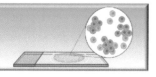

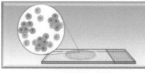
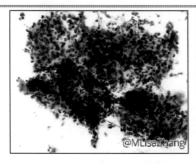
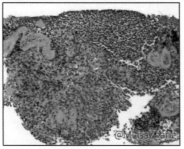

Figure: PAP stain and H&E stain. Splenule: Smear showing blood vessels with admixed lymphocytes. Courtesy M. Lisa Zhang, MD (Twitter: @MLisaZhang)

SPLENULE
CYTOMORPHOLOGY
- Few plasma cell
- Many lymphocytes without tingible body macrophages
- Vascular structure can be seen on cell block
- Numerous platelet aggregates
- Macrophages with hemosiderin
- Mixed inflammatory cells
- CD8 positive endothelial cells highlight sinusoids

LYMPHANGIOMA
CYTOMORPHOLOGY
- Mature appearing lymphocytes
- No epithelial cells
- Thin non-mucinous background
- Immunocytochemistry:
  ➢ CD31/CD34/D2-40
OTHER HIGH YIELD POINTS
- Benign neoplasm
- <0.2 % of pancreatic neoplasms
Common in young women

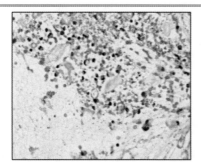

Figure: PAP stain. Pseudocyst: smear showing debris, hematoidin pigments.

CYSTS
PSEUDOCYST:
CYTOMORPHOLOGY
- Thin cloudy or dark turbid fluid on aspirate
- Necrotic debris with mixed inflammatory cells, histiocytes
- Yellow pigments, hemosiderin or hematoidin
- No epithelial elements
- Can show GI contaminants
OTHER HIGH YIELD POINTS
- Elevated amylase with low CEA

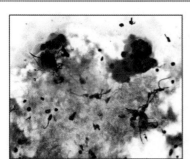
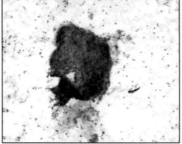

Figure: Diff-Quik stain and PAP stain. Lympho-epithelial Cyst: Smear showing giant cells, keratinous debris (left), stratified squamous epithelium, and lymphocytes (right). Courtesy Syed Z. Ali, MD (Twitter: @sza_jhcyto)

LYMPHO-EPITHELIAL CYST
CYTOMORPHOLOGY
- Background shows keratinous debris, cholesterol crystal
- Aspirate shows lymphocytes, mature squamous cells, anucleate squames
OTHER HIGH YIELD POINTS
- Rare entity
- Common in middle-aged men (4:1, male to female ratio)
- Not location specific within pancreas
- Imaging: uni/multilocular + solid component due to thick debris

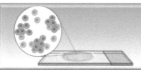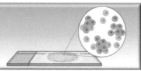
- Elevated CEA and amylase (refer to table: differential diagnosis of pancreatic cystic lesions)
- Absent KRAS or GNAS mutations

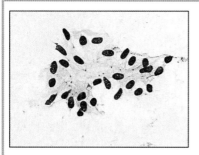

Figure: Diff-Quik stain. Serous cyst adenoma: Paucicelluar smear with abundant clear/glycogen-rich cytoplasm. Courtesy Naomi Hardy (Twitter: @NHardy_path)

SEROUS CYSTADENOMA
CYTOMORPHOLOGY
- Background is clear or hemorrhagic
- Sparsely cellular
- Flat sheets/loose clusters
- The cells are cuboidal cells with clear, finely vacuolated/granular cytoplasm, indistinct borders, naked nuclei
- Nuclei are small round with fine chromatin, containing inconspicuous nucleolus
- PAS positive; PAS-D negative
- Immunocytochemistry
  - α-inhibin, cytoplasmic
  - Glut-1, cytoplasmic

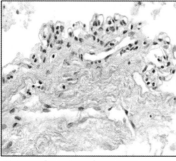
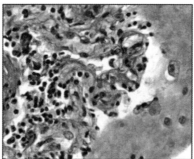

Figure: H&E stain and PAS stain. Serous cystadenoma: showing clusters of bland cuboidal cells with vacuolated cytoplasm (left), containing glycogen (confirmed on PAS-D stain).

HISTOLOGIC FEATURES
- Cysts lined by single layer of cuboidal/ flat epithelium
- Clear to pale cytoplasm with distinct cellular borders
- Uniform small, round to oval nuclei
- PAS positivity in the cells

OTHER HIGH YIELD POINTS
- More common in women
- Mean age, 66 years
- Mostly in body and tail
- Two major variants,
  - Oligocystic, few larger cysts (adult)
  - Microcystic, multiple small cysts (children/young); appear spongy and can be associated with scar
- Rare, unilocular or solid variant
- Almost always benign
- VHL (3p25) gene mutation
- Low CEA and amylase level, cyst fluid

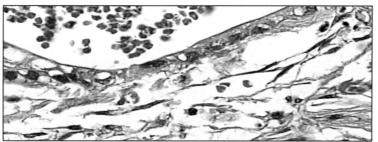

Figure: H&E stain. Serous cyst adenoma (histology): Histologic section showing cyst wall lined by low cuboidal cells with vacuolated cytoplasm.

MUCINOUS CYSTS
MUCINOUS CYSTIC NEOPLASM (MCN)
CYTOMORPHOLOGY
- Background
  - Extracellular mucin
  - Cellular or inflammatory debris within the mucin
- Cellularity:
  - Variable
- Architecture
  - Small cohesive clusters
  - Flat sheets of mucinous epithelium
  - Rare single cells

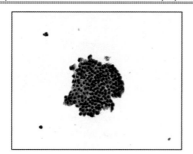

Figure: PAP stain. Mucinous cystic neoplasm: Smear with scanty aspirate showing bland mucinous epithelium.

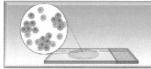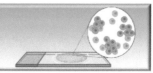

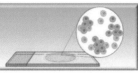

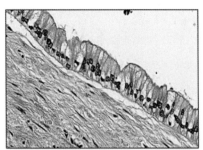

Figure: H&E. Mucinous cystic neoplasm: Histologic section showing bland mucinous epithelium with ovarian type stroma underneath.

- Cellular features:
  - Mucinous cells
  - Low-grade mucinous epithelium with low-grade atypia
  - High-grade epithelium, e.g., high-grade atypia (rare)

OTHER HIGH YIELD POINTS
- Elevated CEA
- Mucinous cysts with mutations:
  - KRAS mutated in IPMN and MCN
  - GNAS mutations in IPMN
  - RNF43 mutations in IPMN and MCN

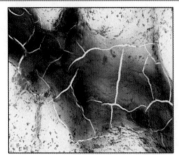

Figure: Diff-Quik stain. IPMN: Smear showing abundant thick mucin.

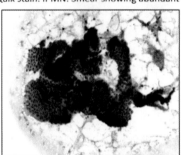

Figure: PAP stain. IPMN: Small papillary frond lined by atypical epithelial cells with moderate nuclear atypia floating in thin mucin.

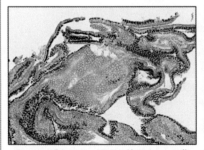 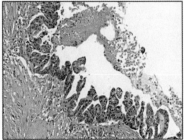

Figure: H&E stains. IPMN: Showing papillary fronds of mucinous epithelium with low grade cytologic atypia. Histologic section showing atypical papillary lesion in duct.

INTRADUCTAL PAPILLARY MUCINOUS NEOPLASM (IPMN)

CYTOMORPHOLOGY
- Background
  - Thick mucin
- Tumor cell features
  - The tumor cells show flat sheets, honeycomb, papilla, isolated columnar mucinous cells
  - Bland columnar mucinous cells to cells with high-grade cytologic atypia, including crowded hyperchromatic nuclei with loss of polarity, irregularity of nuclear membrane
  - Dense oncocytic cytoplasm can be seen rarely

OTHER HIGH YIELD POINT
- 3% to 5% of pancreatic tumors
- Equal incidence in male and females
- Mostly located in the head of the pancreas
- Grows intraluminal, along the pancreatic ducts
- There are three main histologic types:
  - (1) only the main pancreatic duct
  - (2) only the branch-ducts
  - (3) involving both
- CEA (high; >192 ng/ml) with high amylase on cyst fluid
- Can show different histologic grades
- Can show KRAS, GNAS alteration
- P53, SMAD4 and p16 support high risk cyst

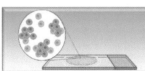

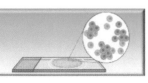

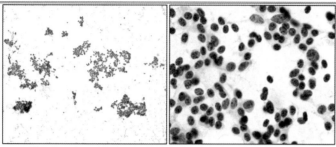

Figure: Diff-Quik stain and PAP stain. NET: Isolated single cells and loosely cohesive clusters of plasmacytoid cells. ©CytoAtlas (left)

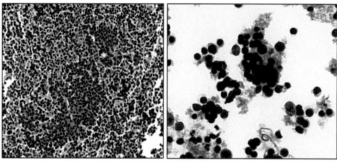

Figure: H&E stain and PAP stain. NET: Cell block showing dense aggregates of plasmacytoid tumor cells. Small cell carcinoma (right) showing crowded groups of plasmacytoid to rounded cells with stippled chromatin, nuclear molding, and scant cytoplasm.

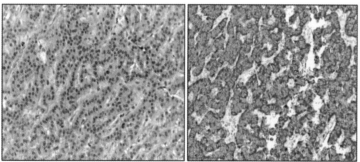

Figure: H&E stain and Chromogranin IHC. NET: Histologic section showing trabecular arrangement of tumor cells (left). Immunohistochemistry for Chromogranin is diffusely positive (right).

NEOPLASTIC AND MALIGNANT LESIONS
PANCREATIC NEUROENDOCRINE TUMOR (NET)

CYTOMORPHOLOGY
- Cellularity
  ➢ Moderate to high
- Architecture
  ➢ Loosely cohesive, isolated single cells, rosette, cell cluster
- Tumor cell features
  ➢ Monomorphic tumor cells, with small to medium sized, plasmacytoid cells
  ➢ Bland uniform nuclei with coarse stippled evenly distributed chromatin, 'salt and pepper'
  ➢ "Endocrine atypia"/pleomorphism
  ➢ Many stripped naked nuclei can be seen
  ➢ Cytoplasm is fairly scanty and dense
  ➢ Rarely, cytoplasm can be clear, vacuolated or oncocytic
  ➢ Mitosis and necrosis are absent to rare
- Immunocytochemistry
  ➢ CAM 5.2, CD 56, synaptophysin, chromogranin, insulinoma associated protein 1 (INSM1)
  ➢ Ki-67 labeling index depends on grade (see grading below)

HISTOLOGIC FEATURES
- Monotonous round cells or plasmacytoid cells, rosettes
- Nuclei with coarse with salt and pepper appearance
- Cytoplasmic variations such as oncocyte, vacuolated lipid-rich variant
- Histology Grading:
  ➢ Grade 1: Mitoses < 2 per 2 mm² &/or Ki-67 index < 3%
  ➢ Grade 2: Mitoses 2-20 per 2 mm² &/or Ki-67 index 3-20%
  ➢ Grade 3: Mitoses > 20 per 2 mm² &/or Ki-67 index > 20%

OTHER HIGH YIELD POINTS
- Associated with Multiple endocrine neoplasia syndrome, von Hippel-Lindau syndrome, Tuberous sclerosis
- Grading controversial on FNA

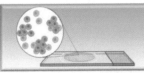

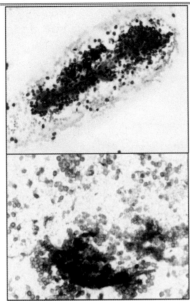

Figure: Diff-Quik stain and beta catenin IHC. SPN: Smear showing papillary core with tumor cells and scattered singly lying tumor cells (upper image). Immunohistochemistry for beta catenin shows nuclear expression (lower image). Courtesy Naomi Hardy, MD (Twitter: @NHardy_path)

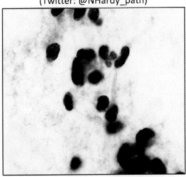

Figure: PAP stain. SPN: Monomorphic tumor cells with occasional nuclear grooves. ©CytoAtlas

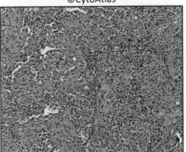

Figure: H&E stain. SPN: Histologic section showing vague pseudopapillary arrangement of tumor cells.

SOLID-PSEUDOPAPILLARY NEOPLASM (SPN)

CYTOMORPHOLOGY

- Background
  - Clear/hemorrhagic debris with foamy macrophages
- Cellularity
  - Fairly cellular
- Architecture
  - Cohesive clusters
  - Cells attached to branching capillaries
  - Papilla composed of delicate fibrovascular cores with myxoid stroma
  - Rare single cells
- Tumor cell features
  - Small uniform cells with mild anisonucleosis
  - Round to oval nuclei with nuclear indentation or grooves with evenly distributed finely granular chromatin and inconspicuous nucleoli
  - Scant to moderate amount of finely granular cytoplasm
  - Occasionally, perinuclear vacuole or intracytoplasmic hyaline globule can be seen
  - No/rare mitotic activity
- Immunocytochemistry
  - Cytoplasmic or perinuclear CD10
  - Nuclear staining with β-catenin, progesterone receptor (PR) , LEF1
  - Synaptophysin

HISTOLOGIC FEATURES

- Pseudopapillae with delicate vessels surrounded by hyalinized or myxoid stroma
- Intracytoplasmic eosinophilic hyaline globules
- Uniform round-oval nuclei with finely dispersed chromatin with occasional nuclear grooves

OTHER HIGH YIELD POINTS

- Missense mutation of CTNNB1 gene
- Most common in young women

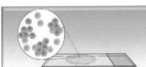
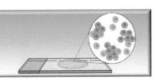

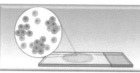
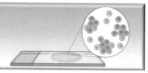
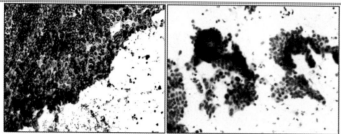

Figure: PAP stain. Pancreatic ductal adenocarcinoma: Drunken honey-comb pattern.
©CytoAtlas

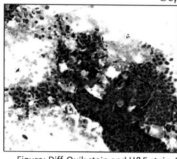
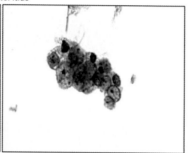

Figure: Diff-Quik stain and H&E stain. Pancreatic ductal adenocarcinoma: Smear showing cohesive clusters of tumor cells.

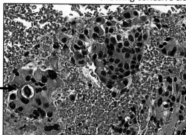
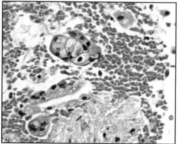

Figure: H&E stain. Pancreatic adenocarcinoma: Cell block (left) showing vague gland formation, cytoplasmic mucin, and high grade cytologic atypia in tumor cells. Cell block showing tumor cell with mucinous features (right).

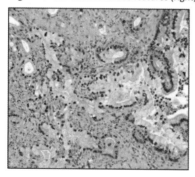

Figure: H&E stain. Pancreatic adenocarcinoma: Sections from pancreatic mass showing ductal type pancreatic adenocarcinoma.

DUCTAL CARCINOMA AND VARIANTS
PANCREATIC DUCTAL ADENOCARCINOMA
CYTOMORPHOLOGY

- Cellularity
  - Moderate to high
- Architecture
  - Irregular clusters
  - Isolated cells
  - Drunken honeycomb - irregular distribution of ductal cells in a sheet
- Tumor cell features
  - Mild to moderate pleomorphism
  - Irregular nuclear contour – notch/groove/convolutions/irregular nuclear membrane
  - 'Drunken honey-comb' pattern: anisonucleosis (> 4:1 variation in diameter in a single sheet) with nuclear enlargement
  - Chromatin clumping with parachromatin clearing
  - Mitotic figures
  - Scant to abundant cytoplasm, mucinous or foamy
- Immunocytochemistry
  - Loss of SMAD4
  - Loss of P16
  - Expression of p53

HISTOLOGIC FEATURES

- Well to moderately differentiated adenocarcinoma
- Reactive myxoid/desmoplastic stroma
- Infiltrating tubular pattern, most common,
- Subtle clues: misplaced glands in fat/next to arteries/perineural location

OTHER HIGH YIELD POINTS

- 90% of all pancreatic neoplasms
- Older age group – 60-80 years
- Imaging: 'double duct sign'
- KRAS mutation
- Risk factors:
  - BRCA2 and BRCA1
  - Family history of pancreatic cancer
  - Hereditary pancreatitis
  - Peutz-Jeghers syndrome
  - Familial atypical multiple mole melanoma syndrome
  - Smoking
  - More common in male

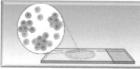
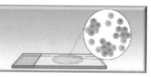

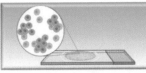

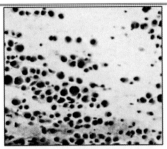

Figure: PAP stain. Colloid carcinoma.

COLLOID CARCINOMA
- Tumor cells suspended in large pools of extracellular mucin
- Diagnostic histologic criteria: Colloid component must be ≥80% of tumor
- Positive for CDX2 and MUC2

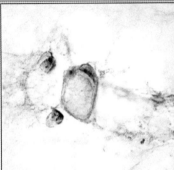 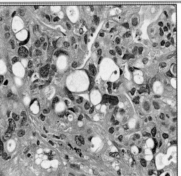

Figure: PAP stain and H&E stain. Pancreatic adenocarcinoma signet ring cell type: Smear showing signet ring cells (left). Courtesy Syed Z. Ali, MD (Twitter: @sza_jhcyto). Histologic section showing pancreatic adenocarcinoma with signet ring cell features (right). Courtesy Binny Khandakar, MD.

SIGNET RING CELL CARCINOMA
CYTOMORPHOLOGY
- Tumor cells with signet ring morphology
- Signet ring cells > 50% of tumor

OTHER HIGH YIELD POINTS
- Very poor prognosis
- Metastasis from other areas (stomach, breast, colon) needs excluded

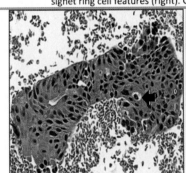 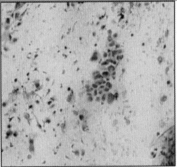

Figure: H&E stain and PAP stain. Pancreatic adenocarcinoma (adenosquamous type): Cell block showing squamous component, evident by intercellular bridges (left), with glandular component, evidenced by intracytoplasmic mucin (arrow). The aspirate smear shows cohesive clusters of atypical cells with squamous features. Courtesy Terrance Lynn, MD (smear)

ADENOSQUAMOUS CARCINOMA
CYTOMORPHOLOGY
- Mixture of malignant glandular and squamous cells (30% each)
- Malignant squamous component: large polygonal to oval cells with a dense or orangeophilic cytoplasm and pyknotic nuclei
- Malignant glandular component: readily identified with vacuolated/mucinous cytoplasm and glandular features (see above)

OTHER HIGH YIELD POINTS
- Extremely poor prognosis
- Immunohistochemistry
  ➤ p63, p40, CK5/6: + squamous component
  ➤ CK7, CK20, CEA: + glandular component

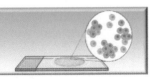

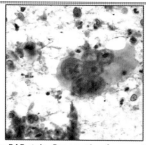
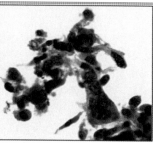

Figure: PAP stain. Pancreatic adenocarcinoma (anaplastic type, left): smear showing marked cytologic atypia with giant cells. Courtesy Syed Z. Ali, MD (Twitter: @sza_jhcyto). Right: Undifferentiated carcinoma with osteoclast like giant cells. Courtesy Laila Nomani, MD.

UNDIFFERENTIATED CARCINOMA ± OSTEOCLASTIC-LIKE GIANT CELLS
CYTOMORPHOLOGY
- Subtypes:
  - Anaplastic giant cell: Pleomorphic tumor cells mixed with bizarre multinucleated giant cells admixed with mononuclear tumor cells
  - Carcinosarcoma: Adenocarcinoma admixed with sarcomatoid spindle cell
  - Undifferentiated carcinoma with osteoclast-like giant cells: pleomorphic tumor cells some with spindle cell morphology, admixed with nonneoplastic osteoclast-like giant cells (usually with >20 nuclei)

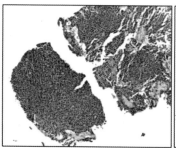

Figure: Diff-Quik stain and PAP stain. Acinar cell carcinoma: Cells have fragile cytoplasm and conspicuous nucleoli (right). Courtesy Susan Shyu, MD (Twitter: @susanshyu)

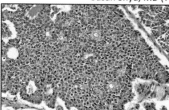
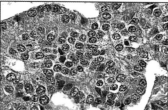

Figure: H&E stain and BCL10 IHC. Acinar cell carcinoma: Solid clusters of tumor cells. Immunocytochemistry for BCL10 shows strong reactivity in the tumor cells. Courtesy Susan Shyu, MD (Twitter: @susanshyu)

Figure: H&E stains. Acinar cell carcinoma: Histologic section showing tumor cells in acinar growth pattern with minimal intervening stroma. Tumor cells have relatively uniform nuclei with finely granular eosinophilic cytoplasm.

ACINAR CELL CARCINOMA
CYTOMORPHOLOGY
- Cellularity
  - High
- Background
  - Naked tumor cell nuclei
  - Granules
- Architecture
  - Loosely cohesive clusters
  - Acinar structures
  - Isolated tumor cells
- Cytologic features
  - Usually, monomorphic cells
  - Round or oval nucleus with smooth nuclear contour containing single prominent nucleolus
  - Cells have delicate fragile granular cytoplasm
- Immunocytochemistry
  - BCL10
  - Trypsin
  - Lipase
  - Chymotrypsin, phospholipase A2
HISTOLOGIC FEATURES
- Solid or acinar architectural patterns
- Uniform nuclei with central conspicuous nucleoli
- Finely granular eosinophilic cytoplasm
- Minimal to moderate finely granular, eosinophilic to amphophilic cytoplasm
- Typically have minimal stroma
OTHER HIGH YIELD POINTS
- < 2% of pancreatic exocrine tumors
- Poor prognosis
- Older patients usually
  - Rare children and adolescents

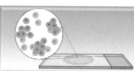
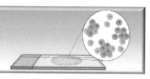

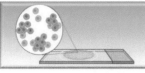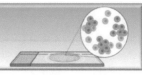
CARCINOMAS WITH MIXED DIFFERENTIATION	
• Commonly diagnosed on histology, as by definition, each component should be at least 30% of total histology. • Subtypes:	➤ Mixed ductal-neuroendocrine carcinoma ➤ Mixed acinar-ductal carcinoma ➤ Mixed acinar-ductal-neuroendocrine carcinoma

PANCREATOBLASTOMA:	

CYTOMORPHOLOGY
• Biphasic tumor
  ➤ Epithelial component: syncytium or isolated monomorphic cell with a moderate cytoplasm; rare squamoid corpuscles/morules (diagnostic)
  ➤ Stromal Component: primitive looking spindle cells; rare heterologous elements, including cartilage
• Immunocytochemistry
	➤ Cytokeratin
	➤ Endocrine markers
	➤ Nuclear β-catenin (squamoid morules)
	➤ Cyclin D1
	OTHER HIGH YIELD POINTS
	• Most common malignant pancreatic neoplasm of childhood
	• Mutations in β-catenin/APC pathway, leading to aberrant activation of Wnt/β-catenin with concurrent dysregulation of IGF2
	• Subset associated with SMAD4 (DPC4) alterations

PANCREATIC CYST FLUID ANALYSIS AND MOLECULAR TESTING:
- Aspirated cyst fluid can be sent for biochemical and molecular analysis
- Minimal amounts of cyst fluid can be triaged for cytology, CEA/amylase analysis

TABLE 1: DIFFERENTIAL DIAGNOSIS OF PANCREATIC CYSTIC LESIONS

DIAGNOSIS	AMYLASE	CEA	CA19-9	CA 72-4
SCA	Low	Low	Low/variable	Low
MCN	Low	High	High/V	High
IPMN	High	High	V	High
PSEUDOCYST	High	Low	High/v	Low/V

TABLE 2: MOLECULAR ALTERATIONS OF PANCREATIC CYSTIC LESIONS

DIAGNOSIS	MOLECULAR ALTERATIONS					
	KRAS	GNAS	3p25 (VHL)	p53	p16	SMAD4
Pseudocyst	-	-	-	-	-	-
SCA	-	-	+	-	-	-
LCA	-	-	-	-	-	-
IPMN	+	+	-	+ (HR)	+ (HR)	+ (HR)
MCN	+	-	-	+ (HR)	+ (HR)	+ (HR)
PNET	-	-	+/-	-	-	-
PAdCA	+	+/-	-	+	+	+

V: variable; SCA: serous cyst adenoma; MCN: mucinous cystic neoplasm; IPMN: intraductal papillary mucinous neoplasm; PNET: pancreatic neuroendocrine tumor; PADCa: Pancreatic adenocarcinoma; hr: high risk

BILIARY BRUSHING

INTRODUCTION:
- Mostly done for biliary strictures
- Most biliary strictures are malignant: pancreatic ductal adenocarcinomas, cholangiocarcinoma, and peri-ampullary carcinoma
- Benign causes of strictures: chronic pancreatitis, stones, primary sclerosing cholangitis, IgG4-related sclerosing disease and post-procedure bile duct injury
- Biliary brushing diagnostic efficacy for malignant lesion:
  ➤ Specificity: >95%
  ➤ Sensitivity: 30% to 85%

ANCILLARY TESTING:
- Immunohistochemistry:
  ➤ P53, S100P, maspin, and claudin-18 expressed in carcinoma
  ➤ Loss of SMAD4 expression
- Molecular tests:
  ➤ Fluorescence in situ hybridization (FISH) increases sensitivity of cytology
    - Combination with UroVysion probe with cytology:
    - Sensitivity: 42.9–63.89% for malignant lesions
    - Detects aneuploidy of chromosomes 3, 7, and 17, deletion of 9p21

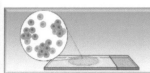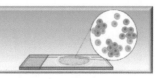

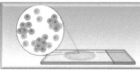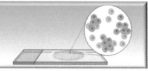
- Polysomy in PSC patients, high chance of cholangiocarcinoma
➢ FISH probes 1q21, 7p12, 8q24, and 9p21:
  - Used for pancreatobiliary samples
  - Sensitivity of 64.7% for detection of carcinoma

➢ Targeted next-generation sequencing with cytology:
  - Sensitivity: 85% for malignant lesions
  - Driver mutations in KRAS, TP53, SMAD4, and CDKN2A (30%), in pancreatobiliary carcinoma

BILIARY BRUSH CYTOLOGY

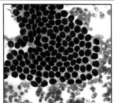 Figure: Diff-Quik stain. Benign bile duct epithelium.	**NORMAL BILE DUCT** CYTOMORPHOLOGY • Flat 'honey-comb' sheet or 'picket fence' • Cohesive clusters or groups of cuboidal to columnar cells • Maintained polarity, basally located nuclei • Cells with well-defined cytoplasmic borders, low nuclear-cytoplasmic ratio with smooth nuclear membranes, and finely distributed chromatin with indistinct nucleoli
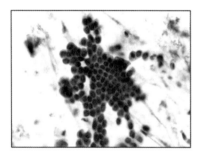 Figure: PAP stain. Reactive bile duct epithelium. ©CytoAtlas	**REACTIVE BILE DUCT EPITHELIUM** CYTOMORPHOLOGY • Background: can show acute inflammation, necrosis • Flat to mildly disorganized clusters • Spectrum of cells can be seen • Mild nuclear enlargement and anisonucleosis with low nuclear-cytoplasmic ratio, evenly distributed fine chromatin, smooth nuclear membranes • Nucleoli can be prominent • In presence of stent: worrisome cytologic features can be present, including marked anisonucleosis (6-fold variation in nuclear size), three-dimensional clusters, coarse chromatin, and isolated malignant-looking cells OTHER HIGH YIELD POINTS • Careful correlation with clinical, radiologic, and molecular findings is helpful
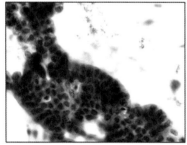 Figure: PAP stain. Dysplasia. ©CytoAtlas	**DYSPLASIA** • Classified as low grade and high grade CYTOMORPHOLOGY • Low grade dysplasia: nuclear stratification, mild nuclear crowding, hyperchromasia, and elongated nuclei with low nuclear-cytoplasmic ratio • High-grade dysplasia: 3-D clusters, nuclear enlargement, irregular nuclear membrane, and coarse chromatin OTHER HIGH YIELD POINTS • High grade dysplasia is indistinguishable from adenocarcinoma on cytology

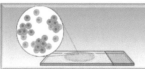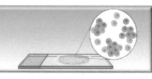

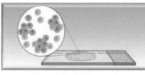
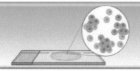

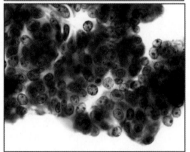

Figure: PAP stain. Adenocarcinoma. ©CytoAtlas

ADENOCARCINOMA

CYTOMORPHOLOGY

- 3-dimensional clusters, hypercellularity, cellular discohesion, two-cell population, cellular pleomorphism (within the same cell group), nuclear molding
- Nuclear enlargement [(≥1:3) in nuclear size], nuclear membrane irregularity nuclear molding, chromatin clumping, increased nuclear-cytoplasmic ratio, prominent nucleoli
- Cytoplasmic vacuoles
- 3 or more of the above-mentioned criteria in combination is helpful for diagnosis of adenocarcinoma

OTHER HIGH YIELD POINTS

- Necrosis and acute inflammation can be seen in the on background, which also can be seen on reactive conditions
- Combination with molecular findings increases sensitivity (see ancillary testing)

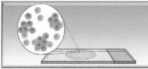
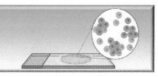

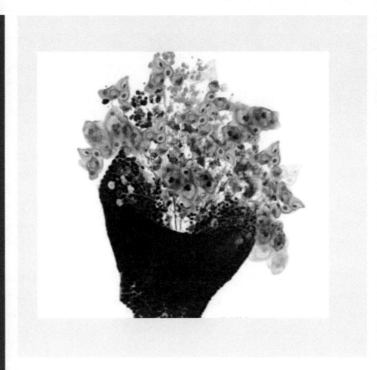

Chapter 10: Salivary Gland Cytology

Abhilasha Borkar, MD

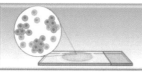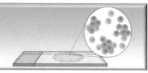

Hayk Melkumyan

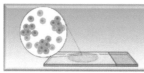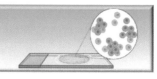

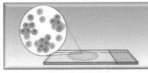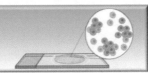
SALIVARY GLAND FNA
INDICATIONS OF FNA
- Postoperative infectious (usually bacterial) lesions
- Mass lesions
- Differentiate salivary gland lesions from non-salivary gland lesions
- Differentiate non-neoplastic from neoplastic and low grade from high grade primary salivary gland neoplasm

ADVANTAGES OF FNA
- Cost-effective
- Fewer complications
- Outpatient procedure

CONTRAINDICATIONS
- Bleeding disorder
- Acute inflammation

RISK OF MALIGNANCY (ROM)
- Parotid- 20-25%
- Submandibular- 40-50%
- Sublingual and Minor salivary glands- 50-81%

- Parotid- 20-25%
- Submandibular- 40-50%
- Sublingual and Minor salivary glands- 50-81%

NONDIAGNOSTIC
CYTOMORPHOLOGY
- < 60 regional cells
- Poorly prepared slides air drying, obscuring blood, poor staining precludes evaluation of cells
- Benign salivary gland elements, in the setting of clinical and radiologic mass lesions
- Non-mucinous cyst fluid without an epithelial component

EXCEPTIONS
- Significant cytologic atypia
- Mucinous cyst fluid without epithelium
- Abundant inflammatory cells without epithelial cells
- Just matrix without epithelium

MILAN SYSTEM OF REPORTING OF SALIVARY GLAND CYTOPATHOLOGY

DIAGNOSTIC CATEGORY	ROM	CLINICAL MANAGEMENT
I Non-Diagnostic	25%	Clinical and radiologic correlation/repeat FNA
II Non-Neoplastic	10%	Clinical follow-up and radiologic correlation
III AUS (Atypia of Undetermined Significance)	20%	Repeat FNA or surgery
IV Neoplasm IVA Benign IVB SUMP (Salivary Gland Neoplasm Of Undetermined Malignant Potential)	<5% 35%	Surgery or clinical follow-up Surgery
V Suspicious for Malignancy (SM)	60%	Surgery
VI Malignant	90%	Surgery

Figure 1.: H&E stain. Normal salivary gland: Normal acinar cells in grapelike clusters with ductal cells. Figure 2.: Diff-Quik stain. Normal salivary gland: Normal acinar cells in grapelike aggregates. Courtesy Bin Xu,MD (Twitter: @BinXu16).

NORMAL SALIVARY GLAND
CYTOMORPHOLOGY
- Acinar cells
- Ductal cells
- Adipose tissue
- Crystals

OTHER HIGH YIELD POINTS
- Acinar cells in grapes on vase pattern
- Ductal cells in flat sheets, honeycomb pattern
- Mature adipose tissue
- Amylase and tyrosine crystals sometimes

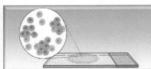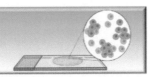

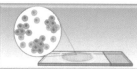
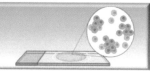
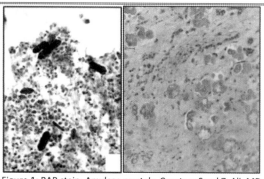

Figure 1: PAP stain. Amylase crystals. Courtesy Syed Z. Ali, MD (Twitter: @Sza_jhcyto) Figure 2: H&E stain. Tyrosine crystals. Courtesy Greta Evaristo, MD (Twitter: @gtevaristomd) and Marc Pusztaseri, MD (Twitter @MarcPusztaseri)

SIALOLITHIASIS

- 80% submandibular salivary duct, 20% parotid duct
- Calcium carbonate, Calcium phosphate

CYTOMORPHOLOGY

- Hypocellular
- Scant acinar cells
- Calcification- stone fragments
- Benign ductal cells and/or metaplastic squamous, ciliated, or mucinous cells
- Inflammation

CRYSTALS

- Amylase- needle-like, nonbirefringent, rhomboid, associated with benign, sometimes with Warthin, pleomorphic adenoma
- Tyrosine - floret shaped, associated with pleomorphic adenoma
- Collagen crystalloid
- Calcium oxalate crystals

ACUTE SUPPURATIVE SIALADENITIS

- Parotid, older, dehydration, poor oral hygiene, diabetes
- Staphylococcus, Streptococcus

CYTOMORPHOLOGY

- Neutrophils, necrotic debris, fibrin
- Granulation tissue later stages

- Scant ductal cells
- Stone fragments

TREATMENT

- Antibacterial agents
- Mumps self-limited

ACUTE NON-SUPPURATIVE SIALADENITIS

- Children, viral infections CMV, mumps, EBV

CYTOMORPHOLOGY

- Abundant neutrophils, neuroinflammatory debris, granulation tissue (later stages), histiocytes

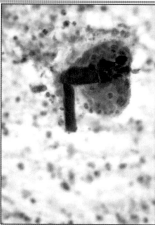
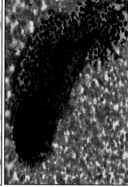

Figure 1: PAP stain. Chronic sialadenitis with amylase crystals. Courtesy Syed Z. Ali, MD (Twitter: @Sza_jhcyto). Figure 2: Diff-Quik stain. Chronic sialadenitis: Predominantly clusters of ductal cells and rare lymphocytes. Courtesy Abeer M. Salama, MD

CHRONIC SIALADENITIS

- Adult, submandibular gland, firm mass (sometimes), m>f
- Associated with stones, radiation, bulimia, trauma, surgery, autoimmune disorders

VARIOUS TYPES

- Chronic obstructive
- Chronic recurrent
- Chronic sclerosing (Kuttner tumor)
- IgG4 type: IgG4, plasma cells, bilateral, firm glands, with elevated serum IgG4

CYTOMORPHOLOGY

- Hypocellular, scant acinar cells, metaplastic basaloid cells, lymphocytes, plasma cells, fibrosis, scant acinar cells

GRANULOMATOUS SIALADENITIS

- Salivary gland or lymph node in salivary gland

CAUSES

- Reaction to extravasated mucin
- Obstructive sialadenitis
- Infections- mycobacteria, actinomycosis, cat scratch disease, toxoplasmosis, tularemia,

- Sarcoidosis
- Rarely Hodgkin's lymphoma, metastasis from nasopharyngeal carcinoma

CYTOMORPHOLOGY

- Hypocellular, groups of epithelioid histiocytes, multinucleated giant cells, acute or chronic inflammation, necrotic background

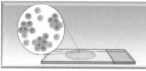
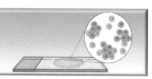

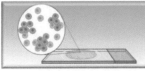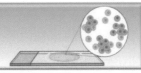
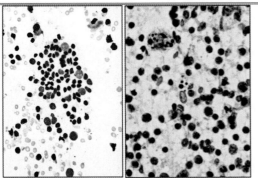

Figure: Diff-Quik stain. Reactive lymph node: Germinal center cells with dendritic cells, small lymphocytes and immunoblasts.
Figure 2: PAP stain. Reactive lymph node with tingible body macrophages in background of lymphocytes. Courtesy Samer Khader, MD (Twitter: @Samkhader)

REACTIVE LYMPH NODE HYPERPLASIA
Intra, peri-salivary gland lymph node
CYTOMORPHOLOGY
- Polymorphous population of lymphocytes
- Tingible-body macrophages, germinal centers, lymphoglandular bodies
RISK OF LYMPHOMA
- Long-standing Sjogren's syndrome
- Multiple, enlarged >3cm lymph nodes

LYMPHOEPITHELIAL SIALADENITIS (LESA)
- Autoimmune, bilateral, parotid, associated with Sjogren's, F>M

CYTOMORPHOLOGY
- Cellular, rare acinar cells, abundant polymorphous lymphocytes, lymphoepithelial lesions, lymphohistiocytic aggregates, tingible body macrophages, reparative ductal cells with squamous metaplasia, lymphoglandular bodies

SIALADENOSIS
- Diffuse, bilateral, noninflammatory, non-neoplastic painless enlargement
- Parotid> submandibular

SYSTEMIC DISEASES
- Diabetes, hypothyroidism, malnutrition, obesity, pregnancy, HIV, cirrhosis, and alcohol abuse
CYTOMORPHOLOGY
- Cellular clusters of enlarged hyperplastic acinar cells, normal cytoarchitecture, stripped acinar nuclei, fibroadipose tissue

ONCOCYTOSIS
- Older patients, oncocytic metaplasia of acinar and ductal cells
- Distinction from oncocytic neoplasm not possible on cytology

CYTOMORPHOLOGY
- Cells with abundant granular eosinophilic cytoplasm
- Normal cytoarchitecture maintained
- Variable benign salivary gland elements

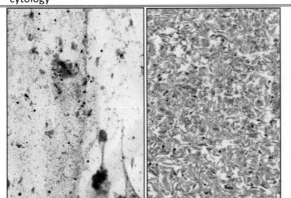

Figure 1: PAP stain. Branchial cleft cyst: Squamous cells in granular debris. Figure 2: H&E stain. Branchial cleft cyst: keratinous debris. Courtesy Abeer M. Salama, MD

SALIVARY GLAND CYSTS
- 5% FNA
NON-NEOPLASTIC
- Congenital
- Acquired
2 TYPES

- Squamous lined
- Mucus-containing
SQUAMOUS LINED CYSTS
CONGENITAL
- Epidermoid
- Branchial cleft cysts

Figure: PAP stain. Epidermoid cyst: Keratinous debris with red blood cells. Courtesy Abeer M. Salama, MD

Figure: Diff-Quik stain. Epidermoid cyst showing anucleate keratin debris. Courtesy Abeer M. Salama, MD

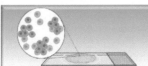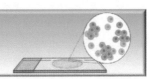

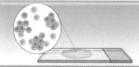
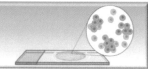

SIMPLE LYMPHOEPITHELIAL CYSTS

- Sporadic
- Middle-aged men
- Unilateral
- Solitary
- Not associated with HIV and Sjogren's syndrome

HIV-ASSOCIATED LYMPHOEPITHELIAL CYSTS

- Bilateral and multiple

CYTOMORPHOLOGY

- Cellular
- Histiocytes
- Keratin debris/ anucleate squames
- Proteinaceous debris

- Small clusters of squamous cells
- Mixed population of lymphocytes
- With or without germinal center fragments with tingible-body macrophages
- Absence of lymphoepithelial islands
- Seen in HIV and cystic LESA

DIFFERENTIAL DIAGNOSIS

- Cystic squamous cell carcinoma
- Warthin tumor
- Acinic cell carcinoma
- Mucoepidermoid carcinoma
- Intraparotid lymph node
-

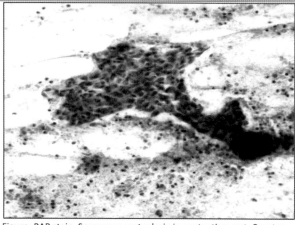

Figure: PAP stain. Squamous metaplasia in a retention cyst. Courtesy Syed Z. Ali, MD (Twitter: @Sza_jhcyto)

MUCIN CONTAINING CYSTS

- Acquired cysts
- Retention cysts lined by either squamous, columnar, or oncocytic epithelium
- Mucocele are pseudocysts (lack epithelial lining)
- More in submandibular and sublingual glands
- Often categorized as AUS according to the MILAN system

CYTOMORPHOLOGY

- Sparsely cellular
- Extracellular mucin
- Histiocytes, amylase crystalloids
- Scattered inflammatory cells

DIFFERENTIAL DIAGNOSES

- Chronic sialadenitis with mucinous metaplasia
- Mucoepidermoid carcinoma

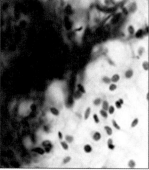

Figure 1: Diff-Quik stain. Pleomorphic adenoma: Fibrillary matrix with embedded myoepithelial cells and epithelial cells. ©CytoAtlas.
Figure 2: PAP stain. Pleomorphic adenoma: Bluish green matrix, with plasmacytoid to spindled myoepithelial cells and scattered ductal epithelial cells. ©CytoAtlas

BENIGN NEOPLASMS

PLEOMORPHIC ADENOMA

- Most common, children and adults, 2/3 rd. in the parotid, 50% of salivary gland tumors
- Often at tail, firm, painless

CYTOMORPHOLOGY

- Epithelial cells
- Myoepithelial cells
- Chondromyxoid matrix
- Tyrosine crystals
- Cohesive groups of epithelial cells in a honeycombing pattern

- Myoepithelial cells in spindle cell, epithelioid, clear cell, or plasmacytoid pattern
- Fibrillary chondromyxoid matrix with myoepithelial cells embedded within
- Sample different areas

PITFALLS

- Matrix poor PA
- Adenoid cystic like matrix
- Cytologic atypia
- Squamous or mucinous metaplasia

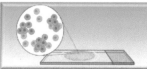
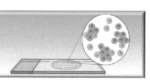

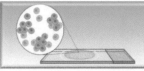

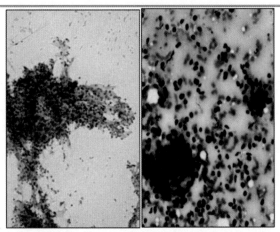

Figure 1: PAP stain. Myoepithelioma: Low power view of cellular monotonous epithelioid cells in a loose aggregate. Figure 2: Diff-Quik. Myoepithelioma: Small ovoid to spindle basaloid appearing cells scattered singly and in loose aggregates. Courtesy Israh Khan Akhtar, MD (Twitter:@israhkhan)

MYOEPITHELIOMA
- Rare, Monomorphic variant of PA
- Clinical history and presentation like pleomorphic adenoma

CYTOMORPHOLOGY
- Loose aggregates and isolated cells
- Lack of honeycomb sheets
- Lack of chondromyxoid matrix

SPINDLE CELL MYOEPITHELIOMA
- Difficult to distinguish from schwannoma
- P63 stain is positive in myoepithelial cells
- S100 is positive in both

PLASMACYTOID MYOEPITHELIOMA
- Lacks clock face nuclear chromatin pattern and perinuclear hof
- Immunocytochemistry and serum electrophoresis helpful

CLEAR CELL MYOEPITHELIOMA
- Resembles epithelial-myoepithelial
- Acinic cell carcinoma
- Mucoepidermoid carcinoma

Figure: PAP stain. Basaloid cells neoplasm was classified as SUMP according to the MILAN system. Differentials include Basal cell adenoma/ Basal cell adenocarcinoma/ solid variant of adenoid cystic carcinoma. Surgical resection specimen showed solid variant of adenoid cystic carcinoma. Courtesy Syed Z. Ali, MD (Twitter: sza_jhcyto)

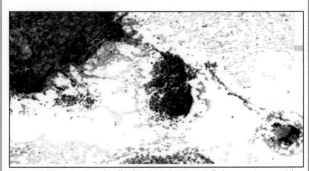

Figure: PAP stain. Basal cell adenocarcinoma: Cellular specimen with small to medium sized cells with peripheral palisading. Courtesy Abeer M. Salama, MD

BASAL CELL ADENOMA
- Most common in the parotid
- Usually mistaken for PA

HISTOLOGIC PATTERN
- Solid
- Tubular
- Trabecular
- Membranous
- Mix

CANALICULAR ADENOMA
- Upper lip

MEMBRANOUS BASAL CELL ADENOMA (DERMAL ANALOGUE TUMOR)
- Associated with autosomal dominant other synchronous skin tumors

CYTOMORPHOLOGY
- Small intermediate cells with peripheral palisading
- Dense, nonfibrillar stroma at the periphery of groups
- Smooth contoured hyaline globules

DIFFERENTIAL DIAGNOSIS OF BASALOID NEOPLASMS

Chronic sialadenitis
- Basal cell adenoma
- Basal cell adenocarcinoma
- Adenoid cystic carcinoma
- Cellular pleomorphic adenoma
- Metastatic basal cell carcinoma
- Metastatic basaloid squamous cell carcinoma
- Small cell carcinoma

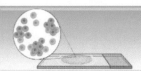
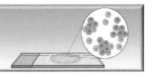

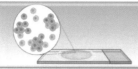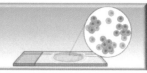
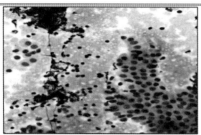

Figure: Diff-Quik stain. Warthin tumor: Oncocytic cells in a background of lymphocytes. ©CytoAtlas

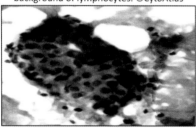

Figure: PAP stain. Warthin tumor: Mostly oncocytic cells are seen in a bloody background. ©CytoAtlas

WARTHIN TUMOR
- Parotid gland tumor
- Second most common
- 5-10%
- 50-79yrs
- M>F
- Can be Bilateral
- Doughy
- Motor oil contents, thick brown-green, granular fluid

CYTOMORPHOLOGY
- Lymphocytes
- Oncocytes
- Granular debris
- Predominant small lymphocytes with scattered large lymphocytes
- Few oncocyte clusters
- Infrequent papillary group double layered
- Abundant granular cytoplasm, round uniform, eccentrically located nucleus with evenly textured chromatin, small nucleoli
- Sometimes only cystic fluid with granular debris and rare viable cells

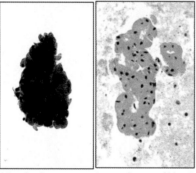

Figure 1: PAP stain. Oncocytoma: Loose clusters of bland epithelioid cells with abundant granular cytoplasm, round to oval, small central nuclei. Figure 2: H&E stain. Oncocytoma: Cells with abundant pink granular cytoplasm. Courtesy Abeer M. Salama, MD

ONCOCYTOMA
- Rare benign
- 1-3%
- Discrete nodule
- Well circumscribed with fibrous capsule
- 7th decade

CYTOMORPHOLOGY
- Cellular
- Oncocytes, clean background
- No lymphocytes

DIFFERENTIAL DIAGNOSIS
- Oncocytoma, Oncocytosis
- WT, PA, Mucoepidermoid carcinoma

- Acinic cell carcinoma
- Oncocytic carcinoma
- Metastatic RCC

MUNOHISTOCHEMISTRY
- Used: oncocytoma vs acinic cell carcinoma
- PTAH: positive in mitochondria of oncocytes; negative in acinic cell carcinoma
- Oncocytes lack PASD resistant granules which are seen in acinic cell carcinoma

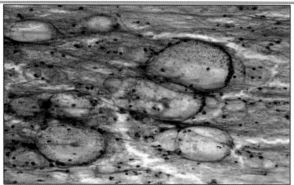

Figure: PAP stain. Low-grade mucoepidermoid carcinoma large mucin vacuoles admixed with mucin containing tumor cells. Courtesy Syed Z. Ali, MD (Twitter: sza_jhcyto)

PRIMARY MALIGNANT SALIVARY GLAND TUMORS
MUCOEPIDERMOID CARCINOMA (MEC)
- Most common primary malignant salivary gland carcinoma
- Both in children and adults
- Major and minor salivary glands

LOW GRADE
- Usually, cystic
- Mucus cells predominant
- Conservative surgery

HIGH GRADE
- Solid, infiltrative
- Epidermoid cells predominate
- Nerve conservating total salivary gland resection surgery often with selective lymph node dissection followed by radiation therapy

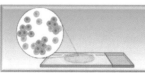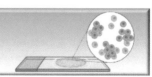

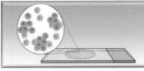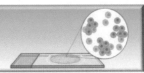
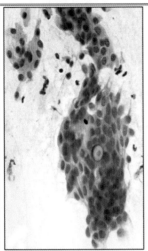
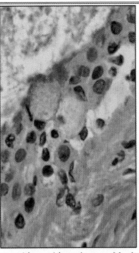

Figure 1: PAP stain. Low-grade mucoepidermoid carcinoma: Mucin vacuoles admixed with squamoid appearing tumor cells. Courtesy Syed Z. Ali, MD (Twitter: sza_jhcyto) Figure 2: H&E stain. Mucoepidermoid carcinoma: Mucin cells admixed with squamoid and intermediate cells. ©CytoAtlas

CYTOMORPHOLOGY
- Combination of mucus cells, squamoid cells, clear cells, and intermediate cells
- Extracellular mucin
- Overt cytologic malignancy (high-grade): mitoses, necrosis, pleomorphism

DIFFERENTIAL DIAGNOSES OF LOW GRADE MEC
- Acquired cysts
- Warthin Tumor with mucinous metaplasia
- Chronic sialadenitis with mucinous metaplasia
- Pleomorphic Adenoma with mucinous metaplasia
- Mammary analogue secretory carcinoma

DIFFERENTIAL DIAGNOSES OF HIGH GRADE MEC
- Carcinoma ex pleomorphic adenoma
- Salivary duct carcinoma
- Metastatic carcinoma

ANCILLARY TESTS
- IHC: positive: PANCK, LMWCK, HMWCK, P63, P40, mucicarmine, ±sox-10, DOG-1, negative: S-100, mammaglobin
- FISH: t (11;19) (q21; p13) CRTC1-MAML2 or t (11;15) (q21; p26) CRTC3-MAML2

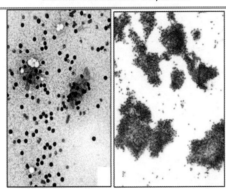

Figure 1: Diff-Quik stain Acinic cell carcinoma: Bland monomorphic tumor cells with naked nuclei and indistinct cytoplasm in pseudo tigroid background. Courtesy Syed Z. Ali, MD (Twitter: sza_jhcyto) Figure 2: Diff-Quik stain. Acinic cell carcinoma (Diff-Quik)-low-power view of loose clusters of bland monomorphic acinic cell carcinoma cells. Courtesy of Samer Khader MD (Twitter : @mycytopathology).

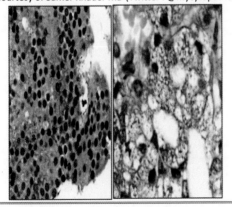

ACINIC CELL CARCINOMA
- Second most common primary salivary gland malignancy
- 4-6% of all salivary gland neoplasms
- Female > Male
- Mean age: 44yrs
- Common in parotid gland
- Can occur in children
- Bilateral: up to 3%
- Low grade
- Slow growing, circumscribed, mobile, sometimes painful

CYTOMORPHOLOGY
- Cellular
- Serous-type acinar cells
- Sheets, crowded clusters or isolated cells
- Large polygonal cells with abundant vacuolated cytoplasm
- Indistinct cell borders
- Bland round nuclei
- Naked nuclei with or without lymphocytes
- Delicate vasculature surrounded by tumor cells

DIFFERENTIAL DIAGNOSES
- Normal salivary gland
- Sialadenitis
- Oncocytoma
- WT
- Mucoepidermoid carcinoma
- Sebaceous carcinoma
- Clear cell neoplasms
- Mammary analogue secretory carcinoma

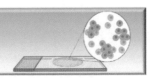

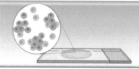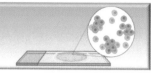
Figure 1: Acinic cell carcinoma. Bland monomorphic tumor cells with bland nuclei and indistinct cytoplasm and cytoplasmic granularity. ©CytoAtlas. Figure 2: PAS-D stain. Acinic cell carcinoma: The cytoplasmic granules are resistant with PAS-D. ©CytoAtlas

ANCILLARY TESTS
- DOG-1
- PAS positive diastase resistant granules
- NRA4A3 nuclear immunostain or break apart FISH (sensitive and specific than DOG-1)

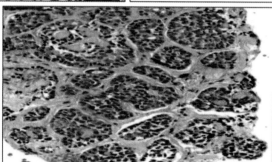

Figure 1: Diff-Quik. Adenoid cystic carcinoma: Tight clusters of basaloid cells with hyalinized stromal material and metachromatic hyaline matrix-globules. ©CytoAtlas. Figure 2: PAP stain. Adenoid cystic carcinoma: Three-dimensional sharp matrix globule surrounded by basaloid tumor cells. Courtesy Abeer M. Salama, MD. Figure 3: H&E stain. Adenoid cystic carcinoma: Cribriform arrangement of basaloid carcinoma cells and hyaline matrix. ©CytoAtlas

ADENOID CYSTIC CARCINOMA
- 3rd most common in the major salivary glands
- Occurs most commonly at submandibular gland
- Frequently invade nerves: present as a painful mass: clue to a malignant diagnosis

HISTOLOGIC VARIANTS

Often in combination of
- Tubular
- Cribriform
- Solid (aggressive/associated with poor prognosis)

CYTOMORPHOLOGY
- Large, acellular, three-dimensional, shar-bordered hyaline matrix globules
- Matrix: sharp cookie cutter like-in globules and cylinders; intense metachromatic in Romanowsky stain and barely visible in Papanicolaou stain
- Basaloid cells: scant cytoplasm with hyperchromatic angulated nuclei: nucleoli, mitosis, necrosis not prominent
- Solid variant: numerous atypical/ typical basaloid cells with scant matrix

DIFFERENTIAL DIAGNOSES
- Pleomorphic adenoma
- Basaloid neoplasms: basal cell adenoma/basal cell adenocarcinoma
- Pleomorphic Low-Grade Adenocarcinoma
- Epithelial-myoepithelial carcinoma
- Eccrine cylindroma of skin appendages

ANCILLARY TESTS
- IHC: Positive: PanCK, HMWCK, LMWCK, DOG-1
FISH: t(6;9)(q22-23; p23-24); MYB-NFIB

MALIGNANT MIXED TUMORS
- Carcinoma ex PA (most common)
- Carcinosarcoma
- Metastasizing mixed tumor

CARCINOMA EX PA
- Significant proportion of long standing unexcised PA: transform to malignancy
- Symptoms: rapid enlargement, pain (neural involvement)
- Usually: high grade malignancy of ductal type
- Estimated risk with PA < 5 years: 1.5%, 9.5% for PA > 5 years

CARCINOSARCOMA
- Rare
- Malignant epithelial and mesenchymal cells
- Differentiated components: most commonly are: chondrosarcoma, osteosarcoma

METASTASIZING MIXED TUMOR
- Cytologically benign PA in a distant site
- Multiple local recurrences at surgical site
- Although benign often fatal

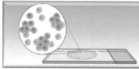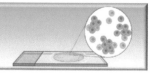

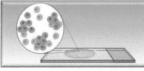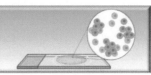
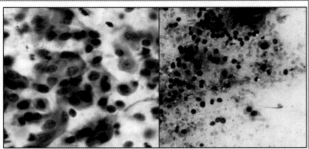

Figure 1: Diff-Quik stain. Salivary duct carcinoma: Pleomorphic malignant cells in clusters and singly. ©CytoAtlas. Figure 2: Diff-Quik stain. Salivary Duct Carcinoma: Moderately pleomorphic malignant cells in loose clusters and singly in a necrotic background. Courtesy Abeer M. Salama, MD

SALIVARY DUCT CARCINOMA
- Uncommon
- Aggressive
- Most common in the parotid
- Elderly male
- Resembles high-grade comedo type ductal carcinoma of the breast

CYTOMORPHOLOGY
- Cellular, overtly malignant
- Polygonal cells with abundant granular, vacuolated cytoplasm
- Sheets, clusters, papillae and cribriform architecture
- Necrosis

ANCILLARY TESTS
- IHCs: positive: panCK, HMWCK, LMWCK, Her-2,
- AR receptor
- FISH for PLAG-1/HMGA2 helpful in cases of secondary salivary duct carcinoma post pleomorphic adenoma

POLYMORPHOUS LOW-GRADE ADENOCARCINOMA
- Low grade
- Perineural invasion (but favorable prognosis)
- Almost exclusively in minor salivary glands
- 2nd most common malignancy in minor salivary glands
- Rare to FNA
- Histologic characteristic: cytologic uniformity and architectural diversity

CYTOMORPHOLOGY
- Tubules, cords, linear cells (mimics lobular carcinoma of breast)
- Acellular matrix globules

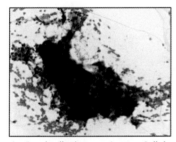

Figure: PAP stain. Basal cell adenocarcinoma: Cellular specimen with small to medium sized basaloid cells with peripheral palisading. Courtesy Abeer M. Salama, MD

RARE MALIGNANT TUMORS

BASAL CELL ADENOCARCINOMA
- Low grade
- Rare
- 2%
- parotid> submandibular and other
- Local recurrence
- Difficult to differentiate from basal cell adenoma on cytology
- Infiltrative growth pattern
- IHC: ß-catenin might be helpful: more diffuse and stronger in basal cell adenoma than in basal cell adenocarcinoma

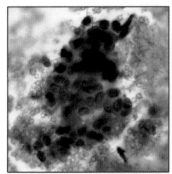

Figure: PAP stain. Epithelial-myoepithelial carcinoma: Biphasic population of darker ductal cells with paler bland appearing myoepithelial cells. Courtesy Samer Khader MD (twitter: @samkhader)

EPITHELIAL-MYOEPITHELIAL CARCINOMA
- 1% of all salivary gland neoplasms
- Parotid >other salivary glands
- F>M; average age 62 years
- Locally aggressive, low grade

CYTOMORPHOLOGY
- 2 cell population
- Smaller inner duct lining cells
- Outer large clear myoepithelial cells
- Peripherally located acellular basement membrane material
- Naked nuclei

DIFFERENTIAL DIAGNOSES
- Adenoid cystic carcinoma
- Basaloid neoplasms
- PA
- PLGA
-

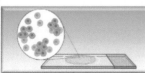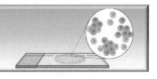

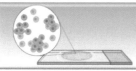
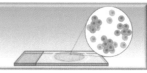

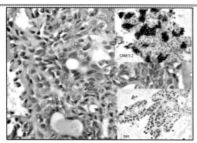

Figure: H&E stain. CAM 5.2 and p63 IHC. Epithelial-myoepithelial carcinoma: Biphasic population of inner ductal cells highlighted by CAM 5.2 (upper left) with paler bland appearing outer myoepithelial cells highlighted by p63 (lower right). Courtesy Samer Khader MD (twitter: @SamKhader)

- Metastatic RCC
- Other clear cell neoplasms

CLEAR CELL CARCINOMA, NOT OTHERWISE SPECIFIED
- Rare
- Diagnosis of exclusion

CYTOMORPHOLOGY
- Clear cytoplasm: can be due to mitochondrial condensation or glycogen, mucin, or fat
- Search for second cell population other than clear cells should be done before the diagnosis
- Special stains for glycogen, mucin, zymogen
- IHC for squamous and myoepithelial differentiation

DIFFERENTIAL DIAGNOSES
- PA
- Myoepithelioma or myoepithelial carcinoma
- Oncocytoma
- Lipoma
- Acinic cell carcinoma
- Epithelial- myoepithelial carcinoma
- Mucoepidermoid carcinoma
- Metastatic renal cell carcinoma
- Sebaceous adenoma
- Sebaceous carcinoma

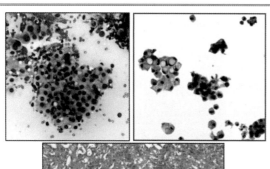
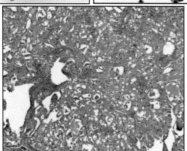

Figure: Diff-Quik stain. MASC: Sheets of monotonous bland appearing tumor cells with cytoplasmic vacuoles. Figure 2: PAP stain. MASC: sheets of tumor cells with abundant vacuolated cytoplasm with signet ring appearance. Figure 3: H&E stain. MASC: Low-power view of uniform appearing cells in cribriform architecture with cytoplasmic and luminal secretions. Courtesy Abeer M. Salama, MD

MAMMARY ANALOG SECRETORY CARCINOMA (MASC)
- Rare
- Resembles the secretory carcinoma of the breast
- M>F
- Parotid>another salivary gland
- Middle aged
- Low grade
- Lymph node metastasis common

CYTOMORPHOLOGY
- Cellular
- papillary, crowded groups
- Large polygonal cells
- Absence of zymogen granules
- Indistinct cell borders
- Bland round nuclei with a distinct nucleolus
- Extracellular mucoid material

ANCILLARY TESTS

FISH: ETV6-NTRK3 gene translocation; t(12;15) (p13q25)

IHC
- Positive: CK7, S100, GATA3, GCDFP15, mammaglobin
- Negative: p63, DOG-1, CK5/6

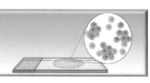

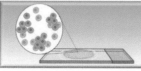
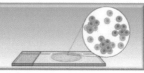
PRIMARY SMALL CELL CARCINOMA

- Rare, 1-2% of all major salivary gland neoplasms
- Small undifferentiated cells, often neuroendocrine features
- Diagnosis of exclusion
- Mean age: 56 years
- M>F
- High-grade neoplasm with poor prognosis

CYTOMORPHOLOGY
- Cellular
- Non-cohesive cells
- Small cells, with round to oval indistinct nuclei
- High N:C ratio, nuclear molding
- Frequent mitoses
- Necrosis

ANCILLARY TESTS
- Dot like positivity for cytokeratin
- Positive for neuroendocrine markers: NSE, synaptophysin, chromogranin, Leu7
- CK20 positive: distinctive for primary lung small cell carcinoma

LYMPHOEPITHELIAL CARCINOMA

- Aggressive and undifferentiated
- Greenland and Southern China
- 0.5% of all salivary gland tumors
- Like nasopharyngeal counterparts

CYTOMORPHOLOGY
- Syncytial sheets of undifferentiated pleomorphic cells
- Pleomorphic vesicular nuclei
- Large nucleoli
- Numerous mitosis
- Lymphocytes
- Plasma cells
- Associated with Epstein-Barr virus

ADENOCARCINOMA NOS

- Adenocarcinoma without specific features are classified as adenocarcinoma- NOS
- Low-grade adenocarcinoma: may not be diagnosed as malignant in cytology as diagnosis relies on histologic infiltrative pattern
- High-grade NOS are cytologically malignant

SQUAMOUS CELL CARCINOMA

- Rare primary
- Metastasis from other primary sites is more common

LYMPHOMA

- 2-5% primary salivary gland neoplasms
- Parotid common
- Most common: B cell Non-Hodgkin type
- MALT
- Follicular
- DLBCL

CYTOMORPHOLOGY
- Extra nodal marginal zone/MALT type
- Low grade
- LESA and Sjogren's
- Monocytic B cells
- Round slightly irregular nuclei
- Occasional immunoblasts
- CD45+, CD20+, CD23-, CD10-, BCL2+, BCL6-, cyclinD1-
- DLBCL
- Large markedly atypical lymphocytes CD45+, CD20+, Keratin-, S100-

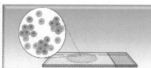

Figure: PAP stain. Metastatic melanoma to salivary gland (Pap). Note the granular melanin pigment in the cytoplasm. Figure 2: PAP stain. Metastatic Melanoma: Plasmacytoid tumor cells with anisonucleosis and bi and multinucleation. Courtesy Syed Z. Ali, MD (Twitter: sza_jhcyto)

METASTATIC TUMORS

- Squamous cell carcinoma
- Melanoma

CHILDREN

- PA: most common neoplasm
- Mucoepidermoid and acinic cell carcinoma most common malignancy

INFANTS

- Hemangioma: most common neoplasm
- Blood and bland spindle cells

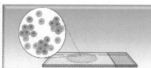
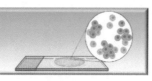

Chapter 11: Thyroid and Parathyroid
Cytology

Abhilasha Borkar, MD

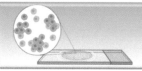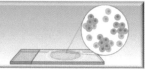
Thyroid FNA Indications

Bethesda System of Reporting

American College of Radiology TIRADS scoring

Benign

Multinodular Goiter

Lymphocytic Thyroiditis

Subacute Thyroiditis

Riedel Thyroiditis

Amyloid Goiter

Radiation Change

Follicular Neoplasm/Suspicious for a Follicular Neoplasm

Follicular Neoplasm, Oncocytic Type

Malignant Tumors

Papillary Thyroid Carcinoma, Variants, and Related Tumors

Poorly Differentiated Thyroid Carcinoma

Undifferentiated (Anaplastic) Carcinoma

Squamous Cell Carcinoma of the Thyroid

Medullary Thyroid Carcinoma

Lymphoma

Metastatic Carcinoma

Parathyroid Cytology

Parathyroid tumors

Medullary Thyroid Carcinoma

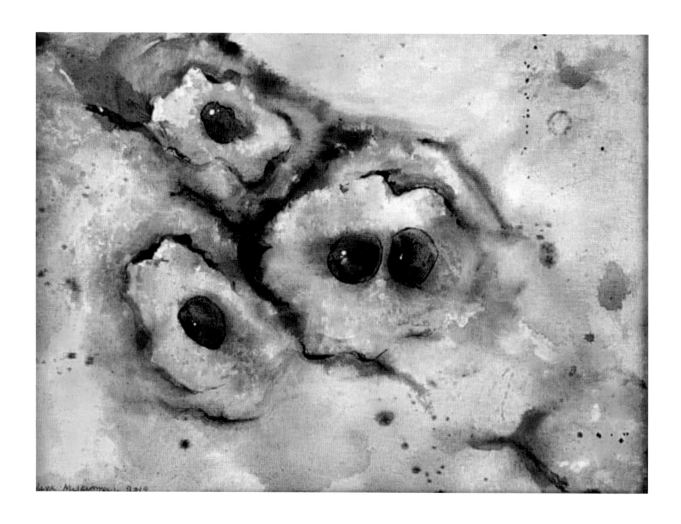

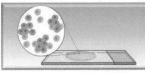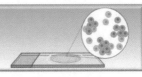
INDICATIONS
- Evaluation of thyroid nodule
- TSH≥ normal, FNA is attempted
- PET avid thyroid nodules should undergo FNA to rule out malignancy

Note: When TSH< normal, radionucleotide scan is attempted first

Aspiration technique
- USG guided FNA is preferred method
- Local lidocaine injection is normally not needed
- 25-gauge needle
- Conventional smears for immediate assessment

Thin layer and liquid-based preparation advantages
- Ease of preparation
- Less time in screening
- Concentrated specimen
- Maintained architecture

Disadvantages
- Immediate assessment is not possible
- Lymphocytic thyroiditis: lymphocytes in is more subtle in differentiating the lymphocytes from blood lymphocytes
- Thin colloid is difficult to identify

PAP stain
- Nuclear stain which provides nuclear details
- Nuclear grooves, chromatin, inclusions well studied

Romanowsky stain (Diff-Quik)
- Commonly used for immediate assessment
- Quick and easy stain
- Cytoplasmic details and background are highlighted
- Colloid has distinctive appearance.

Table 1: Bethesda system of reporting Thyroid cytology (2017)

	Diagnostic category	Risk of Malignancy if NIFTP ≠carcinoma	Risk of malignancy if NIFTP =carcinoma	Usual management
I	Nondiagnostic/ unsatisfactory	5-10%	5-10%	Repeat FNA with ultrasound guidance
II	Benign	0-3%	0-3%	Clinical and sonographic follow up
III	AUS/ FLUS (atypia of undetermined significance/follicular lesion of undetermined significance)	6-18%	10-30%	Molecular tests/repeat FNA in 3 months or lobectomy
IV	Follicular neoplasm/suspicious for follicular neoplasm	10-40%	25-40%	Molecular tests, lobectomy
V	Suspicious for malignancy	45-60%	50-75%	Near total thyroidectomy or lobectomy
VI	Malignant	94-96%	97-99%	Near total thyroidectomy or lobectomy

NIFTP: Non-Invasive Follicular Thyroid Neoplasm with Papillary like Nuclear Features

BETHESDA SYSTEM OF REPORTING THYROID CYTOLOGY
- **Criteria for adequacy:**
  - ➢ 6 groups of at least well visualized 10-12 follicular cells

- **Category I: Nondiagnostic /Unsatisfactory (5-11%)**
  - ➢ Does not meet the minimum criteria for diagnosis
  - ➢ Causes
    - Obscuring blood
    - Thick smears
    - Air Drying
    - Inadequate number of thyroid follicular cells
    - Cyst macrophages only
  - ➢ Satisfactory smears despite less/no follicular cells
    - Abundant colloid
    - Lymphocytic/Hashimoto thyroiditis even if few follicular cells are present
  - ➢ Cyst fluid only (CFO) specimens
    - Cyst fluid only specimens should be repeated FNA

  - 50-88% diagnostic on repeat FNA
- **Category II: Benign (55%-74%)**
  - ➢ 55-74% of thyroid nodules are in this category
  - ➢ Multinodular hyperplasia/multi-nodular goiter
  - ➢ Lymphocytic/Hashimoto thyroiditis
  - ➢ Granulomatous thyroiditis
  - ➢ Colloid nodule
- **Category III: Atypia of Undetermined Significance (AUS) (up to 10%)**
  - ➢ Sparsely cellular with predominant microfollicular pattern
  - ➢ Sparsely cellular with only Hurthle cells
  - ➢ Atypical cyst lining cells
  - ➢ Atypical lymphoid cells

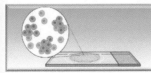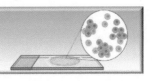

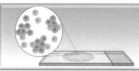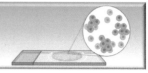
- ➢ Focal marked anisonucleosis
- ➢ Focal nuclear atypia
- **Category IV: Follicular neoplasm/Suspicious for follicular neoplasm**
  - ➢ Follicular cells arranged predominantly in microfollicular pattern with scant or no colloid
  - ➢ Specify if Hurthle cell (oncocytic) type
  - ➢ Management: Molecular test or lobectomy

- **Category V: Suspicious for malignancy**
  - ➢ Suspicious for papillary carcinoma
  - ➢ Suspicious for medullary carcinoma
  - ➢ Suspicious for metastatic carcinoma
  - ➢ Suspicious for lymphoma
  - ➢ Preferred surgery: near total thyroidectomy or lobectomy

- **Category VI: Malignant (2-5%)**
  - ➢ Papillary thyroid carcinoma
  - ➢ Medullary thyroid carcinoma
  - ➢ Poorly differentiated carcinoma
  - ➢ Undifferentiated (anaplastic) carcinoma
  - ➢ Squamous cell carcinoma
  - ➢ Carcinoma with mixed features (specify)
  - ➢ Metastatic carcinoma
  - ➢ Non-Hodgkin lymphoma
- **Ancillary molecular testing**
  - ➢ Helps in Triaging nodule for surgery
  - ➢ *BRAF* and point mutation *RAS*
  - ➢ Gene rearrangement *RET*/PTC, *PAX8–PPARγ*
  - ➢ Commercially available patented test such as Thyroseq, Affirma, Interpace etc.

American College of Radiology (ACR) – Thyroid Imaging and Reporting Data System (TIRADS) Scoring
Introduction:
- A standardized scoring system for reporting thyroid sonographs with recommendations for when to use FNA or ultrasound follow-up of suspicious nodules, and when to safely leave alone nodules that are benign/not suspicious

Sonographic Criteria
- **Composition:** (choose one)
  - ○ Cystic or completely cystic: 0 points
  - ○ Spongiform: 0 points
  - ○ Mixed cystic and solid: 1 point
  - ○ Solid or almost completely solid: 2 points
- **Echogenicity:** (choose one)
  - ○ Anechoic: 0 points
  - ○ Hyper- or isoechoic: 1 point
  - ○ Hypoechoic: 2 points
  - ○ Very hypoechoic: 3 points
- **Shape**: (choose one) (assessed on the transverse plane)
  - ○ Wider than tall: 0 points
  - ○ Taller than wide: 3 points
- **Margin:** (choose one)
  - ○ Smooth: 0 points
  - ○ Ill-defined: 0 points
  - ○ Lobulated/irregular: 2 points
  - ○ Extra-thyroidal extension: 3 points

Note: All findings in the final category are also added to the other four scores in the above 4 criteria.

- **Echogenic foci:** (choose all that apply)
  - ○ None: 0 points
  - ○ Large comet-tail artifact: 0 points
  - ○ Macrocalcifications: 1 point
  - ○ Peripheral/rim calcifications: 2 points
  - ○ Punctate echogenic foci: 3 points

Scoring
- TR1: 0 points
  - ○ Benign
- TR2: 2 points
  - ○ Not suspicious
- TR3: 3 points
  - ○ Mildly suspicious
- TR4: 4-6 points
  - ○ Moderately suspicious
- TR5: ≥7 points
  - ○ Highly suspicious

Recommendations
- TR1: no FNA required
- TR2: no FNA required
- TR3: ≥1.5 cm- follow up, ≥2.5 cm FNA
  - ○ Follow up: 1, 3 and 5 years
- TR4: ≥1.0 cm- follow up, ≥1.5 cm FNA
  - ○ follow up: 1, 2, 3 and 5 years
- TR5: ≥0.5 cm- follow up, ≥1.0 cm FNA
  - ○ annual follow up for up to 5 years

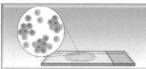

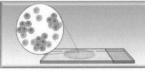

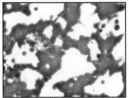
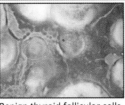

Figure: Diff-Quik and PAP stain. Benign thyroid follicular cells (left). Courtesy Israh (Khan) Akhtar, MD (Twitter: @israhkhan). Colloid (right). ©CytoAtlas

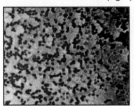
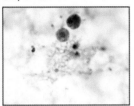

Figure: Diff-Quik and PAP stain. Colloid nodule: purple colloid with mosaic pattern (left). Cyst macrophages, hemosiderin laden macrophages with thin colloid (right). ©CytoAtlas

MULTINODULAR GOITER (MNG)
- Iodine deficient areas
- Female >Male

CYTOMORPHOLOGY
- Low to moderate cellularity
- Micro-follicular, macro- follicular pattern or flat sheets
- Uniform evenly spaced follicular cells with bland nuclear features
- Thick and thin colloid
- Hurthle cells may be seen
- Macrophages often pigment-laden: cystic degeneration

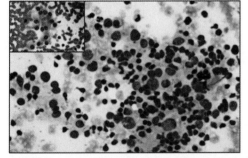

Figure: Diff-Quik stain. Chronic lymphocytic thyroiditis: Hurthle cells with lymphocytes in background (inset: Hurthle cells). Courtesy Smear Khader, MD (Twitter: @SamKhader)

LYMPHOCYTIC THYROIDITIS
- Autoimmune etiology
- Diffuse painless thyroid enlargement (goiter)

CYTOMORPHOLOGY
- Polymorphous population of lymphocytes
- Tingible body macrophages
- Lymphohistiocytic aggregates
- Hurthle cells
- Occasional Hurthle cells with nuclear grooves, nuclear pallor
- Scant to no colloid
- Can demonstrate mild to
- moderate cytologic atypia
- **Differential diagnosis:**
  - Reactive Lymph node
  - MNG with prominent Hurthle cell change
  - Primary thyroid lymphoma
  - Hurthle cell neoplasm
  - Papillary carcinoma

HIGH-YIELD POINTS
- If monotonous or atypical lymphoid population- sample should be submitted for flowcytometry, to rule out primary thyroid lymphoma

SUBACUTE (DE QUERVAIN) THYROIDITIS
- Rare
- Painful thyroid enlargement
- Possible viral etiology
- Self-limited
- Early hypothyroidism

CYTOMORPHOLOGY
- Multinucleated giant cells
- Granuloma(rare)
- Syncytium like aggregates of epithelioid cells with oval/spindled nucleus
- Lymphocytes

RIEDEL THYROIDITIS
- Rare, Hard thyroid mass
- Clinically mimics undifferentiated thyroid carcinoma
- Dense fibrosis replaces thyroid gland and extends beyond thyroid parenchyma

CYTOMORPHOLOGY
- Dry tap due to extensive fibrosis
- Fibrous tissue
- Plump fibroblasts
- Mixed inflammatory infiltrate

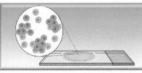
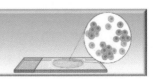

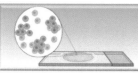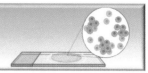
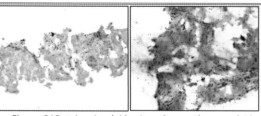
Figure: PAP stains: Amyloid goiter. Smears show amyloid deposits associated with multinucleated giant cells in a case of systemic amyloidosis. Courtesy Charles Sturgis, MD

AMYLOID GOITER
- Diffuse enlargement
- Rapid growth, dysphagia, hoarseness
- Chronic illness predisposing to systemic amyloidosis
- Masses of amyloid with multinucleated giant cells

CYTOMORPHOLOGY
- Amyloid looks like colloid but

- stretched
- Congo Red stain positive
- Apple birefringence under polarized microscopy
- Note: Amyloid is associated with medullary thyroid carcinoma and should be ruled out. (Please refer to image in medullary thyroid carcinoma).

RADIATION CHANGES
- External radiation, I131 Graves' disease, multinodular goiter, a functioning thyroid carcinoma

CYTOMORPHOLOGY
- Sheets (macro-follicle fragments)
- Enlarged nuclei with cytomegaly

- Normal N:C ratio
- Hurthle cells
- Cytoplasmic vacuolization
- Marked nuclear atypia
- Marked size variation
- Hyperchromasia with prominent nucleoli, smudged chromatin

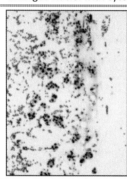
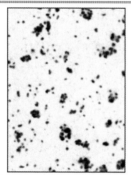
Figure1 &2: Diff-Quik stain and PAP stain. Follicular neoplasm: Highly cellular smear with thyroid follicular cells in sheets and microfollicular pattern. ©CytoAtlas

SUSPICIOUS FOR FOLLICULAR NEOPLASM/ FOLLICULAR NEOPLASM
- Incidence: 10-15%
- Invasion assessed by capsular invasion and/or vascular invasion only on histology, cannot be assessed on cytology FNA

CYTOMORPHOLOGY
- Cellular smears
- Follicular cells in monotonous microfollicular pattern or syncytial sheets
- Scant colloid

- Rare nuclear atypia, mitosis
- **Differential diagnosis**
  - Benign follicular nodule
  - NIFTP (Histology diagnosis only)
  - Papillary thyroid carcinoma
  - Metastatic renal cell carcinoma
  - Parathyroid adenoma: suspicion should be raised when most cells are arranged in microfollicular pattern with no colloid

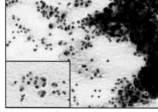
Figure: PAP Stain. Smear showing sheets and syntitial clusters of follicular cells with Hurthle cell change; suspicious for follicular neoplasm, Hurthle cell type. ©CytoAtlas

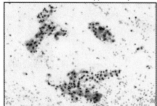
Figure: Diff-Quik Stain. Smear showing sheets Hurthle Cells with abundant amphophilc cytoplasm.

SUSPICIOUS FOR A FOLLICULAR NEOPLASM/ HURTHLE CELL TYPE
- Incidence :3-4%

CYTOMORPHOLOGY
- Follicular, trabecular, and solid pattern-
- Pure Hurthle cell population
- Non-cohesive cells
- Large granular oncocytic cells with prominent nucleolus
- Prominent nucleoli more typical of neoplastic process

Differential diagnosis
- Hashimoto's thyroiditis
- Multi-nodular goiter
- Papillary thyroid carcinoma
- Metastatic RCC
- Medullary carcinoma
- Parathyroid adenoma/carcinoma

- Granular cell tumor
- Hurthle cells in Hashimoto's thyroiditis
- Non neoplastic admixed with numerous lymphocytes
- Admixed with macro follicles and colloid
- Heterogenous mixture of MNG
- Pleomorphic Hurthle cells

Molecular Findings in Follicular Neoplasms including NIFTP:
- RAS gene family (*HRAS, KRAS, and NRAS*) most common
- *PAX8-PPARγ* fusions
- TSH receptors mutations
- *TERT* mutation
- *EIF1AX* and *DICER* mutations
- *THADA/IGF2BP3* gene fusions
- *PTEN* and *TP53* (NIFTP)

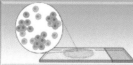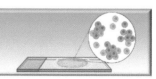

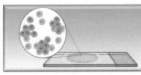
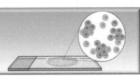

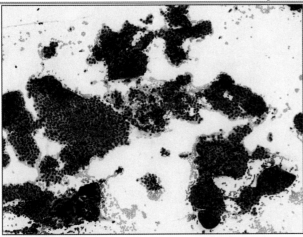

Figure: Diff-Quik stain. Papillary thyoid caricnoma: sheets and papillae.
Figure: Diff-Quik stain and PAP stain. Papillary thyoid carcinoma: cells are arranged in sheets and vauge papillae.

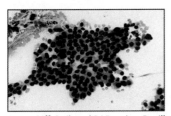
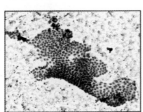

Figure: Diff-Quik and PAP stains. Papillary thyroid caricnoma: pseudo inclusion (left), nuclear grooves (left) and optically clear nuclei (middle panel) with bubble gum colloid (middle panel, inset) and psammoma bodies (right). Courtesy Naomi Hardy

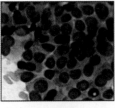
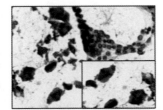

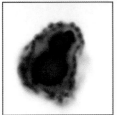
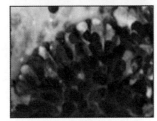

Figure: Diff-Quik stain. High magnification of columnar appearing cells of tall cell variant of PTC. (Twitter: @NHardy_path)

MALIGNANT TUMORS
PAPILLARY THYROID CARCINOMA

- Most common thyroid malignancy
- 80% of thyroid cancers
- 20-50 years
- F>M, 4:1
- Solitary nodule or distinct nodule in MNG or cervical lymphadenopathy

CYTOMORPHOLOGY

- Typical architecture of PTC
  - Papillae
  - Sheets
  - Cellular swirls
- Nuclear changes:
  - Powdery chromatin
  - Grooves
  - Pseudo inclusions
  - Nucleolus
  - Membrane thickening and irregularity
  - Nuclear crowding/molding
- Variable cytoplasm
- Psammoma bodies
- Histiocytes including multinucleated giant cells
- Thick bubble gum colloid
- Psammoma bodies
- **Variants of papillary carcinoma**

- Follicular
- Macrofollicular
- Oncocytic
- Warthin like-with abundant lymphocytic infiltrate
- Clear cell variant
- Solid
- Tall cell variant- aggressive
- Columnar cell variant- aggressive
- Cribriform morular variant- β catenin nuclear positivity
- Fasciitis like stroma
- IHC: thyroglobulin, TTF1, PAX8
- **Molecular**
- Can be classified as BRAF like and RAS like
- *RET*/PTC gene rearrangements and *BRAF/RAS* point mutations are mutually exclusive and accounts for 70% of PTCs
- BRAF v600E most common point mutation
- *TRK* gene rearrangement seen in advanced disease
- RAS like - seen in follicular pattern PTCs
- *TERT* and *TP53* mutation seen in aggressive variants
- **False negative diagnosis**
- Due to cystic change with macrophages with or without hemosiderin
- **Differential diagnosis of PTC**
- Benign follicular nodule Follicular neoplasm

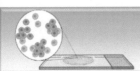
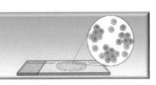

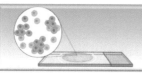
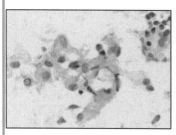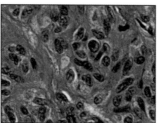

Figure: PAP and H&E stain. Hyalinizing Trabecular tumor: Cells with Intranuclear inclusions and grooves (right). Courtesy: Judith Jebastin, MD Elongated cells with abundant cytoplasm and intranuclear inclusions and grooves. Courtesy Swikrity U Baskota, MD

HYALINIZING TRABECULAR TUMOR
CYTOMORPHOLOGY
- Hypercellular smears with spindle or elongated cells with abundant cytoplasm, intranuclear clearing, nuclear grooves
- Intranuclear inclusions and grooves, like classic PTC
- Cytoplasmic "hyaline bodies" can be seen
- Commonly misdiagnosed as suspicious for papillary carcinoma on cytology
- IHC: Thyroglobulin, TTF-1, characteristic membranous staining of MIB1 monoclonal antibody against Ki-67. Negative for calcitonin.
- Molecular: *PAX8-GLIS3* rearrangement; diagnostic hallmark

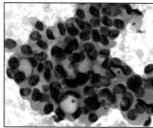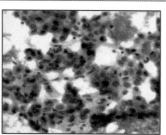

Figure: Diff-Quik (left) and PAP (right) stains: Poorly differentiated thyroid caricnoma: cellular smears with uniform population of cells. Courtesy Charles Sturgis, MD

POORLY DIFFERENTIATED THYROID CARCINOMA
- 4-7%
- Nodal, brain and pulmonary metastasis common
- 5-year survival rate 50%
CYTOMORPHOLOGY
- Highly cellular
- Discohesive cells
- Monomorphic round nuclei
- Mitosis, necrosis
- IHC: Positive for thyroglobulin, TTF-1 and PAX-8
- Molecular: *BRAF, RAS, TERT, EIF1AX*

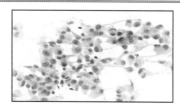

Figure: Pap Stain: Anaplastic thyoid carcinoma: highly atypical epithelioid cells with elongated nuclei and high grade nuclear features.

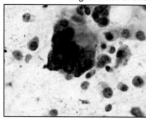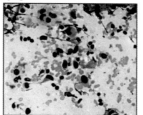

Figure: Diff-Quik Stain. Highly pleomorphic multinucleated cells (left) and many discohesive atypical cells (right) of epithelioid morphology.

UNDIFFERENTIATED THYROID CARCINOMA (ANAPLASTIC CARCINOMA)
- Rare
- Incidence:<5%
- >60 years
- Hoarseness, dysphagia
- Cytomorphology
- Spindle to epithelioid cells with pleomorphic hyperchromatic nuclei,
- Tumor necrosis
- Osteoclast type giant cells may be present
- IHC: positive for keratin and PAX8 negative for TTF1 and thyrogbulin
- Molecular: *TERT, TP53*, less common: *BRAF*
DIFFERENTIAL DIAGNOSIS
- Atypia of cyst lining cells
- 131I treatment
- Sarcoma- desmin, MyoD1, myogenin
- Metastasis

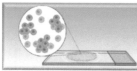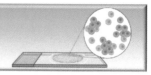

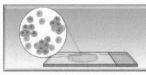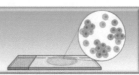
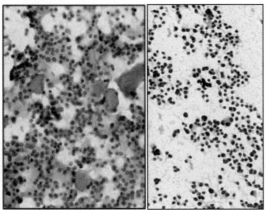

Figure: PAP stain. Medullary thyroid carcinoma with asscociated amyloid.Medually thyroid carcinoma with discohesive single cells.

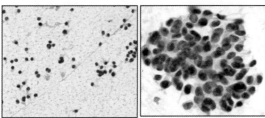

Figure: PAP stain. Medually thyroid carcinoma: plasmcytoid cells with salt and pepper chromatin. Right Image, Courtesy Charles Sturgis, MD

MEDULLARY THYROID CARCINOMA
- 5-10%
- Arising from parafollicular C cells
- 90% cases are sporadic
- Mean age 50 years
- Associated with MEN syndromes
- 90% secrete calcitonin: serum calcitonin level can be helpful
- 50% with regional lymph node metastasis

CYTOMORPHOLOGY
- Non cohesive cells/loose clusters
- Epithelioid, plasmacytoid, and or spindle shaped cells
- Nuclei, round to elongated, granular chromatin, inconspicuous nuclei
- Moderate or abundant cytoplasm with fine granularity
- Amyloid can be seen
- IHC: Calcitonin, TTF-1, CEA, chromogranin positive, negative for thyroglobulin
- Congo red: for amyloid
- Clinical examination and Genetic testing for MEN syndrome; MEN2A: Sipple syndrome: Pheochromocytoma, Medullary carcinoma of thyroid and hyperplasia of parathyroid, MEN2B: Mucosal neuromas: Medullary carcinoma, pheochromocytoma, multiple mucosal neuromas and marfanoid habitus
- Molecular: Germline or somatic *RET* mutations, RAS genes

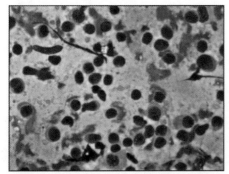

Figure: Diff-Quik stain. Lymphoma with atypical, discohesive cells (©CytoAtlas).

THYROID LYMPHOMA
- 5% of all thyroid cancers: Primary thyroid lymphomas
- Suspected in patient with long standing thyroid thyroiditis with new rapidly enlarging mass
- For cytomorphology refer to lymph node chapter
- Subtypes most seen in thyroid:
  - Extra nodal marginal zone B cell lymphoma
  - Diffuse large B-cell lymphoma (DLBCL)

METASTATIC CARCINOMA
- 0.1-0.3%
- Lung, breast, kidney, and esophagus most common primary
- IHC helpful in distinguishing primary thyroid cancer from metastasis

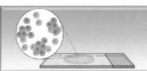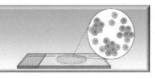

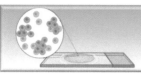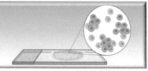
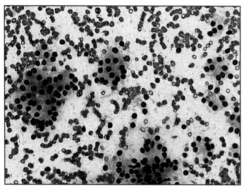

Figure: Diff-Quik Stain. Parathyroid cells with abundant ill-delineated cytoplasm, round to oval small uniform nuclei.

PARATHYROID TUMORS
CYTOMORPHOLOGY
- Cellular smears
- Sheets and micro follicular pattern
- Finely granular cytoplasm
- Small, round nuclei with inconspicuous nucleoli
- Isolated naked nuclei in the background
- Focal nuclear pleomorphism- endocrine atypia
- Absence of colloid
- Not possible to distinguish normal parathyroid from parathyroid adenoma in cytology

IMMUNOHISTOCHEMISTRY
- Parathyroid hormone (PTH)
- GATA3
- Parafibromin (CDC73)

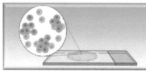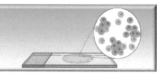

Hayk MELKUMYAN

Chapter 12: Lymph Node Cytology

Siddharth Dalvi, MD
Laila Nomani, MD

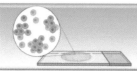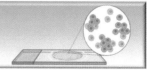

Hayk MELKUMYAN

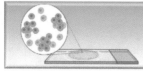

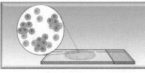 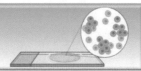

INDICATIONS FOR LYMPH NODE FINE NEEDLE ASPIRATION:
- Clinically enlarged palpable lymph nodes
- Lymphadenopathy of unknown etiology detected on imaging studies
- Staging for malignancies (hematopoietic and non-hematopoietic)
- Monitoring progression, recurrence, and relapse of malignancies

BENEFITS
- Minimally invasive, can be done in outpatient settings
- Rapid onset assessment with triaging for ancillary studies
  ➢ Flow cytometry, microbiology, immunohistochemistry, molecular
- Preliminary results
- Minimal side effects

LIMITATIONS
- Inadequate sampling
- Difficult to distinguish between reactive lymph nodes and low-grade lymphomas
- Follicular hyperplasia vs follicular lymphoma can be challenging in aspiration cytology
- Difficult to accurately classify lymphomas on cytology alone
- Excisional biopsy is still needed for definitive classification

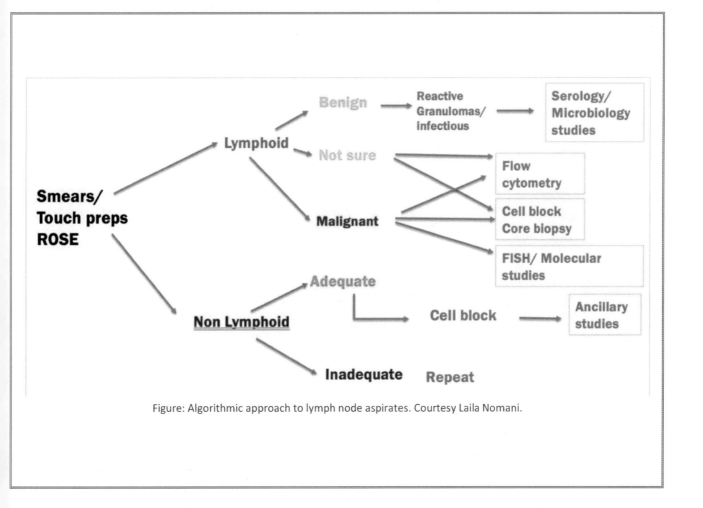

Figure: Algorithmic approach to lymph node aspirates. Courtesy Laila Nomani.

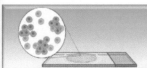 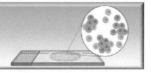

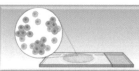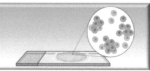
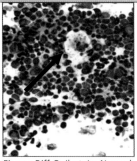

Figure: Diff-Quik stain. Normal lymph node with mixture of small, medium, and large lymphocytes, tingible macrophage (arrow) and lymphoglandular bodies.

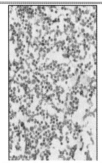

Figure: PAP stain. Reactive lymph node: Heterogenous population of lymphocytes with scattered tingible body macrophages

NORMAL LYMPH NODE
- Centroblasts
- Centrocytes
- Small lymphocytes
- Tingible body macrophages
- Dendritic cells
- Tingible body macrophages

PATTERNS ON LYMPH NODE ASPIRATES
- Monomorphic: Small or large
  ➢ CLL, DLBCL
- Polymorphous
  ➢ Reactive lymph node, mantle cell lymphoma, marginal zone lymphoma, Peripheral T-Cell Lymphoma (PTCL), follicular lymphoma
- Pleomorphic
  ➢ Anaplastic, Hodgkin lymphoma

GRANULOMATOUS LYMPHADENITIS
EITIOLOGY
- Infectious includes mycobacteria, bacteria, fungi, parasites and viruses
- Sarcoid
- Foreign body

CYTOMORPHOLOGY
- Epithelioid histiocytes (grooves, kidney shaped, boomerang shape), lymphocytes
- Multinucleate giant cells
- Necrosis may or may not be identified
- Background lymphocytes

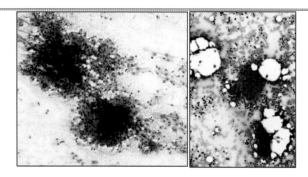

Figure : PAP stain and Diff-Quik stain. Epithelioid histiocytes and admixed lymphocytes consistent with epithelioid granulomas Courtesy Abeer M. Salama, MD and Terrance Lynn, MD

SARCOIDOSIS
CYTOMORPHOLOGY
- Non-necrotizing granulomas with epithelioid histiocytes and multi-nucleated giant cells
- Epithelioid histiocytes show elongated, irregular, or grooved nuclei and often described as "boomerang", "kidney-shaped", or "footprints in sand"
- Background reactive lymphocytes
- Hypocellular aspirate in late fibrotic stage
- Asteroid bodies, Schaumann bodies and Hamazaki-Wesenberg bodies

IMMUNOCYTOCHEMISTRY
- Not contributory

OTHER HIGH YIELD POINTS
- More prevalent in African American population
- Can present with lymphadenopathy, fever, weight loss, skin rash, respiratory symptoms
- Elevated serum calcium, gamma globulins and angiotensin-converting enzyme
- Microbial stains and/or cultures must be performed before diagnosis of sarcoidosis can be suggested; diagnosis of exclusion

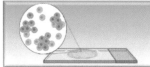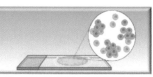

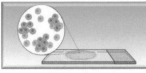

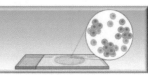

INFECTIOUS LYMPHADENITIS: BACTERIAL AND FUNGAL
CYTOMORPHOLOGY
- Mixed inflammatory infiltrate comprising predominantly neutrophils and lymphocytes
- Necrotizing granulomas in fungal lymphadenitis
- Organisms may be seen

IMMUNOCYTOCHEMISTRY
- Not contributory
- Special stains for organisms (PAS, GMS, mucicarmine) may help identify organisms in cellblocks

OTHER HIGH YIELD POINTS
- More sensitive molecular methods like PCR can be employed if organisms are not detected on microscopy or culture

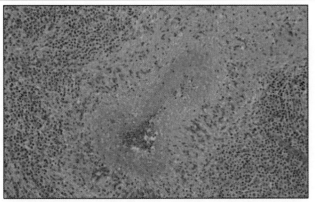

Figure: H&E stain. Central stellate necrosis with peripheral lymphocytes in a case of cat-scratch disease. Courtesy Margaret Compton, MD (@MComptonMD)

CAT SCRATCH DISEASE
CYTOMORPHOLOGY
- Necrotizing granulomas consisting of aggregates of epithelioid histiocytes with surrounding neutrophils
- Necrotic foci enlarge and form stellate microabscesses, a typical histologic feature
- Bacilli can be demonstrated by Warthin-Starry or Steiner stains, but not very sensitive

IMMUNOCYTOCHEMISTRY
- Not contributory

OTHER HIGH YIELD POINTS
- Causative organism is Bartonella henselae, a small Gram-negative coccobacillus
- Acquired through cat bites or scratches
- Tender lymphadenopathy with matted lymph nodes
- Axillary, inguinal, and cervical lymph nodes most affected
- Serologic, culture, or molecular methods may be required for a more definitive diagnosis

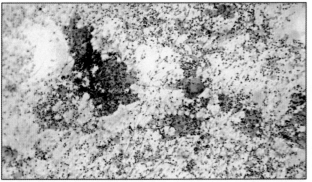

PAP stain. Granulomas with background necrosis and mixed inflammation. Courtesy Eduardo Alcaraz, MD, PhD (Twitter: @edusqo)

MYCOBACTERIAL LYMPHADENITIS
CYTOMORPHOLOGY
- Granulomatous inflammation is the hallmark
- Granulomas (well-formed or loose) may be necrotizing or non-necrotizing
- Background shows variable proportions of necrosis, neutrophils, lymphocytes
- Extra-and intra-cellular bacilli, seen as "ghost" or "negative" image on Romanowsky stains
- Organisms more likely to be associated with necrotic areas

IMMUNOCYTOCHEMISTRY
- Acid fast bacilli can be demonstrated with Ziehl Neelsen, Kinyoun (cold), or Fite-Faraco stains, but suffer from low sensitivity
- Fluorescent staining with auramine-rhodamine can be tried

OTHER HIGH YIELD POINTS
- Causative agents include Mycobacterium tuberculosis and non-tuberculous mycobacteria
- Tuberculin (Mantoux) test, QuantiFERON test, or other similar interferon-gamma release assay (IGRA) tests positive
- Molecular techniques like PCR (or similar target amplification techniques) preferred for diagnosis
- M. marinum: water sources like swimming pools and hot tubs. M. scrofulaceum: isolated cervical lymphadenitis in children (scrofula). M. avium-intracellulare: associated with HIV

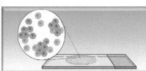

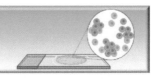

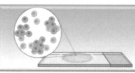
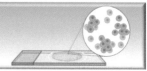

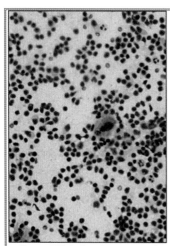
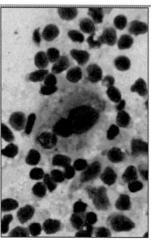

Figure: Diff-Quik stain. Emperipolesis in Rosai-Dorfman disease. Courtesy Terrance Lynn, MD

ROSAI DORFMAN DISEASE (SINUS HISTIOCYTOSIS WITH MASSIVE LYMPHADENOPATHY)

CYTOMORPHOLOGY

- Predominantly small lymphocytes on aspiration
- Spectrum of other reactive lymphoid cells including plasmacytoid lymphocytes and immunoblasts may be seen
- Hallmark of disease is large histiocytes with abundant eosinophilic cytoplasm and engulfed small lymphocyte (emperipolesis)
- Histiocytes have a round to oval vesicular nucleus with prominent nucleolus
- Enlarged reactive lymph nodes with histiocytes distending the sinuses, best appreciated on histology

IMMUNOCYTOCHEMISTRY

- Histiocytes immunoreactive for S-100, CD68, and CD163, but negative for CD1a and langerin (important for distinguishing from Langerhans cell histiocytosis)

OTHER HIGH YIELD POINTS

- Bilateral painless cervical lymphadenopathy most common
- Constitutional symptoms like fever, night sweats, weight loss may be seen
- Other laboratory findings can include leukocytosis and polyclonal hypergammaglobulinemia
- Emperipolesis comprises viable lymphocytes and plasma cells surrounded by a cytoplasmic halo and "passing through" or "wandering through" the cytoplasm, distinct from phagocytosis

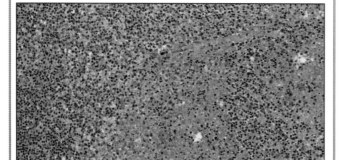

Figure: Diff-Quik stain. Necrotizing lymphadenopathy showing numerous apoptotic cells without any granulocytes. Courtesy Laila Nomani, MD

KIKUCHI FUJIMOTO LYMPHADENITIS (NECROTIZING HISTIOCYTIC LYMPHADENITIS)

CYTOMORPHOLOGY

- Background proteinaceous and karyorrhectic debris
- Numerous histiocytes with crescent-shaped and irregular, angulated nuclei
- Cytoplasm of histiocytes contains karyorrhectic debris
- Increased plasmacytoid dendritic cells and reactive immunoblasts
- Neutrophils and plasma cells are characteristically absent or scant

IMMUNOCYTOCHEMISTRY

- Plasmacytoid dendritic cells immunoreactive for CD123
- Histiocytes may aberrantly express myeloperoxidase

OTHER HIGH YIELD POINTS

- Typically seen in young Asian women
- Tender cervical lymphadenopathy, which may be accompanied by fever and peripheral lymphocytosis with atypical lymphocyte
- SLE lymphadenitis can have a similar cyto-histologic appearance, and hematoxylin bodies typical of lupus may always be seen; so serologic studies are important in ruling out lupus

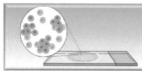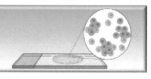

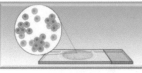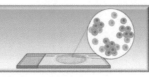
INFECTIOUS MONONUCLEOSIS

CYTOMORPHOLOGY

- May resemble reactive lymphoid hyperplasia, but shows numerous immunoblasts and centroblasts, along with small lymphocytes and plasmacytoid lymphocytes
- Reactive centroblasts and immunoblasts may resemble mononuclear Reed-Sternberg cells of Hodgkin disease; however, they have smaller and more basophilic nucleoli
- Binucleate Reed-Sternberg-like cells may be rarely seen

IMMUNOCYTOCHEMISTRY

- In situ hybridization for EBV-encoded RNA (EBER-ISH) may show scattered immunoreactive cells
- Reed-Sternberg-like immunoblasts may be immunoreactive for CD30, but negative for CD15
- Immunocytochemistry and flow cytometry reveal lack of light chain restriction, ruling out a clonal neoplasm

OTHER HIGH YIELD POINTS

- Classical presentation includes tender cervical lymphadenopathy, fever, pharyngitis, rash, malaise, splenomegaly
- Peripheral blood lymphocytosis with atypical reactive lymphocytes

Positive heterophile (Monospot) test

DERMATOPATHIC LYMPHADENOPATHY

CYTOMORPHOLOGY

- Melanin pigment-laden macrophages
- Background small and large lymphocytes
- Paracortical nodules comprising lymphocytes, dendritic cells, and pigment-laden macrophages on histology

IMMUNOCYTOCHEMISTRY

- Pigment-laden macrophages can be highlighted by Fontana-Masson stain for melanin
- T-cell receptor gene rearrangement studies may be performed to rule out lymph node involvement by mycosis fungoides

OTHER HIGH YIELD POINTS

- Reactive lymph node changes seen in association with, and usually up-stream, of dermatologic disorders like psoriasis, other inflammatory dermatoses, mycosis fungoides, injuries, tattoos
- Tender lymphadenopathy, most commonly involving axillary or inguinal lymph nodes

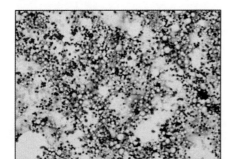
Figure: Diff-Quik stain. Silicone granuloma with epithelioid histiocytes.

SILICONE LYMPHADENITIS

CYTOMORPHOLOGY

- Non-necrotizing granulomas
- Foreign body-type giant cells
- Foamy macrophages with intracytoplasmic vacuoles

IMMUNOCYTOCHEMISTRY

- Not contributory

OTHER HIGH YIELD POINTS

- Caused by rupture of silicone breast implants, resulting in leakage of silicone and subsequent reactive changes in axillary lymph nodes
- Painless lymphadenopathy, in association with history of breast implants

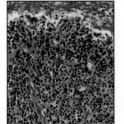
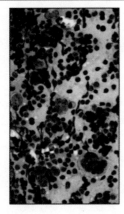

HODGKIN LYMPHOMA

CYTOMORPHOLOGY

- Binucleate (Reed Sternberg) or mononuclear variants (Hodgkin cells) with macronucleoli are the neoplastic cells, usually few
- Reed Sternberg cells in NLP Hodgkin have less prominent nucleoli, but large, folded, multilobate nuclei (LP cells or popcorn cells)
- Background of mixed inflammatory infiltrate comprising small lymphocytes, neutrophils, eosinophils, plasma cells, histiocytes, fibroblasts in classical HL
- Background cells in NLP HL comprise predominantly small B- and T-lymphocytes without other inflammatory cells
- Small, poorly formed granulomas may be seen

IMMUNOCYTOCHEMISTRY

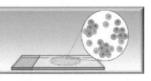

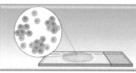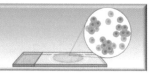

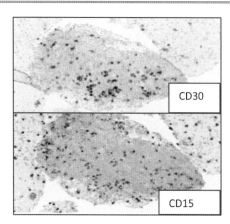

Figure: Diff-Quik, H&E stain, and CD30 and CD15 IHC. Large Reed-Sternberg cells in a background of small lymphocytes. The large cells show dual positivity for CD30 and CD15. Courtesy Laila Nomani, MD.

- RS cells of classical Hodgkin lymphoma positive for CD15, CD30, PAX-5, MUM1, and negative for CD45
- RS cells of NLP Hodgkin lymphoma positive for CD20, CD45, OCT2, BOB1, BCL6 and negative for CD15 and CD30

OTHER HIGH YIELD POINTS
- Accounts for up to 30% of all lymphomas
- Bimodal age distribution: a peak at 15-35 years of age, and a smaller peak in older individuals
- Classical HL accounts for more than 90-95% of all HL
- NLP HL accounts for up to 5% of all HL; more common in young males
- Painless lymphadenopathy: cervical, axillary, inguinal
- Systemic symptoms like fever, night sweats, weight loss
- Flow cytometric analysis is usually inconclusive as neoplastic cells are outnumbered by non-neoplastic reactive cells

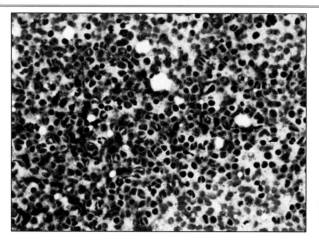

Figure: Diff-Quik stain. Cleaved small cells of follicular lymphoma. Courtesy Terrance Lynn, MD

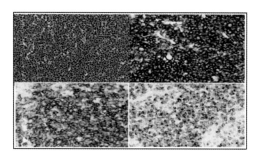

Figure: H&E stain, CD20, CD10 and BCL-2 IHC. Follicular lymphoma (clockwise) CD20, CD10 & BCL2 immunostains.

FOLLICULAR LYMPHOMA
CYTOMORPHOLOGY
- Mixture of small, cleaved cells (centrocytes; more in low grade) and large cleaved or non-cleaved cells (centroblasts; more in high grade)
- Centrocytes have irregular angulated or clefted nuclei with clumped chromatin and inconspicuous to absent nucleoli, with scant cytoplasm
- Centroblasts have large, vesicular nuclei with 1 to 3 small, but prominent nucleoli, usually closely opposed to the nuclear membrane (peripheral)
- Lymphoglandular bodies in background
- Tingible body macrophages absent or rare
- Lymphoid aggregates or vague follicular pattern may be appreciated in the background, but rare

IMMUNOCYTOCHEMISTRY
- Positive markers: B-cell markers, CD10, BCL2, BCL6
- Negative markers: CD5, CD43, CD200, Cyclin D1
- High Ki-67 proliferation index usually correlates with higher grade
- Characteristic t(14;18) translocation seen in up to 95% cases, more in Grade 1 FL and less in Grade 3; translocation results in juxtaposition of bcl-2 gene next to IgH locus

OTHER HIGH YIELD POINTS
- Most common small B-cell non-Hodgkin lymphoma, accounting for up to 35% of all non-Hodgkin lymphomas
- More than 80% patients present with disseminated disease involving multiple lymph node groups, bone marrow and other organs
- Up to one-third of patients show progression to large cell lymphoma, most commonly, diffuse large B-cell lymphoma
- In limited material, detection of t(14;18) translocation by FISH is more sensitive than immunostaining or flow cytometry

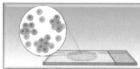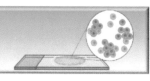

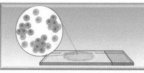 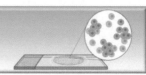

- Grading of FL into low (WHO Grade 1-2) versus high grade (WHO Grade 3) prognostically important, but should be avoided on aspirate smears, unless no other specimen is available from the patient.
- Centroblasts comprising less than 20% of total cellularity favors low grade FL, while centroblasts over 40-50% of total cellularity favors high grade FL. Grade cannot be assigned for centroblast percentage between 20 and 40
- Rare variant morphology may be occasionally encountered such as FL with monocytoid cells and FL with signet ring cells (can be mistaken for signet ring cell carcinoma)

MARGINAL ZONE LYMPHOMA (MZL)
CYTOMORPHOLOGY

- Polymorphous population of small to medium sized lymphocytes with slightly irregular nuclei
- Plasmacytoid lymphocytes
- Plasma cells show intranuclear inclusions (Dutcher bodies) and intracytoplasmic inclusions (Russell bodies)
- Monocytoid cells with irregular nuclei and moderate to abundant cytoplasm,
- Large transformed immunoblast-like cells
- Variable reactive T-cells in the background
- Other non-lymphoid cells include tingible body macrophages and follicular dendritic cells
- Lymphoglandular bodies in the background
- Characteristic lympho-epithelial lesions are usually not seen

IMMUNOCYTOCHEMISTRY

- Typically, CD5- CD10-
- Aberrant expression of CD43 in about half of cases
- t(11;18)(q21;q21): lung and stomach MZL
- t(14;18)(q32;q21): eye and salivary gland MZL
- t(3;14)(p14.1;q32): skin, thyroid, eye MZL

OTHER HIGH YIELD POINTS

- Strong association with autoimmune disorders (Hashimoto thyroiditis, Sjogren's syndrome) and certain infectious agents (Helicobacter pylori, Chlamydia trachomatis, Borrelia burgdorferi)
- Specific subtypes such as gastric MALT lymphoma can be treated with antibiotic therapy for eradication of H. pylori
- Differentiation from reactive lymphoid hyperplasia may be difficult on morphology
- Flow cytometric demonstration of light chain restriction is extremely helpful for diagnosis of lymphoma

DIFFERENTIAL DIAGNOSIS:
LYMPHOPLASMACYTIC LYMPHOMA (LPL)

- Spectrum of cells including small lymphocytes, plasmacytoid lymphocytes, plasma cell, immunoblast-like transformed cells
- Neoplastic cells with intranuclear (Dutcher bodies) or cytoplasmic (Russell bodies) immunoglobulin inclusions
- Frequent mast cells, eosinophils and histiocytes in the background

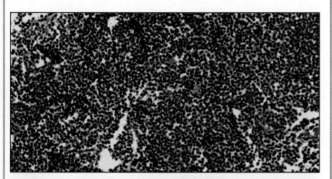
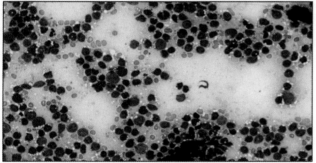

Figure: Diff-Quik stain and H&E stain. Marginal zone lymphoma showing polymorphous population of lymphocytes. Courtesy Laila Nomani, MD

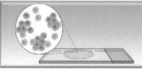 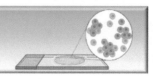

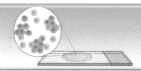
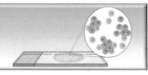

- Vast majority show MYD88 L265P mutation
- Waldenstrom macroglobulinemia (WM): bone marrow involvement by LPL and monoclonal IgM paraprotein in serum
- Paraprotein can rarely be IgG or IgA
- B-cell component positive markers: CD19, CD20, PAX-5 Plasmacytoid/plasma cell component positive markers: CD38, CD138

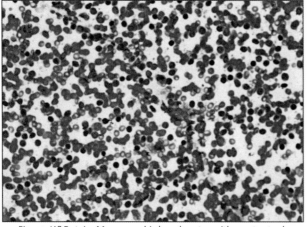

Figure: H&E stain. Monomorphic lymphocytes with scant cytoplasm and regular nuclei with clumped chromatin. Courtesy Terrance Lynn, MD

SMALL LYMPHOCYTIC LYMPHOMA (SLL)
CYTOMORPHOLOGY
- Monomorphic
- Small to medium-sized lymphocytes with round, regular nuclei, and clumped or clotted ("soccer-ball") chromatin, absent nucleoli, and scant cytoplasm
- Numerous smudge cells in the background
- Transformed cells include prolymphocytes and paraimmunoblasts with less clumped chromatin, prominent nucleoli, and more abundant cytoplasm; increased numbers may indicate progression to large cell lymphoma
- Background lymphoglandular bodies
- Tingible body macrophages absent or rare

IMMUNOCYTOCHEMISTRY
- Positive markers: CD5+ (dim), CD20+ (dim), CD23+, CD43+, CD200+, LEF1+
- Prognostic markers: Expression of CD49d, ZAP70 and CD38 in over 30% cells and unmutated IgH gene locus correlates with poor prognosis
- FISH: del 13q (most common), trisomy 12, del 11q, del 17p (worse prognosis)

OTHER HIGH YIELD POINTS
- Progression to large B-cell lymphoma (Richter transformation) seen in up to 10% of patients
- SLL can rarely transform to Hodgkin lymphoma
Proliferation centers in SLL may be immunoreactive with cyclin D1

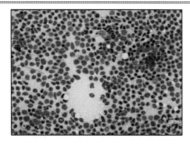

Figure: Diff-Quik stain (top), H&E stain, CD20, CD5 and cyclin D1 IHC. Mantle cell lymphoma with small irregular lymphocytes (Top).

Lymph node excision. Courtesy Terrance Lynn (smear) and Laila Nomani, MD (excision)

MANTLE CELL LYMPHOMA (MCL)
CYTOMORPHOLOGY
- Monomorphous population of small to intermediate-sized cells with slightly irregular nuclei with fine, less condensed chromatin, inconspicuous to absent nucleoli, and scant cytoplasm
- Transformed cells are not seen, unlike in other small B-cell lymphomas
- Epithelioid histiocytes with eosinophilic cytoplasm (but no tingible body macrophages)
- Background lymphoglandular bodies
- Blast-like cells or highly pleomorphic cells seen in blastoid and pleomorphic variants, respectively

IMMUNOCYTOCHEMISTRY
- Positive markers: CD5 (bright), CD20 (bright), CD43, cyclin D1, SOX11
- FISH: t(11;14)(q13;q32), involving cyclin D1 (BCL1) and IGH
- Elevated Ki-67 proliferation index bad prognostic factor

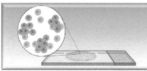
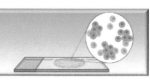

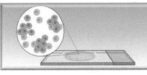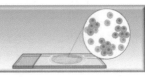
OTHER HIGH YIELD POINTS

- Usually, extensive disease at the time of diagnosis
- Extra-nodal disease, including peripheral blood involvement, more common than nodal involvement
- The only small B-cell lymphoma that does not have larger transformed cells
- The only small B-cell lymphoma that does not progress to a large B-cell lymphoma (rarely transform into blastoid variant)

DIFFUSE LARGE B-CELL LYMPHOMA (DLBCL)

CYTOMORPHOLOGY

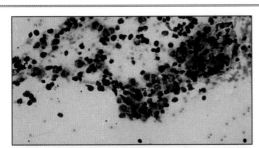

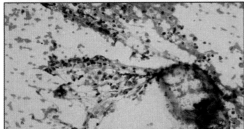

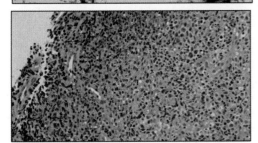

Figure: Diff-Quik stain, PAP stain and H&E stain. Diffuse large B-cell lymphoma. Courtesy Laila Nomain, MD

- Large cells, defined as nuclei 3-5 times the size of small lymphocyte, or larger than histiocyte nucleus, with scant to moderate cytoplasm, fine chromatin, and conspicuous nucleoli
- Cell morphology varies from case to case, and can resemble centroblasts, immunoblasts, or pleomorphic cells
- Varying proportion of reactive small lymphocytes, mostly T-cells
- Background lymphoglandular bodies

IMMUNOCYTOCHEMISTRY

- Positive markers: Pan-B-cell markers (CD20, CD79a, PAX-5)
- Variable expression: CD10, BCL6, MUM1 used to classify DLBCL into germinal center versus non-germinal center (activated B-cell) phenotypes (Hans algorithm)
- FISH for MYC, BCL2, and BCL6 translocations to prognostically separate other high-grade B-cell lymphomas from DLBCL
- Immunoreactivity for MYC and BCL2 and/or BCL6, without corresponding translocations defines "double or triple expressor" lymphoma
- CD5 positivity in up to 10% of DLBCL correlates with more aggressive behavior

OTHER HIGH YIELD POINTS

- Flow cytometry for diagnosis of DLBCL may be inconclusive as the large neoplastic B-cells may not be gated as lymphoid cells or may be too fragile to survive processing
- In general, for prioritizing limited specimens, flow cytometry is preferred for diagnosis of small B-cell lymphomas, whereas more tissue to be conserved for cell blocks and histology for diagnosis of large B-cell lymphomas

BURKITT LYMPHOMA

CYTOMORPHOLOGY

- Hypercellular smears
- Uniform medium-sized cells with high N:C ratio
- Round uniform nuclei with "intermediate" chromatin: less clumped than the soccer-ball chromatin of CLL/SLL, but more mature than the chromatin of a blast
- Several small nucleoli, or chromocenters
- Scant, deeply basophilic cytoplasm
- Cytoplasmic vacuoles
- Increased mitotic figures
- Tingible body macrophages
- Apoptotic bodies and necrotic debris in the background

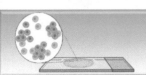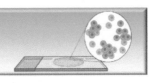

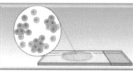
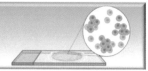

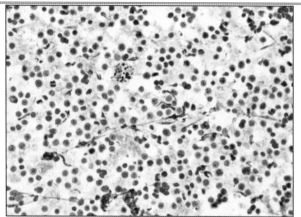

Diff-Quik stain and Pap stain. Intermediate sized lymphocytes with tingible body macrophages (starry sky). Courtesy Terrance Lynn, MD

IMMUNOCYTOCHEMISTRY
- Positive markers: Pan B-cell markers, CD10, BCL6, c-myc, Ki-67 (nearly 100%)
- Negative markers: BCL2, TdT
- FISH: t(8;14)(q24;q32) (most common), others: t(8;22)(q24;q11), t(2;8)(p12;q24)

OTHER HIGH YIELD POINTS
- 3 forms: Endemic (African and Asian children; almost always EBV-associated); sporadic (Children in western countries; less frequent association with EBV); immunodeficiency-related (immunocompromised adults; less frequent association with EBV)

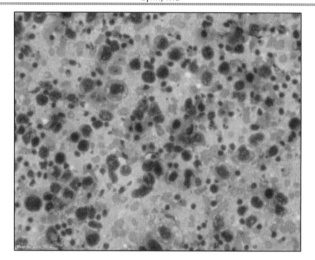

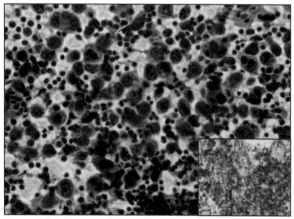

Figure: Diff-Quik stain, H&E stain, and CD30 IHC. Anaplastic large cell lymphoma with large, atypical cells with prominent nucleoli and CD30 positive IHC. Courtesy Melissa Hogan, MD and Terrance Lynn, MD

ANAPLASTIC LARGE CELL LYMPHOMA

CYTOMORPHOLOGY
- Moderately to highly cellular smears
- Mixture of large, intermediate, and small cells
- Large cells show highly irregular, polylobated, pleomorphic nuclei with prominent nucleoli: hallmark cells, donut (or bagel) cells, embryoid or kidney-shaped cells
- Reed-Sternberg-like cells (with smaller and less prominent nucleoli)
- Background necrosis and inflammation with neutrophils and histiocytes
- Rare subtypes include lymphohistiocytic type with increased non-neoplastic histiocytes, small cell, and sarcomatoid types

IMMUNOCYTOCHEMISTRY
- Can be T-cell phenotype (with aberrant loss of one or more pan-T-cell antigens) or null-cell phenotype (with no phenotypic evidence of T-cell markers)
- Positive markers: CD30, EMA, ALK
- Subset of ALCL, especially in pediatric population can be negative for ALK; worse prognosis in adult ALK-negative lymphomas
- Usually EBV- but subset of ALK- lymphomas can be EBV+
- FISH: various ALK translocations including t(2;5) (ALK/NPM; most common; up to 75% of cases; nuclear and cytoplasmic staining on IHC), t(2;17) with granular cytoplasmic staining; and t(2;X) with membranous staining

OTHER HIGH YIELD POINTS
- Accounts for up to 3% of all NHL in adults; greater proportion in children
- Male predominance
- Extra-nodal involvement common
- Good response to chemotherapy

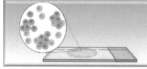
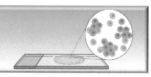

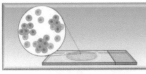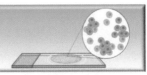
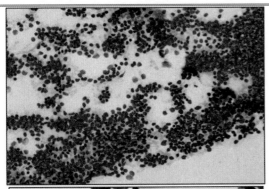

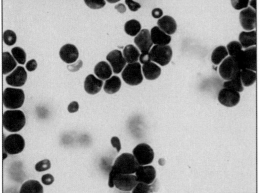

Figure: Diff-Quik stains. Lymphoblasts showing high nuclear to cytoplasmic ratio, inconspicuous nucleoli, and scant cytoplasm. Courtesy Terrence Lynn, MD (upper) and @Cytoatlas (lower)

LYMPHOBLASTIC LYMPHOMA
CYTOMORPHOLOGY
- Hypercellular smears
- Monotonous population of lymphoblasts
- Nuclei 1.5 to 2 times the size of mature small lymphocytes (intermediate-sized)
- Nuclei round and uniform or slightly irregular and indented
- Fine chromatin with inconspicuous nucleoli
- Scant cytoplasm, with or without vacuoles
- Mitotic figures and tingible body macrophages may be seen in the background

IMMUNOCYTOCHEMISTRY
- 90% cases are T-cell and 10% are B-cell LBL
- Common positive markers: TdT, CD10, CD99, CD34
- Positive in T-cell LBL: Pan-T-cell markers
- Positive in B-cell LBL: Pan-B-cell markers

OTHER HIGH YIELD POINTS
- More common in children; up to half of NHL in pediatric population
- More common in males
- Most common presentation: anterior mediastinal mass (80%)
- Translocation t(9;22) (BCR-ABL1) positive in up to a third of adult B-LBL

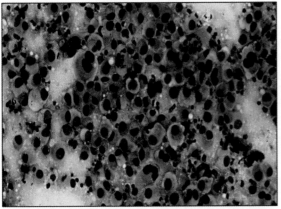

Figure: Diff-Quik stain. Plasmacytoid and discohesive cells of melanoma. Courtesy Laila Nomani, MD

METASTATIC MELANOMA
CYTOMORPHOLOGY
- Loosely cohesive or singly dispersed cells
- Epithelioid, small cell, or spindle cell pattern
- No lymphoglandular bodies in the background
- Eccentric nuclei with relatively abundant cytoplasm (plasmacytoid appearance)
- Binucleate cells
- Prominent cherry-red macronucleoli
- Intranuclear cytoplasmic inclusions
- Cytoplasmic melanin pigment in up to half of cases
- Foamy cytoplasm with small vacuoles

IMMUNOCYTOCHEMISTRY
- Positive markers: S100, SOX10, HMB-45, Melan-A

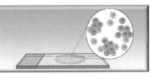

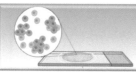
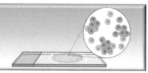

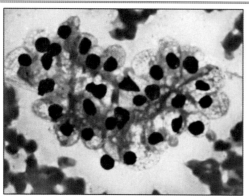

Figure: Diff-Quik stain. Metastatic clear cell renal cell carcinoma.

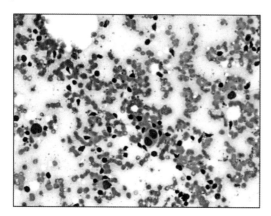

Figure: Diff-Quik stain. Metastatic lobular breast carcinoma.

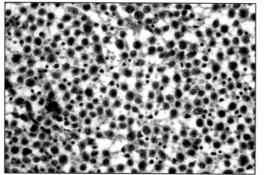

Figure: PAP stain. Seminomatous GCT metastatic to lymph node. Uniform round to oval cells with prominent nucleoli and ill-defined clear cytoplasm and lymphocytes in the background. Courtesy Syed Z. Ali, MD (@sza_jhcyto)

METASTATIC CARCINOMA

CYTOMORPHOLOGY

- High N:C ratio
- Hyperchromatic nuclei
- Irregular nuclear membranes
- Vesicular chromatin with prominent and irregular nucleoli
- Malignant cells usually seen in cohesive clusters, but can be poorly cohesive in poorly differentiated carcinomas
- No lymphoglandular bodies in the background
- Prominent necrosis: colorectal carcinoma and small cell carcinoma commonly, but can be seen in any high-grade carcinoma
- Signet ring cells: stomach, breast, colon
- Clear cells: Ovary, kidney, lung
- Plasmacytoid cells: breast, melanoma, neuro-endocrine
- Intra-nuclear inclusions: melanoma, papillary thyroid carcinoma
- Squamous cell carcinoma: keratinized orangeophilic cells, necrotic parakeratotic cells, tadpole cells, dense glassy cytoplasm
- HPV-associated carcinoma: basaloid immature cells with fine chromatin, inconspicuous nucleoli, scant cytoplasm, mitotic figures
- Urothelial carcinoma: cercariform cells
- Prostate carcinoma: acinar pattern with relatively bland morphology

IMMUNOCYTOCHEMISTRY

- Generally, always positive for cytokeratins
- Panel of different cytokeratins may be used, as all carcinomas are not positive for all keratins: AE1/AE3, MNF-116, CK7, CK20, CAM5.2, high molecular weight cytokeratins
- Appropriate panels of additional IHC to be performed for definite diagnosis of site of origin

METASTATIC GERM CELL TUMOR

CYTOMORPHOLOGY

- Seminomatous and non-seminomatous mixed GCT
- Background: Tigroid background (due to intracellular collagen) with lymphoglandular bodies (due to background lymphocytes)
- Mixture of large cells and small cells
- Large round to polyhedral cells with round to oval nuclei, finely granular chromatin, one or two prominent nucleoli and abundant, eosinophilic or slightly foamy cytoplasm
- Small cells are T-lymphocytes
- Granulomas may be seen

IMMUNOCYTOCHEMISTRY

- Positive markers: PLAP, CD117, Oct3/4, D2-40, SALL4, NANOG, SOX17
- Negative markers: cytokeratin (may be focal or weak), EMA, α-fetoprotein, HCG (may be positive in syncytiotrophoblasts), inhibin-α, CD30, glypican-3, SOX2

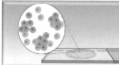
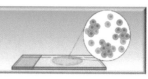

Chapter 13: Head and Neck Cytology

Deepa Iyer Kotari, MD

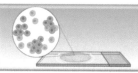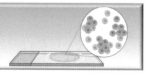

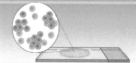

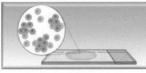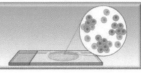
CYSTS OF HEAD AND NECK:

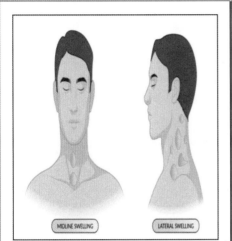

INTRODUCTION

Epidemiology

- Cystic lesions of head and neck area may be congenital or acquired
- >70% of the congenital cysts present in the first two decades of life
- Acquired cystic lesions can present at any age

Table 1: ANATOMICAL LOCATION OF CONGENITAL NECK CYSTS

LOCATION	NAME OF THE ENTITY
Midline	Thyroglossal cyst
	Dermoid cyst
	Ectopic thyroid
	Teratoma
	Plunging ranula
Lateral	Branchial cyst
Midline/ Lateral	Cystic hygroma
	Ectopic thymus/ Thymic cyst
	Cervical bronchogenic cyst

THYROGLOSSAL CYST (TGC)

CYTOMORPHOLOGY

- Clear to mucoid aspirate with colloid like material, pauci-cellular smears
- May contain respiratory epithelium or squamous metaplastic cells
- ± Thyroid epithelial cells (rare), background may contain inflammatory cells, macrophages & cholesterol crystals

OTHER HIGH YIELD POINTS

- Midline painless cyst of about 2-4 cm size, moves with deglutition and
- protrusion of tongue
- Differentiation from branchial cyst: Midline TGC vs lateral branchial cyst
- Presence of thyroid epithelial cells in thyroglossal cyst clinches the diagnosis

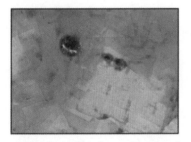

Figure: PAP stain. Aspirate from a thyroglossal cyst showing cholesterol crystals and macrophages.

DERMOID CYST

CYTOMORPHOLOGY

- Aspirate may be greasy and foul smelling
- Smears show mature and anucleate squames, keratinized and adnexal cells
- Background looks dirty and contains inflammatory cells and debris
- Cyst rupture may produce foreign body giant cell reaction, long standing cases may show calcium granules

OTHER HIGH YIELD POINTS

- Found along embryonic closure lines, common in periorbital area & can erode the frontal or orbital bone to evade dura
- Epidermoid cyst differs from dermoid in the absence of adnexal elements like hair, sebaceous and sweat glands

Figure: Diff-Quik and PAP stain. Epidermoid cyst showing anucleate squamous cells, note lack of adnexal elements.

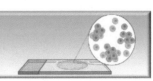

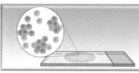
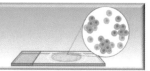

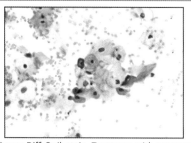

Figure: Diff-Quik stain. Teratoma with squamous cells, anucleate squamous cells and debris.

TERATOMA
CYTOMORPHOLOGY
- Cellular smears with keratinized squames, anucleate squames and hair shaft derivatives
- Glandular epithelium may be seen
- Background shows debris ± inflammatory cells
- Foreign body giant cell reaction may be seen
- Presence of immature neural elements predominate in immature/ malignant teratoma

OTHER HIGH YIELD POINTS
- Usually benign in childhood and more likely to be malignant in adults
- Well differentiated squamous cell carcinoma
- SCC usually occurs in older adults
- Cells lack cohesion in SCC and appear as dispersed pleomorphic squames
- Teratoma has cohesive clusters of squames with low N/C ratio

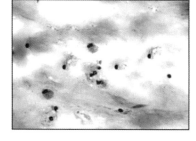

Figure: Diff-Quik stain. Plunging ranula with thick mucinous material and macrophages.

PLUNGING RANULA
CYTOMORPHOLOGY
- Sticky viscous aspirate with pools of mucin and salivary gland cells
- Background has histiocytes and inflammatory cells

OTHER HIGH YIELD POINTS
- Simple ranulas are usually at the floor of the mouth involving sublingual salivary gland while plunging ranula extends to the neck in the midline after dissecting through the muscles of the floor of the mouth
- Extravasated mucin is PAS +
- Simple ranula is a pseudo cyst with focal epithelial lining limited to the floor of the mouth while plunging ranula extends to the neck

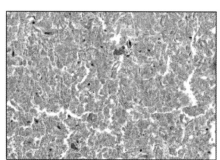

Figure: PAP stain. Branchial cleft cyst aspirate showing mature and degenerating squamous cells with scattered inflammatory cells.

LATERAL CYSTS
BRANCHIAL CYST/ BRANCHIAL CLEFT CYST
CYTOMORPHOLOGY
- Mature squamous cells and degenerating squamous cells with inflammatory cells in the background
- Rarely respiratory epithelial cells may be seen, no cytological atypia

OTHER HIGH YIELD POINTS
- Also called cervical lympho-epithelial cysts or lateral neck cysts
- Bilateral masses suggest syndromic association
- Excellent prognosis after complete excision with a recurrence rate of <3 %
- Presence of atypia in a middle aged and older patient should raise suspicion of metastatic oropharyngeal carcinoma
- p16 immunostaining is a potential pitfall in such cases as more than half of branchial cysts also express p16
- History of radiation to the neck for another lesion also can cause atypia in branchial cyst lining cells

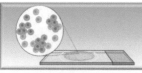
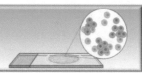

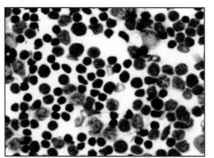

Figure: Diff-Quik stain. Aspirate from ectopic thymus showing population of lymphoid cells and scattered thymocytes.

ECTOPIC THYMUS/ THYMIC CYST:
CYTOMORPHOLOGY
- Ectopic thymus aspirates are cellular with small lymphocytes, monocytes and thymocytes
- Thymic cysts have serosanguinous aspirate with inflammatory cells, RBCs, occasional cholesterol crystals and calcium deposits, few squamous, spindled or ciliated epithelial cells

OTHER HIGH YIELD POINTS
- Ectopic thymic tissue is usually seen in children < 10 years of age, usually seen in the anterior triangle of neck
- On Immunocytochemistry B and T cell show thymic phenotype
- Surgical excision is the treatment of choice
- Thymic cysts may be closely approximated to the carotid sheath CT/ USG -guided aspiration is ideal in such cases

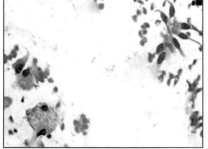

Figure: PAP stain. Bronchial cyst with respiratory epithelium and background macrophages.

CERVICAL BRONCHOGENIC CYST
CYTOMORPHOLOGY
- Aspirate is serous or mucinous with ciliated columnar and occasional squamous metaplastic cells ± elements of cartilage/muscle
- Inflammatory cells and macrophages may be seen in the background

OTHER HIGH YIELD POINTS
- Also called bronchial cyst, rare malformation of the ventral foregut CK7 +
- Can be mistaken for branchial cleft cyst
- Presence of muscle/ cartilage elements points towards bronchogenic cyst

CUTANEOUS LESIONS OF THE HEAD AND NECK

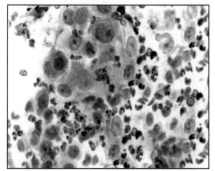

Figure: Diff-Quik stain. Cutaneous squamous cell carcinoma with marked pleomorphism, central nuclei, prominent nucleoli and perinuclear halo, in a necrotic background.

SQUAMOUS CELL CARCINOMA (SCC)
CYTOMORPHOLOGY
- Non- keratinizing SCC shows solid cohesive bits
- Individual cells have round to oval nuclei
- Keratinizing SCC have scattered single cells with eosinophilic refractile cytoplasm, nuclei show marked pleomorphism, hyperchromatic and homogenous chromatin with perinuclear halo, large pleomorphic nucleoli and mitotic figures
- Bizarre tadpole shapes, spindled cells with caudate nuclei may be seen
- Necrosis is prominent with mixed inflammatory infiltrates and keratin pearls
- PAP stain can be used to differentiate orangeophilic keratinization from necrosis

OTHER HIGH YIELD POINTS
- Usually seen in elderly, risk factor is sun exposure, prior radiotherapy, Xeroderma pigmentosum and Epidermolysis bullosa
- IHC is required for poorly differentiated and spindle cell variants: CK5/6, p63, p40
- Cystic variants may be mistaken for branchial cleft cyst, epidermal inclusion cyst or teratoma
- Branchial cleft cyst occurs at younger age, lack keratin pearls, lack prominent nucleoli, perinuclear halo and marked pleomorphism that are seen in SCC
- Epidermal inclusion cyst has squames with low N/C ratio
- Spindle cell SCC resembles mesenchymal tumor and spindle cell melanoma
- Keratotic BCC may mimic SCC, more marked pleomorphism and higher N/C ratio and lack of nuclear palisading prompts towards SCC

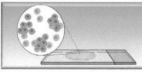
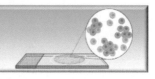

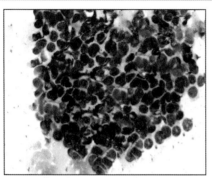

Figure: Diff-Quik stain. Basal cell carcinoma smear showing tight cluster of basaloid cells with hyperchromasia, nuclear overlapping and vague palisading at the edges, background shows necrotic debris.

BASAL CELL CARCINOMA (SCC)
CYTOMORPHOLOGY
- High cellularity in the aspirates with cohesive tight clusters with smooth edges, clear outline and occasional budding & palisading of the nuclei at the edges
- High N/C ratio of the monomorphic round to oval nuclei with crowding, overlapping and hyperchromasia, inconspicuous nucleoli
- No intercellular bridges, single cells may also be seen in the background with scant cytoplasm, occasional Langerhans cells and melanocytes may be seen in the background
- Keratotic BCC shows hair like differentiated cells with elongated nuclei and eosinophilic to amphiphilic cytoplasm with few horn cysts
- Cystic BCC shows sebaceous differentiation with solid BCC fragments admixed with sebaceous cells
- Adenoid BCC shows apocrine differentiation with tubule like areas and central secretions
- Granular cell BCC shows granular cells alone ± classical BCC pattern
- Pigmented BCC shows melanophages, melanocytes and tumor cells with melanin

OTHER HIGH YIELD POINTS
- Also called Rodent ulcer or basal epithelioma
- BCC is a tumor of sun exposed hair bearing area of the skin unlike SCC which may occur in lips and mucosal areas, usually seen in 4th to 8th decade of life
- BCC almost never metastasizes (rarely to lymph node)

VARIANT	CLINICAL PRESENTATION
Superficial	Erythematous macule
Nodular	Raised translucent nodule ± pigmentation and ulceration
Morpheaform/ sclerosing	Shiny resembling scleroderma
Basosquamous	Resembles SCC with keratotic appearance and ulceration
Fibroepithelioma of pinkus	Pink plaque, Back > Head & neck

- Immunocytochemistry shows CK AE1/AE3 , CAM 5.2, p53, p63, BerEP4 p63, AR,
- 34β E12, BCL2 (diffuse staining), CD10 (+ in only tumor cells, - in stroma)
- Granular cell tumor resembles granular variant of BCC
- Non keratinizing SCC can be differentiated from BCC by lack of cohesion and presence of intercellular bridges in the SCC
- Cytological differentiation of trichoepithelioma and BCC cannot be done based
- on morphology
- **Syndromes associated with BCC**
  - ➢ Xeroderma pigmentosum
  - ➢ Gorlin syndrome
  - ➢ Occulocutaneous albinism
  - ➢ Muir-Torre syndrome
  - ➢ Bazex-Dupre'-Christol syndrome

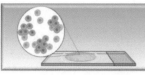
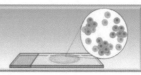
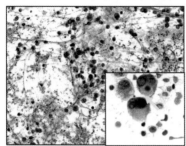

Figure: PAP stains. Melanoma with discohesive cells with large pleomorphic nuclei with nuclear pseudo-inclusions (inset arrow).

MELANOMA:

CYTOMORPHOLOGY

- Large discohesive cells of varying sizes and shapes
- Large pleomorphic nuclei with clumped chromatin and prominent eosinophilic nucleoli
- Nuclear pseudo-inclusions may be seen
- Cytoplasm may vary from scant to abundant ± melanin pigment
- Background may show melanophages ± dispersed melanin ± giant cells

OTHER HIGH YIELD POINTS

- Predisposition to melanoma includes fair skin, family history, sun exposure, Dysplastic nevus syndrome, immunosuppression, germline mutations of TERT, CDK4, CDKN2A, MITF, MIC1R, BAP1 gene
- IHC: Positive for S100, Melan A, HMB-45, tyrosinase

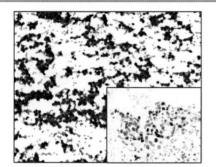

Figure: Diff-Quik stain and MCPyV IHC. Merkel cell carcinoma with monotonous small round blue cells, Inset: MCPyV IHC positivity.

MERKEL CELL CARCINOMA:

CYTOMORPHOLOGY

- Smears are cellular with monotonous small round cell population with poorly defined cell borders, scant cytoplasm and salt and pepper chromatin
- Frequent mitotic figures may be seen
- Background may have stripped nuclei, syncytial fragments and necrosis

OTHER HIGH YIELD POINTS

- Also called cutaneous neuroendocrine carcinoma, nearly 50% occur in head and neck region
- IHC: Positive CD56, NSE, chromogranin, synaptophysin, NKX 2.2, INSM1, neurofilament protein, CK20(peri-nuclear dot like)
- CM2B4 antibody shows nuclear positivity for Merkel cell polyoma virus-MCPyV
- Negative: CK7, S100, TTF 1, HMWCK, LCA
- Prognosis is generally poor (5-year survival < 50%)
- Immune check point inhibitors like anti PDL-1 monoclonal antibody & Avelumab are administered in advanced/ unresectable cases
- Recurrence rate after excision is 30% and 80% in isolated and metastatic cases respectively
- Differential diagnosis of Merkel cell carcinoma includes all the small round blue cell tumors of head and neck

NASAL CAVITY AND PARANASAL SINUSES

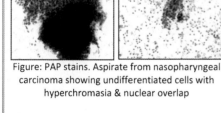

Figure: PAP stains. Aspirate from nasopharyngeal carcinoma showing undifferentiated cells with hyperchromasia & nuclear overlap

NASOPHARYNGEAL CARCINOMA

CYTOMORPHOLOGY

- Aspirate shows irregular clusters/ sheets of large cells with fragile cytoplasm and hyperchromatic large nuclei with nuclear overlap and prominent nucleoli
- Background usually has lymphocytes and plasma cells
- Lympho-epitheliomatous variant may show large cohesive sheets of cells resembling lymphoma
- Keratinized cells may also be seen

OTHER HIGH YIELD POINTS

- Occupational exposure to chemical fumes, consumption of smoked fish with nitrosamine content has been implicated as the cause
- Usually located in fossa of Rosenmuller and posterior wall of nasopharynx
- IHC: Positive P63, HMWCK, pancytokeratin, Negative: EMA, CK7, CK20
- EBER-ISH
- Mainstay in treatment is radiation ± Chemotherapy
- Keratinizing variant is less responsive to radiation and therefore has poorer prognosis than the non-keratinizing variant

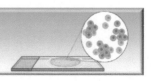

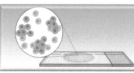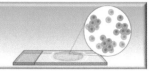
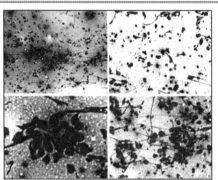
Figure: Diff-Quik stains. SNUC showing small to medium sized cells with high N/C ratio.

SINONASAL UNDIFFERENTIATED CARCINOMA
CYTOMORPHOLOGY
- Aspirates are cellular with small to medium sized cells with ill-defined cell borders and scant cytoplasm and high N/C ratio
- Nucleus has coarse chromatin with prominent nucleoli and may resemble small cell neuroendocrine tumors
- Frequent mitosis and crush artefacts
OTHER HIGH YIELD POINTS
- Highly aggressive rare tumor with uncertain pathogenesis
- IHC: Positive for epithelial markers like CAM 5.2, AE1/AE2, OSCAR
- Negative or focal for CK 5/6, CK14, p40 and p63
- Overall prognosis is poor with a median survival of less than 20 months
- A small subset of SNUC include IDH mutant subtype

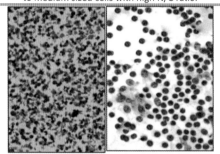
Figure: PAP stains. Esthesioneuroblastoma showing monomorphic small round blue cells that are loosely cohesive, note rosette formations.

ESTHESIONEUROBLASTOMA
CYTOMORPHOLOGY
- Aspirate is cellular with monomorphic small round blue cells that are loosely cohesive
- Cells appear to have delicate cytoplasm with central nucleus with salt and pepper chromatin and indistinct or absent nucleolus, rosettes/ pseudo-rosettes
OTHER HIGH YIELD POINTS
- Also called olfactory neuroblastoma
- Occurs in 5th to 6th decades, Usual location is in ethmoid sinus and cribriform plate as a glistening mass of about 1 cm size
- IHC: Positive neuroendocrine markers, S100 and GFAP
- Negative: Desmin, myogenin, CD99, p63, FLI 1
- Extensive craniofacial resection with adequate margins including the removal of the cribriform plate is followed usually by radiotherapy
- Silver stains can highlight neurosecretory granules

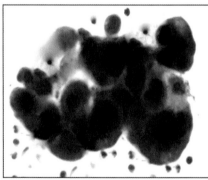
Figure: Diff-Quik stain. Metastatic carcinoma (Photo from a primary in the breast)

METASTASIS
CYTOMORPHOLOGY
- Cytological diagnosis is done when there is high clinical suspicion
- Aspirate smears resemble the primary tumor
OTHER HIGH YIELD POINTS
- RCCs are the commonest tumors metastasizing to paranasal sinus
- Lymphomas, breast carcinomas, lung carcinomas and salivary gland carcinomas, neuroendocrine tumors also metastasize to paranasal sinuses
- Maxillary sinus is most frequently affected
- IHC is done for confirmation
OROPHARYNGEAL SQUAMOUS CELL CARCINOMA: HPV POSITIVE
CYTOMORPHOLOGY
- Cellular smears, cohesive clusters or sheets of tumor cells
- Pleomorphic nuclei, prominent nucleoli
- Uncommon squamous differentiation or keratinization (as it is non-keratinizing)
OTHER HIGH YIELD POINTS
  - M>F, elderly, high socioeconomic status
  - Site: Base of tongue and tonsils
  - >90% cases due to HPV16
  - Associated with oral sex
  - Present at advanced stage with cystic neck lymph node metastasis

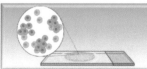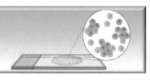

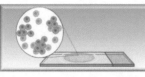
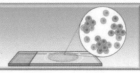
	➤ IHC: Positive: p16, HR-HPV-ISH ➤ More common PIK3CA mutation or gene amplification ➤ Better survival compared to HPV-SCC
	OROPHARYNGEAL SQUAMOUS CELL CARCINOMA: HPV NEGATIVE CYTOMORPHOLOGY • Keratinizing squamous cell carcinoma with sheets and clusters of squamous cells • Dense orangeophilic cytoplasm • +/- necrosis OTHER HIGH YIELD POINTS • Affects palate > base of tongue or tonsils • Smoking related • Worse prognosis than HPV positive SCC • IHC: Negative for p16 or hrHPV-ISH P53 expression (mutant)

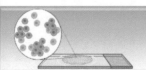
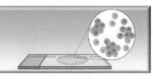

Chapter 14: Breast and Nipple Cytology

Deepak Donthi, MD

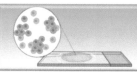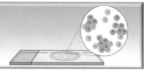

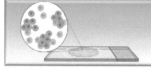

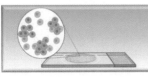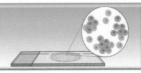
SPECIMEN TYPES

FNA

- To evaluate palpable breast masses and cysts
- To evaluate palpable and non-palpable mammographic abnormalities
- Useful in recurrent lesions
- Limitations
  - Not appropriate for < 1 cm lesions
  - Can't distinguish in situ from invasive carcinoma
  - False negative error: sampling issue, interpretation, and/or both

ADEQUACY: (5-6 GROUPS OF WELL-PRESERVED BEING DUCTAL CELLS)

REPORTING TERMINOLOGY

- Insufficient/inadequate
  - < 6 clusters of cells each contain 5-10 cells
  - < 10 intact bipolar cells per 10 (x200) medium power fields.

- Benign
- Atypical
- Suspicious
- Malignant

NIPPLE DISCHARGE CYTOLOGY

	BENIGN NIPPLE SECRETIONS	MALIGNANT NIPPLE SECRETIONS
	PAP stain.	Diff-Quik stain.
Smears	Hypocellular	Hypercellular, necrotic debris
Cell types	Few ductal, many histocytes with vacuolated cytoplasm RBCs and inflammatory cells	Ductal cells
Arrangement	Usually, single cells, loose or tight clusters	Isolated and large clusters
Nucleus	Monomorphic, small	Variable size and shape, nucleoli, naked nuclei

SPECIMEN EVALUATION:

ARCHITECTURAL PATTERNS				
Sheets	**3-D clusters**	**Loose clusters**	**Papillary**	**Isolated cells**
Fibrocystic changes	Fibroadenoma and Phyllodes	Invasive carcinoma	Fibroadenoma	Carcinoma
Fibroadenoma	Intraductal papilloma	Ductal carcinoma in-situ (DCIS)	Intraductal Papilloma	Lactation
Lobular carcinoma in-situ (LCIS)	Mucinous carcinoma		Papillary carcinoma	Lymphoma

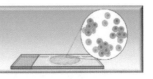

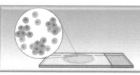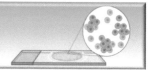
BACKGROUND	
Mucin	**Blood**
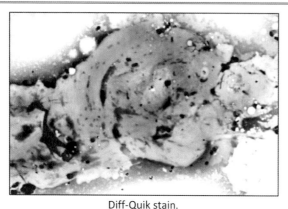	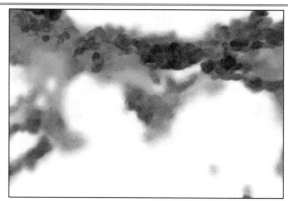
Diff-Quik stain.	H&E stain.
Mucocele, Fibroadenoma and mucinous carcinoma	Intraductal papilloma, angiosarcoma and papillary carcinoma

BENIGN LESIONS OF THE BREAST

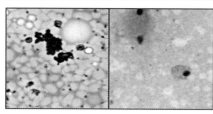

Figure: Diff-Quik and PAP stain. Fibrocystic change: Benign ductal cells and foamy histiocytes against a proteinaceous background. ©CytoAtlas

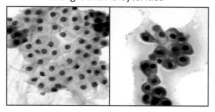

Figure: PAP stain. Fibrocystic change: Cells with apocrine change. ©CytoAtlas

FIBROCYSTIC CHANGES

CYTOMORPHOLOGY

	Proliferative	Non-proliferative
Smears	Hypercellular	Hypocellular
Cell types	Ductal and myoepithelial cells	Apocrine, foam and small ductal cells

OTHER HIGH YIELD POINTS
- Simple cysts (without septations) collapse easily on aspiration; the procedure can be therapeutic
- Complex cysts (with septations) are more resilient to collapse on aspiration and have a greater association with abscess formation and malignancy
- Granular cell tumors can morphologically resemble apocrine cells, but can be identified by their labelling with S-100

RADIATION INDUCED CHANGES

CYTOMORPHOLOGY
- FNA yields hypocellular smears

- Cells show bizarre shapes, increase in nuclear and cytoplasmic size with preservation of N/C ratio, prominent nucleoli, and increased cytoplasmic vacuolation, multinucleation

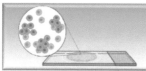

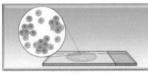

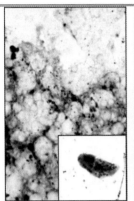
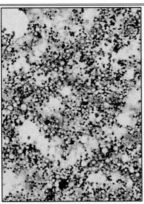

Figure 1: PAP stain. Fat Necrosis: Pap stain showing degenerated and necrotic adipocytes (loss of nuclei), and foamy macrophages. Inset: Multinucleated histiocytic giant cell. ©CytoAtlas. Figure 2: Silicone granuloma. Courtesy Terrance, MD

FAT NECROSIS

CYTOMORPHOLOGY

- Sparsely cellular aspirates show necrotic or degenerated adipose tissue (with loss of nuclei) against a proteinaceous background
- Foamy macrophages with oval nuclei and abundant, extensively vacuolated cytoplasm are seen either as single cells or in small clusters
- Multinucleated giant cells and inflammatory cells like neutrophils (early stages) can be seen

Differential diagnoses of fat necrosis	
Diagnosis	**Cytomorphology**
Subareolar abscess	<ul><li>Anucleate squames with keratin debris</li><li>Acute inflammation</li></ul>
Acute mastitis	<ul><li>Abundant acute inflammation</li></ul>
Silicon mastitis	<ul><li>Intracytoplasmic refractile material within histiocytes</li><li>Relevant history</li></ul>

PAPILLOMA

CYTOMORPHOLOGY

- Moderately cellular smears showing sheets or cohesive 3-D clusters with fibrovascular cores
- The fibrovascular cores are lined by cuboidal to columnar cells along with myoepithelial cells
- +/- Apocrine cells, foam cells and inflammation

HISTOLOGIC FEATURES

- Multiple fibrovascular cores with arborizing finger like fronds, located within a central fibrotic duct
- Myoepithelial cells present in the fibrovascular cores and the wall
- Can undergo infarction, necrosis, hemorrhage, and calcification

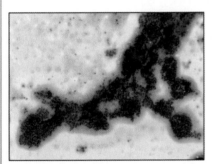

Figure: PAP stain. Papillary lesion of breast.

OTHER HIGH YIELD POINTS

- Usually affects younger (<35 years) age group
- Typical presentation is a unilateral single mass under usually the nipple with serosanguinous discharge
- While symptomatic papillomas are excised, asymptomatic lesions require no further excision
- Myoepithelial markers such as p63 and CK5/6 help differentiate benign intraductal papillomas from papillary DCIS and papillary carcinoma
- FNA cannot always differentiate with total accuracy between intraductal papillomas and papillary neoplasms – a diagnosis of atypical/suspicious papillary neoplasm can be suggested

Clues to differentiate papillary neoplasms	
Intraductal papilloma	**Atypical/suspicious papillary neoplasms**
Cohesive, tight papillary clusters with rare, isolated cells	Frond-like clusters with non-cohesive, single, scattered tumor cells
Numerous myoepithelial cells seen as bipolar naked nuclei	Monomorphous population of columnar tumor cells (i.e., absence of myoepithelial cells)
	Hemorrhagic background with hemosiderin laden macrophages

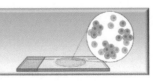

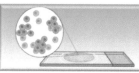
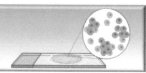

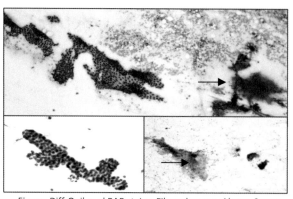

Figure: Diff-Quik and PAP stains. Fibroadenoma: Above -Smear showing stag-horn shaped epithelial groups and metachromatic stromal fragments (arrow); below: Benign ductal cells and fibromyxoid matrix (arrow). ©CytoAtlas

FIBROADENOMA
CYTOMORPHOLOGY

- Hypercellular smears showing cohesive, crowded, complex papillary fronds (seen in a stag horn pattern)
- Characteristic dual population of cells in the groups: ductal epithelial cells and numerous myoepithelial cells (seen as bipolar, spindled, naked nuclei)
- Prominent cellular stroma can take on a myxoid appearance
- Metachromatic stromal fragments can be seen on Diff-Quik stain
- Features such as cytologic atypia, loss of cohesion, and a hemorrhagic background suggest a diagnosis other than fibroadenoma

OTHER HIGH YIELD POINTS

- Most common breast tumor seen in reproductive age group women
- Presents as a firm, mobile, slow-growing, painless, palpable mass in breast parenchyma

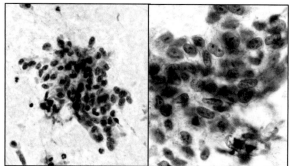

Figure: Diff-Quik stain. Phyllodes tumor: Hypercellular stromal fragment ©CytoAtlas

Figure: PAP stains. Phyllodes tumor: Left: Aspirate showing epithelial and stromal cells with few dispersed stromal cells (left) and high-power view of atypical stromal cells (right). ©CytoAtlas

PHYLLODES TUMOR
CYTOMORPHOLOGY

- Biphasic tumor that yields moderately to highly cellular smears
- Even though high stromal cellularity and increased stroma to epithelial ratio favors malignancy, accurate distinction of benign, borderline, and malignant phyllodes tumors needs resection sample for classification
- Atypia can be present even in the epithelial component

Features favoring diagnosis of Phyllodes tumor over Fibroadenoma
Higher cellularity with greater stromal cellularity
Presence of large, atypical, or dispersed spindle cells within the stromal component
Cohesive groups of fibroblasts showing "pavement"-like pattern
Presence of marked stromal atypia, stromal mitoses, or epithelial atypia
Presence of malignant heterologous elements (such tumors are classified as malignant Phyllodes tumor by definition)

Differential diagnoses for Phyllodes tumors	
Fibroadenoma	See table above
Invasive ductal carcinoma	• Presence of stromal component and few benign ductal elements favors diagnosis of Phyllodes tumor
Metaplastic carcinoma and soft tissue tumors	• Atypical spindle cell component can be misleading on cytology • Presence of benign ductal component suggests a diagnosis of Phyllodes tumor

OTHER HIGH YIELD POINTS
- Much less common than fibroadenomas (1% of breast tumors)
- Higher incidence in the 4th and 5th decade

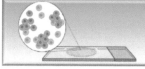
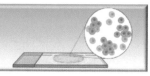

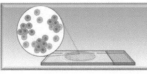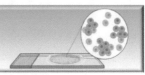
MALIGNANT LESIONS OF THE BREAST

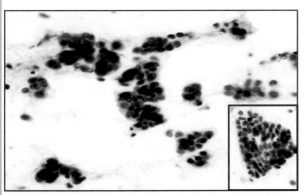

Figure: Diff-Quik stain. Ductal Carcinoma: Aspirate showing clusters and isolated tumor cells; Inset: high magnification view shows plasmacytoid malignant cells with enlarged nuclei; cytoplasmic vacuolations are due to lipid that dissolves during processing. ©CytoAtlas

Figure: PAP stain. Ductal Carcinoma: Low (Inset) and high magnification mages show clusters of tumor cells with enlarged, irregular nuclei and prominent nucleoli. ©CytoAtlas

INVASIVE DUCTAL CARCINOMA

CYTOMORPHOLOGY

- Ductal carcinomas yield hypercellular smears with cells seen in clusters or as single cells
- Tumor cells tend to have large, pleomorphic, hypo- to hyperchromatic nuclei with fine or coarse granular chromatin
- High degree of variation in nuclear size and shape
- Nuclei may show protrusion from the cytoplasm ("Comet cells")
- Nucleoli can be prominently large or small, and can show irregular nucleolar borders and crowding
- Cytoplasm can flow towards one side (based on the smearing pattern) giving it a pulled-out appearance
- Increased mitotic activity
- Background may be clean, or may show karyorrhectic debris and acute inflammation

OTHER HIGH YIELD POINTS

- Most common malignant neoplasm in breast FNACs
- Epithelial and myoepithelial IHC markers along with proliferation markers can be used on cell blocks
- Calcifications can be present in both in-situ as well as invasive carcinoma

Differential diagnoses for Invasive duct carcinoma	
DCIS	• Cannot reliably differentiate in-situ from invasive carcinoma on cytology
Fibroadenoma	• Features favoring a fibroadenoma are presence of a stromal component showing bipolar cells in pairs, and the presence of small ductal cells with single, uniform nuclei
Phyllodes tumor	• Presence of stromal component and few benign ductal elements favors diagnosis of Phyllodes tumor
Lactation-related changes	• Can show scattered, single cells with prominent nucleoli, but lack the hyperchromatic nuclei and anisonucleosis seen in carcinoma
Changes with nuclear atypia	• Nuclear atypia can be seen in fat necrosis, inflammatory conditions, and radiation-related changes • Unlike in carcinoma, the atypia tends to be focal and mild

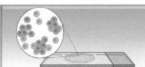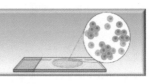

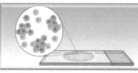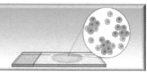
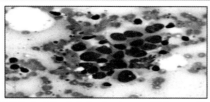

Figure: Diff-Quik stain. Lobular Carcinoma: High magnification view of a Diff-Quik stained aspirate showing a small cluster of lobular carcinoma cells with enlarged irregular nuclei; a mitotic figure can be seen. ©CytoAtlas

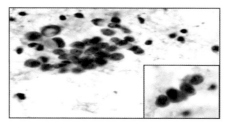

Figure: PAP stain. Lobular Carcinoma: Pap-stained aspirates showing poorly formed clusters of carcinoma cells with intracytoplasmic mucin; Inset: Single file pattern. ©CytoAtlas

INVASIVE LOBULAR CARCINOMA

CYTOMORPHOLOGY

- Sparsely cellular smears due to desmoplastic stroma
- Tumor cells are usually single, or can be seen in linear chains and small clusters
- Cellular morphology can range from plasmacytoid (with eccentric nucleus), to signet-ring type (with prominent intracytoplasmic mucin vacuole)
- Nucleoli are usually indistinct
- Pleomorphic lobular carcinoma tends to yield more cellular smears against a necrotic background with larger nuclei, marked pleomorphism, easily identifiable nucleoli, and apocrine change

OTHER HIGH YIELD POINTS

- Invasive and in-situ lobular carcinoma cannot be differentiated on cytology alone
- Intracytoplasmic mucin vacuoles seen in lobular carcinoma can be highlighted by mucicarmine or PAS
- Radiation changes can mimic invasive lobular carcinoma due to cytoplasmic vacuolation
- Metastasis of lobular carcinoma to the brain is an important cause "carcinomatous meningitis"

MUCINOUS (COLLOID) CARCINOMA

CYTOMORPHOLOGY

- Smears show tightly packed clusters or irregular glandular arrangements of tumor cells floating in extracellular pools of mucin
- Tumor cells display low grade atypia with uniform nuclear membranes, small nuclei, and fine chromatin
- Tumor cells can show plasmacytoid morphology and neuroendocrine differentiation
- Branching capillaries can be seen within the mucinous background

OTHER HIGH YIELD POINTS

- Benign lesions that can yield mucinous material on aspiration include lactational breast parenchyma, mucoceles, fibroadenomas, and aspiration of gel used in augmentation procedures
- Background mucin is red on Romanowsky stains and green on pap stain
- FNA cannot accurate discriminate between pure mucinous carcinomas and mixed mucinous carcinomas

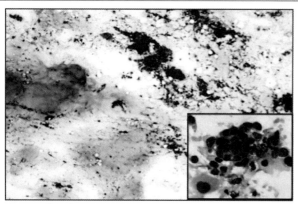

Figure: Diff-Quik stain. Mucinous Carcinoma: Aspirate showing small sheets of malignant cells in a background of mucin. Inset: High power view shows plasmacytoid tumor cells with low grade atypia. ©CytoAtlas

Differential diagnoses for Mucinous carcinoma	
Fibroadenoma	• Cellular component in fibroadenoma shows a branching architecture • Presence of stromal elements and bipolar cells favors fibroadenoma
Mucocele	• Lacks the three-dimension cellular balls seen in mucinous carcinoma
Lobular carcinoma	• Dispersed single cells seen without a mucinous background

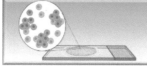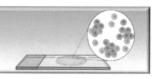

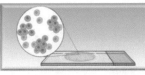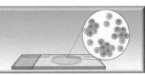
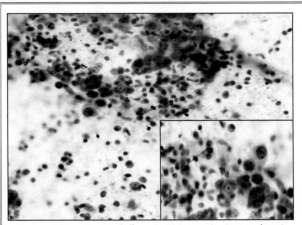

Figure: PAP stain. Medullary Carcinoma: Aspirates showing pleomorphic tumor cells in a lymphoplasmacytic background.
©CytoAtlas

MEDULLARY CARCINOMA
CYTOMORPHOLOGY
- Hypercellular smears with loose clusters and single cells
- Cells have large, vesicular nuclei with irregular membranes, and a large, irregular nucleolus
- Mitotic figures can be numerous
- Lymphocytes and plasma cells associated with tumor cells

OTHER HIGH YIELD POINTS
- Usually triple negative subtype (ER, PR, Her-2 negative)
- These tumors have a better prognosis than ductal carcinoma

Differential diagnoses for Medullary carcinoma	
Chronic mastitis	• Lacks atypical tumor cells
Large cell lymphoma	• Medullary carcinoma cells are larger with greater pleomorphism and clustering • IHC for CD45 and EMA can be useful
Ductal carcinoma	• FNA alone might not be able to separate medullary carcinomas from poorly differentiated ductal carcinomas
Lactating adenoma	• Lactating adenomas can show cells with enlarged nuclei and vacuolated cytoplasm against a proteinaceous background, but lack the syncytial pattern seen in medullary carcinomas

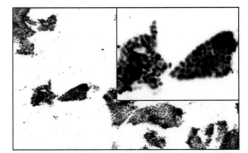

Figure: PAP stained. Tubular Carcinoma: Low and high magnification views of a aspirates showing angulated and pointed groups with cells showing minimal nuclear atypia.
©CytoAtlas

TUBULAR CARCINOMA
CYTOMORPHOLOGY
- Hypocellular smears due stromal fibrosis
- Comma shaped, well-defined, angular and pointed (arrowhead like) tightly packed glands
- Tumor cells have round to uniform nuclei with fine granular chromatin and indistinct nucleoli
- Mitotic figures are rare

OTHER HIGH YIELD POINTS
- True tubular carcinomas (with over 90% composed of tubular structures) associated with a good prognosis
- Cases of ductal or lobular carcinoma with a tubular component would require a biopsy diagnosis

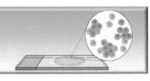

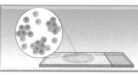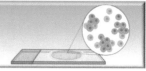

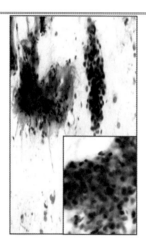

Figure 1: PAP stain. Metaplastic Carcinoma: Aspirate showing pleomorphic tumor cells with spindle and epithelioid morphology. Figure 2: PAP stain. Metaplastic Carcinoma: Aspirate showing epithelial and mesenchymal elements; Inset: High magnification view shows cells with high grade atypia and several mitotic figures. ©CytoAtlas

METAPLASTIC CARCINOMA

CYTOMORPHOLOGY

- Rare tumor with squamous and mesenchymal differentiation
- Tumor cells seen as single cells or in clusters
- Large, pleomorphic spindle cells with a range of atypical features
- Malignant glandular and squamous cells may be seen
- Malignant cartilage and bone may be seen in rare cases
- Background of inflammatory debris

OTHER HIGH YIELD POINTS

- Differential diagnoses include abscess formation (shows squamous and inflammatory cells), post- radiation or surgical changes (shows atypical squamous cells), phyllodes tumor (shows malignant mesenchymal elements), primary breast sarcoma (indistinguishable on cytology alone), and angiosarcoma of the breast
- Tumor cells can show variable labelling with broad spectrum cytokeratin, high molecular weight cytokeratin, and p63
- TRPS1 is a new IHC and is positive in >90% of metaplastic breast carcinomas

DIFFERENTIALS FOR TUMORS METASTATIC TO BREAST	
Adult	Pediatric

- Hematological malignancies
 - Carcinoma
    ➤ Lung
    ➤ Ovarian
    ➤ Gastric
    ➤ Renal
    ➤ Rectal
    ➤ Papillary thyroid
    ➤ Cervix
    ➤ Prostate (male)
 - Sarcomas
    ➤ Leiomyosarcoma
    ➤ Rhabdomyosarcoma
    ➤ Liposarcoma
 - Melanoma
 - Carcinoid tumors
 - Mesothelioma
 - Contralateral breast
	- Hematological malignancies
	 - Rhabdomyosarcoma

METASTATIC LESIONS

- Account for around 1-2% of all breast malignancies
- Cytological diagnosis is done when there is high clinical suspicion (such as known extramammary primary tumor)
- Thorough clinical history, review, and comparison of primary tumor, and immunocytochemical work up are necessary before sign-out
- Presence of bilateral or multiple lesions should raise suspicion of a possible metastasis to breast

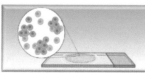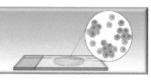

Chapter 15: Soft Tissue and Bone
Cytology

Lynh Nguyen. MD

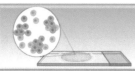 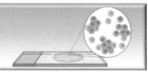

Adipocytic Neoplasms
- Angiolipoma
- Lipoma
- Atypical Lipomatous Tumor/
- Well-Differentiated Liposarcoma
- Myxoid Liposarcoma
- Pleomorphic Liposarcoma
- Dedifferentiated Liposarcoma

Myxoid Neoplasms
- Intramuscular Myxoma
- Myxofibrosarcoma
- Low-Grade Fibromyxoid Sarcoma
- Extraskeletal Myxoid Chondrosarcoma

Spindle Cell Neoplasms
- Leiomyoma
- Leiomyosarcoma
- Synovial Sarcoma
- Solitary Fibrous Tumor
- Desmoid Fibromatosis
- Nodular Fascitis
- Gastrointestinal Stromal Tumor

Fibrohistiocytoid Neoplasms
- Tenosynovial Giant Cell Tumor

Round Cell Neoplasms
- Ewing Sarcoma
- Desmoplastic Small Round Cell Tumor

Rhabdomyosarcoma
- Alveolar Rhabdomyosarcoma
- Embryonal Rhabdomyosarcoma

Epithelioid Neoplasm
- Clear Cell Sarcoma
- Epithelioid Hemangioendothelioma

Notochordal Tumors
- Chordoma

Cartilagenous Tumors
- Chondroblastoma
- Chrondrosarcoma

Osteogenic Tumors
- Osteosarcoma

Hayk MELKUMYAN

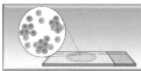

SOFT TISSUE AND BONE CYTOLOGY

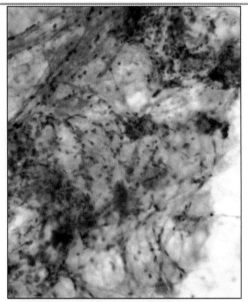

Figure: PAP stain. Angiolipoma: Moderately cellular smear with vascular structures running through adipocytes. ©CytoAtlas

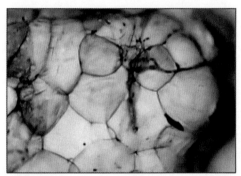

Figure: Diff-Quik stain. Lipoma: Mature uni-vacuolated adipocytes with no associated vasculature. Courtesy Karen Phelps, RVT (Twitter: @jumpinglegacy)

ADIPOCYTIC NEOPLASMS

ANGIOLIPOMA

CYTOMORPHOLOGY
- Moderately cellular smears
- Mature adipocytes admixed with vascular structures

LIPOMA

EPIDEMIOLOGY
- 40-60 y/o; rarely children
- Location: subcutaneous and deep soft tissue
- Often painless unless compressing peripheral nerves

HISTOLOGIC FEATURES
- Lobules of mature uniform adipocytes indistinguishable from adipose tissue
- No associated chicken-wire vascular network
- Variable fat necrosis and myxoid change

CYTOMORPHOLOGY
- Tissue fragments of uniformly sized large adipocytes
- Uni-vacuolated
- Nuclei are small and bland without atypia
- Occasional capillaries
- Foamy macrophages may be seen in cases with fat necrosis

ANCILLARY STUDIES
- IHC: MDM2-
- Cytogenetics: 12q14.3 rearrangement (*HMGA2*)

ATYPICAL LIPOMATOUS TUMOR/WELL-DIFFERENTIATED LIPOSARCOMA

EPIDEMIOLOGY
- 6th decade

SYNONYMOUS TERMS
- Atypical lipomatous tumors refer to lesions of the trunk and extremities; not likely to recur
- Well-differentiated liposarcoma applies to deep-seated lesions (mediastinum, retroperitoneum, and spermatic cord) that recur or are locally aggressive after resection

CYTOMORPHOLOGY
- Fragments of vacuolated lipogenic cells of varying sizes
- Occasional large multilobulated hyperchromatic nuclei with coarse chromatin and abundant cytoplasm
- Lipoblasts – smaller multivacuolated cells with atypical, scalloped nuclei
- Atypical stromal cells with atypical hyperchromatic nuclei
- Rarely can see Floret cells – multinucleated giant cells with hyperchromatic nuclei arranged in wreath-like configuration
- Pleomorphic/spindle cell fragments may suggest dedifferentiation

ANCILLARY STUDIES
- IHC: MDM2+, CDK4+
- Cytogenetics: supernumerary ring and giant marker chromosomes from amplification of chromosome 12q13-15 (*HMGA2/MDM2/CDK4*)

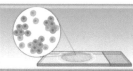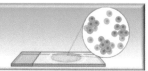
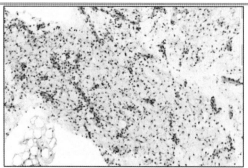

Figure: PAP stain. Myxoid liposarcoma: Note the arborizing vasculature associated with myxoid background. Courtesy Abeer M. Salama, MD

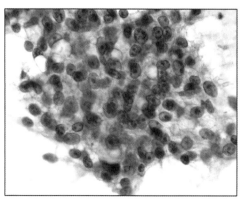

Figure: PAP stain. Pleomorphic liposarcoma: Clusters of pleomorphic cells with prominent nucleoli and atypical lipoblasts. Courtesy Syed Z. Ali, MD (Twitter: @sza_jhcyto)

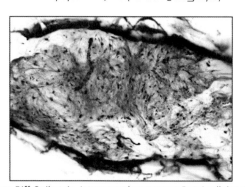

Figure: Diff-Quik stain. Intramuscular myxoma: Pauci-cellular smear with rare bland spindle cells and abundant myxoid matrix. Courtesy Naomi Hardy, MD (Twitter: @NHardy_path)

MYXOID LIPOSARCOMA
EPIDEMIOLOGY
- 4-5th decades
- Location: lower extremities, especially thigh; rarely retroperitoneum and subcutaneous tissue
CYTOMORPHOLOGY
- Markedly cellular smear
- Abundant myxoid background matrix
- Arborizing (chicken-wire) capillaries
- Monomorphic cells with round/ovoid nuclei, finely granular chromatin, and occasional small cytoplasmic vacuoles
- Univacuolated or bivacuolated lipoblasts (signet-ring-like) associated with vessels
- High grade tumors demonstrate larger and predominantly round cells with central nuclei, vesicular chromatin, and multiple prominent nucleoli; poor prognosis
CYTOGENETIC ABERRATIONS
- t(12;16)(q13;p11)/(DDIT3-FUS); 90%
- t(12;22)(q13;q12)/(DDIT3-EWSR1)

PLEOMORPHIC LIPOSARCOMA
EPIDEMIOLOGY
- Elderly
- Location: extremities and trunk
- Frequent metastasis
CYTOMORPHOLOGY
- Hypercellular smears with markedly pleomorphic cells
- Nuclei with coarse chromatin and prominent nucleoli
- Highly atypical multi-vacuolated lipoblasts
- Frequent mitoses and necrosis
ANCILLARY STUDIES
- IHC: S100+, SMA+, desmin focally +; however, MDM2-, HGMA2-, CDK4-
- Cytogenetics: complex rearrangements, but not diagnostic

DEDIFFERENTIATED LIPOSARCOMA
EPIDEMIOLOGY
- No sex predilection
- Location: retroperitoneum, extremities, rarely subcutaneous tissue
- Large painless mass
- Closely associated with well-differentiated liposarcoma component
- Commonly occurs de novo; most cases are not lipogenic, although presence of true lipoblasts is helpful in diagnosis
- Variable morphology, resembles myxofibrosarcoma or undifferentiated pleomorphic sarcoma
CYTOMORPHOLOGY
- Moderate-highly cellular smears
- Moderately atypical spindle cells, occasionally vacuolated
- Occasional binucleated or multinucleated tumor cells
- Rare lipoblasts
- Granular myxoid matrix and thick-walled arborising vessels (only in myxofibrosarcoma-like dedifferentiated liposarcoma)

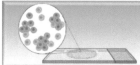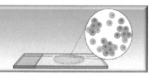

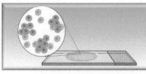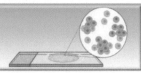
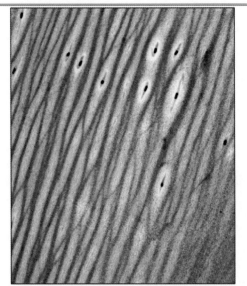

Figure: Diff-Quik stain. Low-grade myxofibrosarcoma: Abundant granular myxoid matrix with mildly atypical spindle cells. Courtesy Syed Z. Ali, MD (Twitter: @sza_jhcyto)

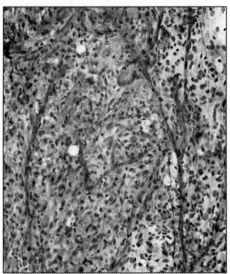

Figure: Diff-Quik. High-grade myxofibrosarcoma: Hypercellular smear with marked nuclear pleomorphism and multinucleation and streaming curvilinear vessels. Courtesy Syed Z. Ali, MD (Twitter: @sza_jhcyto)

ANCILLARY STUDIES
- IHC: MDM2+, CDK4+
- Cytogenetics: supernumerary ring and giant marker chromosomes from amplification of chromosome 12q13-15 (*HMGA2/MDM2/CDK4*)
- FISH: MDM2 amplification

MYXOID NEOPLASMS
INTRAMUSCULAR MYXOMA
EPIDEMIOLOGY
- 40-70 yo; F>M
- Location: thigh, shoulder, buttocks, upper arm
- Benign, painless, circumscribed, but unencapsulated

CYTOMORPHOLOGY
- Paucicellular smear
- Granular myxoid matrix
- Rare bland spindle cells with long cytoplasmic processes and macrophages
- Sparse vascular component
- Skeletal muscle fibers

ANCILLARY STUDIES
- Cytogenetic aberration: GNAS1 point mutation

MYXOFIBROSARCOMA
EPIDEMIOLOGY
- Elderly, 6-8th decade
- Location: extremities, dermis and subcutaneous tissue
- High grade lesions likely metastasize to bones, lungs, and lymph nodes

CYTOMORPHOLOGY
- Variable depending on grade
- Low-grade
  - Abundant myxoid stroma
  - Wavy, spindle and stellate cells
  - Moderate atypia
  - Vacuolated cytoplasm
  - Occasional curvilinear vasculature
- High-grade
  - Marked pleomorphism
  - Prominent bi- or multinucleation
  - Vacuolated cytoplasm (pseudo-lipoblasts)
  - Less myxoid stroma
  - Necrosis

ANCILLARY STUDIES
- IHC: Focal staining for MSA and SMA indicate myofibroblastic differentiation; Claudin-6 in 65%
- Cytogenetic aberration: Highly complex karyotype

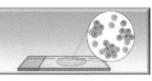

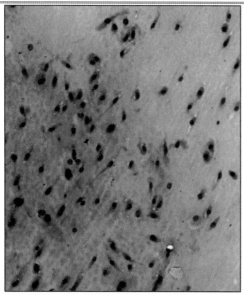

Figure: Diff-Quik stain. Low-grade fibromyxoid sarcoma: uniform bland fibroblasts embedded in myxoid matrix. Courtesy Terrance Lynn, MD

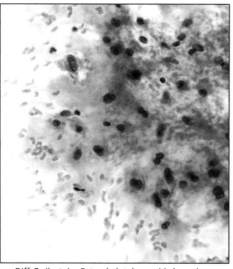

Figure: Diff-Quik stain. Extraskeletal myxoid chrondrosarcoma: Moderately cellular smears with distinct fibrillary chondromyxoid matrix and cells with long cytoplasmic extensions. Courtesy Vikram Deshpande, MD (Twitter: @Vik_deshpandeMD)

LOW-GRADE FIBROMYXOID SARCOMA
EPIDEMIOLOGY
- Young adults; 3-5th decade
- Location: deep soft tissue of proximal extremities (thigh) or trunk
- After long indolent course may metastasize
CYTOMORPHOLOGY
- Myxoid matrix
- Uniform ovoid-spindle cells
- Mild atypia
ANCILLARY STUDIES
- IHC: MUC4+
- Cytogenetic aberration
  - t(7;16)(q34;p11)/ (FUS-CREB3L2); 90%
  - t(11;16)(p11;p11)/(FUS-CREB3L1)

EXTRASKELETAL MYXOID CHONDROSARCOMA
EPIDEMIOLOGY
- Median age: 50 years
- Location: deep soft tissue of proximal limbs (thigh and popliteal fossa)
- Uncertain differentiation despite the name
CYTOMORPHOLOGY
- Moderately cellular smears
- Chondromyxoid fibrillary matrix (bright magenta) on Romanowsky stain
- Monotonous epithelioid-spindle cells with long cytoplasmic extensions arranged in cords or lace-like pattern
- Very little pleomorphism
- Variable lacuna formation without definite cartilage differentiation
ANCILLARY STUDIES
- Stain: PAS+, cytokeratin-, S100+ in <20% cases
- Cytogenetic aberrations
  - t(9;22)(q22;q12)/ (EWSR1-NR4A3); 75%
  - t(9;17)(q22;q11)/ (NR4A3-TAF15)
  - t(9;15)(q22;q21)/(TCF12-NR4A3)
  - t(3;9)(q12;q22)/ (TFG-NR4A3)
  - These mutations are not found in conventional myxoid chondrosarcoma of bone

SPINDLE CELL NEOPLASMS
- Includes neoplasms with smooth muscle, neural, myofibroblastic or other mesenchymal differentiation
LEIOMYOMA
EPIDEMIOLOGY
- Benign smooth muscle tumor commonly found in the uterus
- Can also be found in the GI tract, skin, vasculature, and subcutaneous tissue
CYTOMORPHOLOGY
- Bland spindle cells arranged in loose bundles
- Round-ovoid nuclei that may be pushed peripherally or indented by cytoplasmic vacuoles
- No necrosis or mitoses

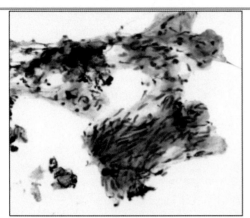

Figure: PAP stain. Leiomyoma: Fragments of tissue composed of spindle cells with cigar-shaped nuclei and fibrillary cytoplasm. ©CytoAtlas

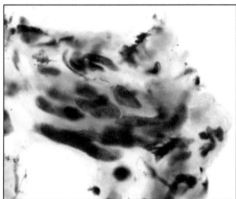

Figure: PAP stain. Leiomyoma: Some nuclei can show fine chromatin and nuclear indenting. ©CytoAtlas

Figure: Diff-Quik stain. Leiomyosarcoma: Tissue fragment composed of pleomorphic spindle cells with hyperchromatic nuclei. ©CytoAtlas

- Degenerative changes: sclerosis, hemorrhage, cystic change, calcification
ANCILLARY STUDIES
- IHC: desmin+, h-caldesmon+, SMA+; S100-

LEIOMYOSARCOMA
EPIDEMIOLOGY
- Adults
- Location
  - Older women: retroperitoneum, mesentery, omentum
  - Common metastasis: liver and lung
  - Males more commonly: subcutaneous, deep soft tissue of extremities (thigh)
  - Muscular vessels (IVC, pulmonary artery, and large veins of lower extremities)
CYTOMORPHOLOGY
- Spindle cells with cigar-shaped nuclei, often indented and homogenous cytoplasm arranged in fascicles
- Increased mitoses
- Variable pleomorphism, multinucleation, and necrosis depending on grade
- Naked nuclei
ANCILLARY
- IHC: desmin+, h-caldesmon+, SMA+; myoglobin-, S100-

SYNOVIAL SARCOMA
EPIDEMIOLOGY
- Occurs at any age, but mainly 10-35yo
- Equal sex predilection
- Location: commonly deep soft tissue of lower extremities adjacent to joints and tendon sheaths (thigh), but can occur anywhere
HISTOLOGIC VARIANTS
- Monophasic (spindle or round cells)
- Biphasic (spindle and epithelial components)
CYTOMORPHOLOGY
- Hypercellular smears
- Cell clusters alternating with dispersed cells
- Branching vessels can be seen in the tissue clusters
- Monophasic: uniform small-medium sized spindled cells with oval or comma-shaped nuclei and delicate, tapering cytoplasm arranged in sheets or fascicles
- Biphasic: may see epithelial component (glands, papillae, cords, nests, etc.) – ovoid cells with abundant cytoplasm and prominent nucleoli
- Mitoses, occasional necrosis
- Mast cells
ANCILLARY STUDIES
- IHC
  - SS18 (specific), CD99+ (>60%), S100+ (30%), TLE1+ (non-specific)
  - Epithelial component: keratin+, EMA+
  - Spindle: BCL2+
- Cytogenetic aberration: t(X;18) (p11;q11)/(*SS18-SSX*)

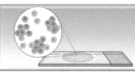
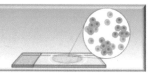

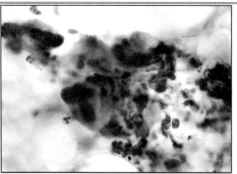

Figure: Diff-Quik stain. Leiomyosarcoma: Highly pleomorphic cells with nuclear crowding, some showing multinucleation. ©CytoAtlas

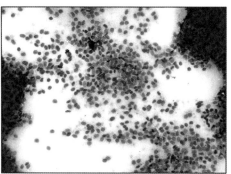

Figure: Diff-Quik stain. Synovial sarcoma (monophasic): Dispersed cells alternating with cohesive clusters. Courtesy Syed Z. Ali, MD (Twitter: @sza_jhcyto)

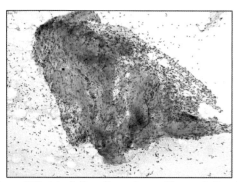

Figure: PAP stain. Solitary fibrous tumor: Plump spindle cells dispersed singly or in syncytial tissue fragments associated with dense ropey collagen. Courtesy Susan Shyu, MD (Twitter: @susanshyu)

SOLITARY FIBROUS TUMOR
- Formerly known as hemangiopericytoma
EPIDEMIOLOGY
- Adults
- Location: pleura, peritoneum, mediastinum, retroperitoneum, upper respiratory tract, orbit, deep soft tissue
CYTOMORPHOLOGY
- Scant-moderately cellular smear
- Ropy collagen fibers
- Hemorrhagic background
- Irregular fascicles of monomorphic spindle cells
- Single cells
- Staghorn-like vessels on cell-block sections
ANCILLARY STUDIES
- IHC: CD34+, STAT6+, CD99+; actin-, desmin-, keratin-, S100-
- Cytogenetic aberration: inv(12)/(*NAB2-STAT6*)

DESMOID FIBROMATOSIS
EPIDEMIOLOGY
- Children and adults
- Locally aggressive, often recurs, does not metastasize
- Location: abdominal (common in reproductive age women), extra-abdominal, intraabdominal
- In children can be manifestation of familial adenomatous polyposis or Gardner syndrome
CYTOMORPHOLOGY
- Pauci-cellular to variable cellular smear
- Fascicular clusters of bland fibroblasts
- Ovoid nuclei often with crush artifact
- Collagenous stroma
- Skeletal muscle present if infiltrative
- No atypia, rare mitoses
ANCILLARY STUDIES
- IHC: beta-catenin+ (nuclear), SMA (variable); CD34-, CD117-, desmin-, S100-
- Cytogenetic aberration: *CTNNB1* or *APC* mutation

NODULAR FASCIITIS
EPIDEMIOLOGY
- All ages, most commonly young adults
- Location: upper extremities, trunk, head, neck
- Rapid growth within 2 months, 2-3 cm size
CYTOMORPHOLOGY
- Myxoid stroma
- Inflammatory cells
- Polymorphic spindle-shaped myofibroblasts arranged in tissue culture pattern
- No atypia
- Branching vessels
ANCILLARY STUDIES
- IHC: SMA+; S100-, desmin-
- Cytogenetic aberration: t(17;22)(p13.1;q12.3)/(*USP6-MYH9*)

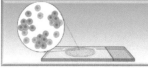
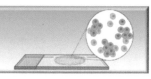

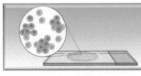
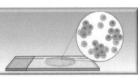

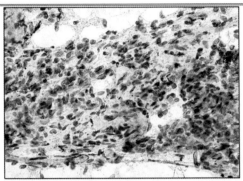

Figure: PAP stain. Solitary fibrous tumor: Monomorphic spindle cells with bland nuclei dispersed Courtesy Susan Shyu, MD (Twitter: @susanshyu)

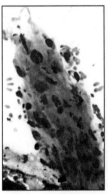
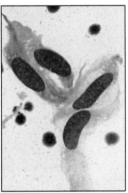

Figure: Diff-Quik. Stain. Desmoid fibromatosis: Fascicle of fibroblasts with mild atypia that stain for beta-catenin. Courtesy MyCytopathology (Twitter: @MyCytopathology)

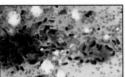
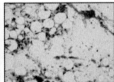

Figure: Diff-Quik stain. Nodular fasciitis: Numerous myofibroblasts in a myxoid background. Courtesy Hubert Lau, MD (Twitter: @HubertLauMD) (left); Terrance Lynn, MD (right)

GASTROINTESTINAL STROMAL TUMOR
EPIDEMIOLOGY
- All ages, median age 65 at diagnosis; M=F
- Location: GI tract (stomach > small intestine >colon and rectum); rarely esophagus, appendix, gallbladder, omentum, mesentery, retroperitoneum, perineum
- Origin: interstitial cells of Cajal
CYTOMORPHOLOGY
- Large tissue fragments of crowded, spindle cells; occasionally epithelioid cells (esp. if lacking c-KIT mutation)
- Wispy cytoplasm with extensions
- Stripped nuclei
- Occasional mitoses and necrosis
ANCILLARY STUDIES
- IHC: CKIT+, DOG1+ (useful in cases lacking c-KIT mutation)
- Cytogenetic aberrations
    - KIT mutation; 75-80%
    - PDGFRA mutation; epithelioid type, 7-15%

FIBROHISTIOCYTOID NEOPLASMS
TENOSYNOVIAL GIANT CELL TUMOR
EPIDEMIOLOGY
- Adult; 30-50 years; F>M
- Location: fingers, wrist, ankle, foot, knee
- Painless swelling
- Clinical Variants
    - Localized type
        - Slow growing
        - Circumscribed, partially encapsulated
        - Adjacent to synovium of hands and feet
    - Diffuse type (formerly pigmented villonodular synovitis)
        - Locally destructive
        - Infiltrative growth
        - Intraarticular (knee, hip, ankle, elbow, shoulder) and extraarticular sites
        - Younger patients, local recurrence
CYTOMORPHOLOGY
- Ovoid-round mononuclear cells with moderate vacuolated cytoplasm
- Osteoclast-like giant cells (up to 50 nuclei)
- Hemosiderin-laden macrophages
- Vascular stroma, hemorrhagic background

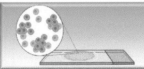
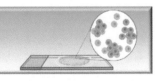

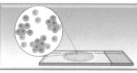

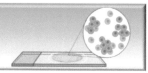

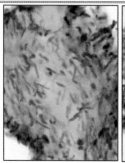
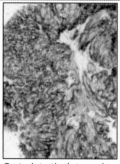

Figure: PAP stain and CD117 IHC. Gastrointestinal stromal tumor – Tissue fragment composed of spindle cells that are immunoreactive for CD117 (c-KIT). ©CytoAtlas

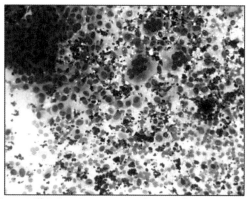

Figure: Diff-Quik stain. Tenosynovial giant cell tumor: Mixture mononuclear cells, multinucleated giant cells, and macrophages. Courtesy Syed Z. Ali, MD (Twitter: @sza_jhcyto)

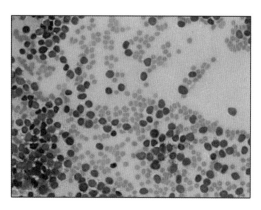

Figure: Diff-Quik stain. Ewing sarcoma with uniform neoplastic cells with smaller dark cells and larger light cells and subtle tigroid background due to glycogen. ©CytoAtlas

ANCILLARY STUDIES
- IHC: CD68+, CD163+, PU.1+
- Cytogenetic aberration: t(1;2)(p13-21;q37)/(*COL6A3-CSF1*), gains of chromosome 5 and 7

ROUND CELL NEOPLASMS
EWING SARCOMA (Formerly PRIMITIVE NEUROECTODERMAL TUMOR)
EPIDEMIOLOGY
- Children and young adults; first two decades of life; M=F
- Location: deep soft tissue, thigh, pelvis, paravertebral, foot
- Rapidly enlarging painful mass

CYTOMORPHOLOGY
- Highly cellular smears
- Large ovoid cells with high N:C ratio and vacuolated cytoplasm (glycogen)
- Finely granular chromatin
- Naked nuclei
- Nuclear molding, crush artifact
- Tigroid background
- Light (viable) and dark (dying) cells
- Rarely pseudorosettes
- Frequent tumor necrosis

ANCILLARY STUDIES
- IHC: CD99+ (membranous), FLI1+, NKX2.2+, synaptophysin+, chromogranin+, cytokeratin+/-; SMA-, desmin-, CD45-, Tdt-
- Cytogenetic aberrations
  - t(11;22)(q24;q12)/(*EWSR1-FLI1*); 85-90%, favorable
  - t(21;22)(q22;q12)/(*EWSR1-ERG*); 5-10%
  - t(2;22)(q33;q12)/(*EWSR1-FEV*)
  - t(7;22)(q22;q12)/(*EWSR1-ETV1*)
  - t(17;22)(q12;q12)/(*EWSR1-ETV4*)
  - t(20;22)(q13;q12)/(*EWSR1-NFATC*)

DESMOPLASTIC SMALL ROUND CELL TUMOR
EPIDEMIOLOGY
- Adolescents and young adults; 15-35 years; M>F
- Location: Serosal surfaces, intraabdominal, pelvis, pleura, retroperitoneum, scrotum

CYTOMORPHOLOGY
- Clusters or nests of small-medium sized round cells
- High N:C ratio, finely granular chromatin
- Inconspicuous nucleoli; however, single cells can show conspicuous nucleoli post-chemotherapy
- Nuclear molding
- Desmoplastic stromal fragments

ANCILLARY STUDIES
- IHC: low molecular weight keratin+, EMA+, synaptophysin+, chromogranin+, desmin+ (dot-like), WT1+, CD99+ (variable and cytoplasmic)
- Cytogenetic aberration: t(11;22)(q13;q12)/(*EWSR1-WT1*)

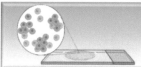

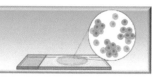

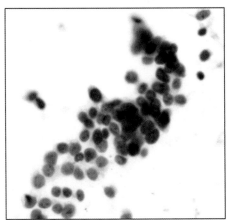

Figure: PAP stain. Ewing sarcoma: Small round blue cells with finely granular chromatin. ©CytoAtlas

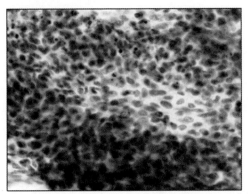

Figure: PAP stain. Desmoplastic small round cell tumor: Cellular smear composed of small round blue cells with vacuolated cytoplasm. ©CytoAtlas

RHABODYMYOSARCOMAS
EPIDEMIOLOGY
- Children
- Location: head and neck (including meninges and orbit), genitourinary tract (bladder), trunk
- Cytologic distinction between embryonal and alveolar rhabdomyosarcoma difficult; however, significant prognostic implications; relies on molecular findings

ALVEOLAR RHABDOMYOSARCOMA
EPIDEMIOLOGY
- Adolescents
- Location: limbs, trunk, head, and neck
- Poor prognosis
CYTOMORPHOLOGY
- Hypercellular smears
- Uniform large round-polygonal cell with irregular nuclei
- Infrequent myxoid or tigroid background
- Multinucleated cells with nuclei arranged in wreath-like formation
- Mitoses common
ANCILLARY STUDIES
- IHC: desmin+, MSA+, myoD1+, myogenin+
- Cytogenetic aberrations
  - t(2;13)(q35;q14)/(*PAX3-FOXO1A*); 60%, unfavorable
  - t(1;13)(p36;q14)/(*PAX7-FOXO1A*); 20%, favorable
  - 2q35 rearrangements

EMBRYONAL RHABDOMYOSARCOMA
- More favorable prognosis compared to alveolar rhabdomyosarcoma
CYTOMORPHOLOGY
- Predominantly isolated cells, occasional loose clusters
- Infrequent myxoid or tigroid background
- Primitive small-medium sized round/spindle cells with eccentric nuclei and elongated tadpole-shaped cytoplasm
- Pronounced pleomorphism
- May show myogenic differentiation (cross-striations or cytoplasmic condensation)
CYTOGENETIC ABERRATIONS
- Chromosome gains 2, 8, 11, 12, 13, and 20
- Loss of heterozygosity at 11p15; results in inactivation of tumor suppressor genes (*GOK*, *H19*, *CDKN1C*, *HOTS*, and *IGF2*)

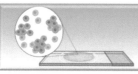

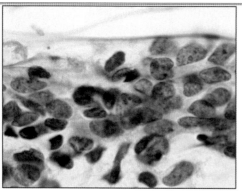

Figure: PAP stain. Desmoplastic small round cell tumor (high power): Round-ovoid nuclei with irregular nuclear contour, granular chromatin, and nucleoli. ©CytoAtlas

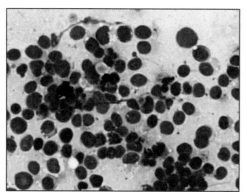

Figure: Diff-Quik stain. Alveolar Rhabdomyosarcoma: Relatively monomorphic round cells with vacuolated cytoplasm. ©CytoAtlas

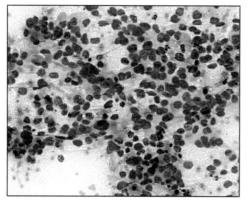

Figure: Diff-Quik stain: Embryonal rhabdomyosarcoma: Mixture of round and elongated cells. Note cytoplasmic condensation suggesting myogenic differentiation. Courtesy Syed Z. Ali, MD (Twitter: @sza_jhcyto)

EPITHELIOID NEOPLASMS
CLEAR CELL SARCOMA
EPIDEMIOLOGY
- Adolescents, young adults; 3-4th decade
- Location: extremities (foot, ankle), associated with fascia, tendons, aponeuroses; lacks skin involvement
- Rare sarcoma with melanocytic differentiation
- Slowly enlarging, painful deep tissue mass, <5 cm
CYTOMORPHOLOGY
- Cellular smear
- Clean or tigroid background
- Predominantly isolated cells, occasional small clusters
- Round, polygonal, or fusiform cells of varying sizes
- Round-ovoid eccentric nucleus with unevenly distributed or vesicular chromatin and a single prominent central nucleolus
- Intranuclear cytoplasmic pseudo-inclusions
- Binucleated and multinucleated cells may be present
- Abundant pale cytoplasm, sometimes vacuolated
- Macrophages with melanin pigment
ANCILLARY STUDIES
- IHC: S100+, SOX10+, HMB45+, MITF+
- Cytogenetic aberrations
  - t(12;22)(q13;q12)/(*EWSR1-ATF1*); 50%
  - t(2;22)(q33;q12)/(*EWSR1-CREB1*); 25%
  - Not found in melanoma

EPITHELIOID HEMANGIOENDOTHELIOMA
EPIDEMIOLOGY
- Adults >20 years
- Location: bone, extremities, head and neck, mediastinum, trunk, visceral organs (liver, lung), medium-large veins
- Often multicentric
CYTOMORPHOLOGY
- Variably cellular smear
- Metachromatic, hyaline or chondroid stroma
- Predominantly isolated cells; occasional loose rosette or acinar-like structures
- Monomorphic cells with round, ovoid or polygonal nuclei and moderate dense cytoplasm
ANCILLARY STUDIES
- IHC: CD31+, FLI1+, ERG+
- Cytogenetic aberration: t(1;3)(p36.3;q25)/(*CAMTA1-WWTR1*)

15.7 NOTOCHORDAL TUMORS
15.7.1 CHORDOMA
EPIDEMIOLOGY
- Peaks at 6th decade; M>F
- Location: rare malignant midline lesion involving the axial skeleton (sacrococcygeal and spheno-occipital); rarely extremities and posterior mediastinum

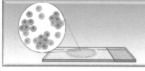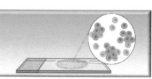

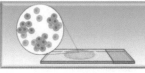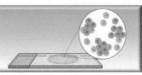
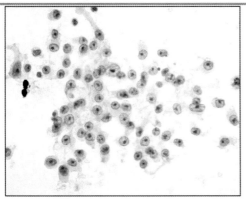

Figure: PAP stain. Clear cell sarcoma: Dispersed round cells with vesicular chromatin and single prominent nucleoli. Intranuclear cytoplasmic pseudo-inclusions can occasionally be seen. Courtesy Syed Z. Ali, MD (Twitter: @sza_jhcyto)

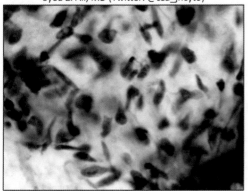

Figure: PAP stain. Epithelioid hemangioendothelioma: Round-polygonal epithelioid cells with dense cytoplasm. Intracytoplasmic lumens containing RBCs may be helpful in making the proper diagnosis. ©CytoAtlas

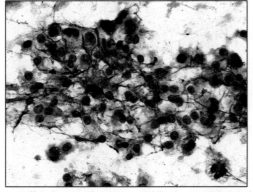

Figure: Diff-Quik stain. Chordoma – Mildly pleomorphic round-ovoid cells with characteristic physaliphorous cytoplasm and metachromatic fibrillary myxoid stroma. Courtesy Susan Shyu, MD (Twitter: @susanshyu)

- Indolent with multiple recurrences
- Large lytic mass with soft tissue extension

CYTOMORPHOLOGY
- Clusters or cords of round-cuboidal cells
- Mild nuclear pleomorphism
- Physaliphorous or abundantly vacuolated/bubbly cytoplasm
- Abundant metachromatic granular and fibrillary myxoid matrix

ANCILLARY STUDIES
- IHC: S100+, EMA+, brachyury+, keratin+; CEA-

CARTILAGINOUS TUMORS
CHONDROBLASTOMA
EPIDEMIOLOGY
- Children and adolescents (10-25 years); M>F
- Location: Epiphysis of long bones around knee (distal femur or proximal tibia), small tubular bones of the hands and feet, calcaneus and patella, skull base and temporal bones in adults
- Painful solitary lesion
- Radiology: Small, well-defined, intramedullary, lytic lesion occupying < ½ the epiphysis
- Recurrence <20%

CYTOMORPHOLOGY
- Uniform chondroblasts in clusters
- Central or eccentric, round-ovoid nucleus with prominent nuclear grooves and well-defined cytoplasm
- Admixed with osteoclast-like giant cells
- Chondroid matrix

ANCILLARY STUDIES
- Cytogenetic aberration: *H3F3B* or *H3F3A* mutations; 95%

CHONDROSARCOMA
EPIDEMIOLOGY
- Any age; 5-7th decades
- Location: trunk (pelvis, ribs, scapula), hip (acetabulum, proximal femur), shoulder girdle (proximal humerus)
- Diaphysis and metaphysis
- Radiology: aggressive lytic lesion with endosteal scalloping and cortical thickening; high grade lesions show cortical destruction and soft tissue infiltration
- Mesenchymal chondrosarcomas: aggressive tumors in younger patients (15-35 years) arising in bone, not soft tissue. Located in the head, neck, and ribs

CYTOMORPHOLOGY
- Cells in lacunae in bright magenta chondroid matrix on Romanowsky stain
- Uneven dispersed, binucleated cells
- Round nuclei and central prominent nucleoli
- Well-defined cytoplasmic borders
- Grading dependent on cellularity
  - Low-grade lesions are indistinguishable from enchondroma cytologically

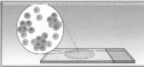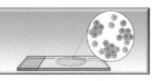

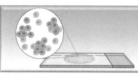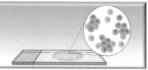
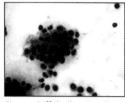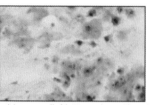

Figure: Diff-Quik stain. Chondroblastoma (left): Note the uniformity of chondroblasts with occasional nuclear grooves present in a magenta chondroid background. Courtesy Sara E. Wobker, MD (Twitter: @SaraEWobker). Diff-Quik stain. Chondrosarcoma: Chondrocytes with well-defined cytoplasmic borders embedded in metachromatic chondroid matrix (right).

- High-grade lesions are more cellular with atypical chondrocytes, more prominent myxoid (not chondroid) matrix
- Mesenchymal chondrosarcomas: highly cellular smears with primitive small round blue cells, hyaline cartilage, osteoclast-like giant cells. Ossification present. Necrosis occasionally.

ANCILLARY STUDIES
- Cytogenetic aberration
    - IDH1/2 point mutations seen in benign and malignant cartilage forming tumors; not useful
    - Mesenchymal chondrosarcoma: t(8;8)/(HEY1-NCOA2)

OSTEOGENIC TUMORS
OSTEOSARCOMA
EPIDEMIOLOGY
- Primarily intramedullary bone producing malignancy, but can occur in soft tissue
- Teenagers and young adults (10-20 yo), and older adults (>50 yo) with history of Paget's disease, radiation, chemotherapy, or orthopedic implants; M>F
- Location: metaphysis of distal femur, proximal tibia, upper humerus
    - Older patients: pelvis and axial skeleton
Radiology: ill-defined intramedullary lytic lesion with cortical destruction, periosteal reaction, focal mineralization/ossification
CYTOMORPHOLOGY
- Varying epithelioid to pleomorphic cells
    - Osteoblasts: eccentric nucleus with central hof
    - Osteoclast-like giant cells
    - Chondroblasts: mono- or binucleated mononuclear cells
- Background: osteoid or chondromyxoid
- Necrosis and numerous mitoses

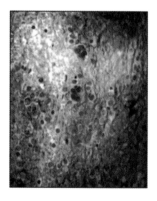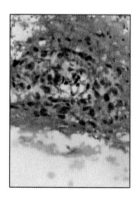

Figure: Diff-Quik stain and PAP stain. Osteosarcoma: Pleomorphic cells composed of osteoclast-like giant cells and malignant mononuclear osteoblasts. Background shows chondromyxoid matrix. Courtesy Syed Z. Ali, MD (Twitter: @sza_jhcyto) (Diff-Quik) and Terrance Lynn, MD (PAP)

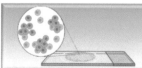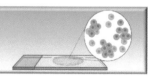

Chapter 16: Kidney and Adrenal
Cytology

Swikrity U Baskota, MD

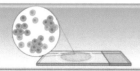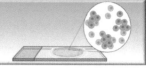

Hayk MELKUMYAN

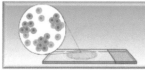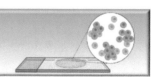

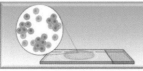
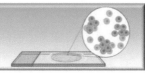
Renal cytology

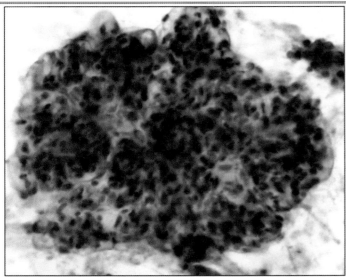

Figure: Glomerulus: Diff-Quik stain. Dense globular structure with cytologically bland cells with capillary loops at the periphery. ©CytoAtlas

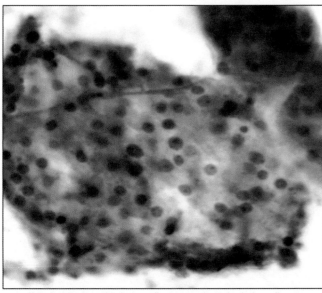

Figure: Diff-Quik stain. Renal Tubular cells: Proximal renal tubular cells arranged in flat cells with granular cytoplasm, round to oval nuclei, prominent nucleoli, and not well-demarcated cytoplasmic borders. ©CytoAtlas

KIDNEY FNA
INDICATIONS:

- In patients where radical nephrectomy is contraindicated: clinical suspicion of metastasis, end stage renal disease, wide-spread lesion, investigational treatment
- Small lesion/decreased renal function or a young patient: where partial nephrectomy can be considered
- Equivocal radiologic findings
- Clinical concern of an infectious process

Accuracy:

- FNA can distinguish benign vs malignant process in 73%-94% of cases
- Accuracy of correct subcategorization of different subtypes of RCC approximates close to 99% with the use of immunohistochemical stains

Adequacy

- No adequacy criteria established
- Repeat FNA can be helpful in non-diagnostic cases which ranges up to 30%

NORMAL ELEMENTS OF KIDNEY FNA
GLOMERULI
CYTOMORPHOLOGY

- Cellular, but cytologically bland dense globular structure with scalloped edges
- Can be confused with papillary renal cell carcinoma

RENAL TUBULAR CELLS
CYTOMORPHOLOGY

- Proximal and distal tubular cells both can be seen
- Proximal tubular cells mostly in flat sheets, have abundant granular cytoplasm, round to oval nuclei, prominent small nucleoli
- Distal tubular cells are seen in clusters, cohesive group with less cytoplasm, well defined cell borders and inconspicuous nucleolus

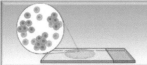
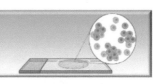

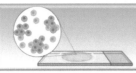
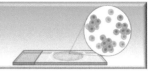

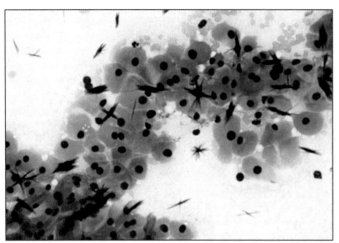

Figure: Diff-Quik stain. Oncocytoma: Cellular smear with discohesive cells in sheets with well-defined cell borders, abundant granular cytoplasm, small round to oval eccentric nuclei. ©CytoAtlas

BENIGN LESIONS
ONCOCYTOMA
CYTOMORPHOLOGY
- Usually highly cellular smears
- Nests (cell block) or cohesive or singly scattered cells in the smears
- Abundant cytoplasm with uniform granularity
- Well-delineated cytoplasmic border
- Round eccentric nucleus with single prominent nucleolus

High-Yield Points
- Electron microscopy: abundant mitochondria; hence granular cytoplasm in light microscopy
- Most common cytogenetics: Loss of Chromosome 1 and Y
- Differentials: hepatocytes, RCC eosinophilic variant of clear cell RCC, papillary RCC and other oncocytic renal neoplasms
- Hale's colloidal iron: Negative or apical in
- Oncocytoma, diffuse cytoplasmic staining in chromophobe RCC
- CK7: Scattered single cell positive in Oncocytoma versus diffuse in chromophobe RCC

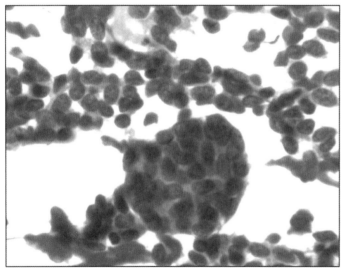

Figure: PAP stain. Metanephric adenoma: Cellular specimen of cells arranged in spheres and cords, small uniform appearing cells with round nuclei, with scant cytoplasm. Courtesy of Pepe Jime`nez Heffernan, MD (Twitter: @pepeheffernan)

ANGIOMYOLIPOMA
CYTOMORPHOLOGY
- Benign triphasic tumor composed of smooth muscles, adipocytes and thick-walled vessels
- Usually pauci-cellular smears
- Bland or atypical spindle cells and/or fat cells
- Stringy cytoplasm
- Very rare thick-walled blood vessels on smears
- Epithelioid angiomyolipoma: epithelioid cells with atypia

High-Yield Points
- Immunostains: Co-expression of melanocytic (HMB-45, Melan-A) markers and smooth muscle markers (SMA) by neoplastic spindle or fat cells
- Epithelioid angiomyolipoma: has metastatic potential
- Differentials: Sarcomatoid renal cell carcinoma, sarcomas

MIXED EPITHELIAL AND STROMAL TUMOR (MEST OR CYSTIC NEPHROMA)
CYTOMORPHOLOGY
- Atypical epithelium lining small cysts or stroma
- Usually hypocellular, contains cells with vacuolated cytoplasm, irregular nuclear

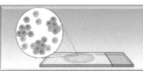

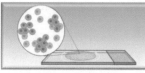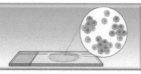
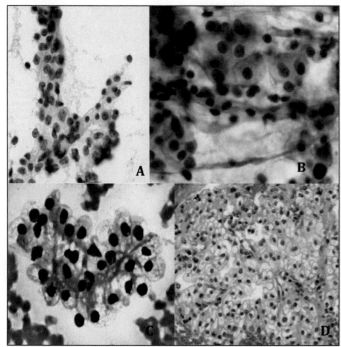

Figure: PAP stain (A,B), Diff-Quik stain (C), H&E stain (D). Clear Cell Renal Cell Carcinoma: A, B: (PAP stain, low power and high power): The carcinoma cells appear round to oval with ill-defined cytoplasmic borders and inconspicuous nucleoli, note the traversing blood vessels in image A-B. C: Vacuolated cytoplasm of the carcinoma cells can be appreciated. D: Cell block: Note the bloody background, with large cohesive clusters of clear cells. ©CytoAtlas

membrane and intracytoplasmic vacuole resembling fat
- Differentials: RCC, angiomyolipoma or sarcoma

METANEPHRIC ADENOMA
CYTOMORPHOLOGY
- Usually, cellular specimens
- Cells arranged in sheets, tubules, or balls
- Small cells with uniform appearing round nuclei, small prominent nucleoli, and scant cytoplasm

High-Yield Points
- Immunostains: Like Wilms Tumor: Nuclear WT-1 positive, BRAF+, CD57+ (specific, negative in Wilms tumor), negative for EMA, CK7, AMACR
- Normal Karyotype
- Differentials: Epithelial predominant Wilms Tumor low grade papillary RCC, metastatic tumor

RENAL ABSCESS/INFARCT/XANTHOGRANULOMATOUS PYELONEPHRITIS
CYTOMORPHOLOGY
- Usually, necrotic material
- Inflammatory cells including neutrophils and eosinophils
- Xanthoma cells and multinucleated giant cells in xantho-granulomatous pyelonephritis
- Rare, atypical cells can be confused with clear cell RCC, papillary RCC in xantho-granulomatous pyelonephritis due to granular foamy cytoplasm

MALIGNANT LESIONS
CLEAR CELL RENAL CELL CARCINOMA
CYTOMORPHOLOGY
- Bloody preparations
- Large cohesive clusters
- Cytoplasmic vacuoles with abundant wispy cytoplasm
- Ill-defined cell borders
- Eccentrically placed large nuclei with varying pleomorphism
- Bare or extruded nuclei
- WHO/ISUP grade depends on nucleolar size
- Rarely, sarcomatoid or rhabdoid cells

High-Yield Points
- Most common cytogenetics: 3p deletion
- Immunostains: Positive for PAX-8, CAIX, CD10, AMACR (focal), CAM5.2, vimentin. Negative for CK7, CD117, HMB45, Melan-A

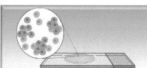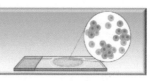

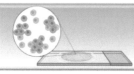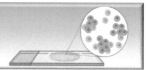
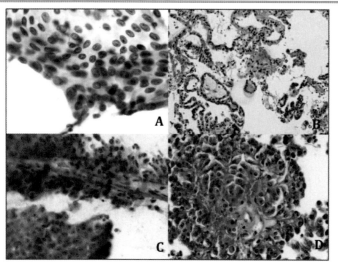

Figure: Diff-Quik stain (A), H&E stain (B & D), and PAP stain (C). Papillary Renal Cell Carcinoma Type I (A&B) is characterized by round to small oval uniform appearing nuclei with minimal pleomorphism and inconspicuous nucleoli. The cell block preparations (B) also show presence of foamy macrophages. Type II Papillary RCC is characterized by large round to oval nuclei with single large prominent grade 3 nucleolus and abundant granular cytoplasm. ©CytoAtlas

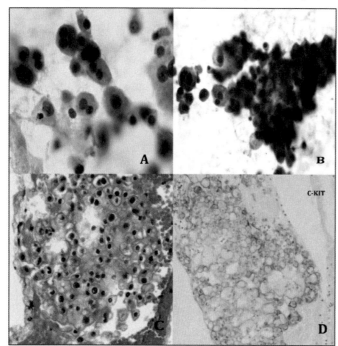

Figure: PAP stain (A), Diff-Quik stain (B), H&E stain (C),and C-Kit IHC (D). Chromophobe renal cell carcinoma is characterized by abundant granular to clear cytoplasm and well-defined cytoplasmic border (plant cell like cell membrane). The nuclei are round to oval, often binucleated, exhibit pleomorphism and perinuclear vacuolated zone (koilocytoid). C-kit stain is positive in these lesions. ©CytoAtlas

- Differentials: Renal tubular cells, hepatocytes, reactive macrophages, adrenal cortical cells, oncocytoma, MEST, angiomyolipoma, papillary RCC, Chromophobe RCC, Sarcoma

PAPILLARY RENAL CELL CARCINOMA

CYTOMORPHOLOGY OF TYPE 1/ LOW-GRADE

- Arranged in papillae with true fibrovascular cores, spherules, or tubules
- Uniform small to medium cuboidal cells
- Scant to moderate cytoplasm
- Round nuclei and inconspicuous nucleoli
- Intracytoplasmic hemosiderin pigment
- Foamy macrophages

CYTOMORPHOLOGY OF TYPE 2/HIGH-GRADE

- Resembles mostly with high grade clear cell RCC
- Often impossible to distinguish based on cytomorphology
- Large cells with abundant granular cytoplasm
- Usually, large single prominent grade 3 nucleolus

High-Yield Points

- Cytogenetics: Most common: Trisomy 7 and 17, loss of Y chromosome
- Immunostains: Positive for PAX-8, CK7, AMACR, CD10, EMA, low molecular weight CKs, Negative for WT-1, CAIX, CD117
- Differentials: Distal renal tubular cells, glomeruli, metanephric adenoma, papillary hyperplasia, clear cell RCC

CHROMOPHOBE RENAL CELL CARCINOMA

CYTOMORPHOLOGY

- Highly cellular preparations
- Trabecular architecture, loose sheets
- Koilocytoid cells
- Abundant irregular granular cytoplasm
- Well-defined cell borders
- Anisonucleosis, hyperchromasia, nuclear pseudoinclusions and irregular nuclear border, mitoses, no nucleoli
- Perinuclear vacuolated zone

High-Yield Points

- Most common cytogenetics: multiple monosomies
- Immunostains: Positive: Hales Colloidal Iron, CK7, CK20, PAX8, CD117; Negative: AMACR, CD10, S100a1, vimentin, HNF1β
- Differentials: Oncocytoma, tubulocystic RCC, clear cell RCC, succinate dehydrogenase-deficient RCC,

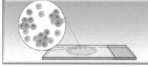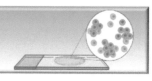

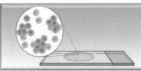
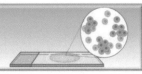

Hereditary Leiomyomatosis RCC, Birt-Hogg-Dube syndrome tumors

MiT FAMILY TRANSLOCATION RENAL CELL CARCINOMA
CYTOMORPHOLOGY

- Cellular preparations
- Papillary architecture or in sheets
- Clear cells or cells with granular voluminous cytoplasm
- Focal calcification

High-Yield Points

- TFE3 Translocation by FISH
- Young age
- Immunostains: Positive: TFE3, PAX8, CAIX, cathepsin K, AMACR; Negative: Cytokeratins, EMA, CK7
- Differentials: clear cell RCC, papillary RCC, and other RCCs

OTHER MALIGNANT TUMORS
MUCINOUS TUBULAR AND SPINDLE CELL CARCINOMA
CYTOMORPHOLOGY

- Mixture of spindle and tubular cells
- Myxoid background
- Immunostains: Positive for EMA, AMACR and CK7
- Differentials: Metastasis from other sites, low-grade clear cell and papillary RCC

COLLECTING DUCT CARCINOMA
CYTOMORPHOLOGY

- High grade cytology: hyperchromatic, polymorphous cells with marked anisonucleosis and scant cytoplasm
- Immunostains: Positive for high molecular weight keratins 34βE12
- Differentials: Metastasis from other sites

RENAL MEDULLARY CARCINOMA
CYTOMORPHOLOGY

- High grade cytology-similar to collecting duct carcinoma
- Large pleomorphic cells with prominent nucleoli and occasional mucin containing cytoplasmic vacuoles
- Immunostains: Positive for PAX-8, OCT3/4 and CK7 and show loss of INI-1
- Centered on renal medulla, often presents with metastasis
- Associated with sickle cell trait or other hemoglobinopathies
- Differentials: Metastasis from other sites

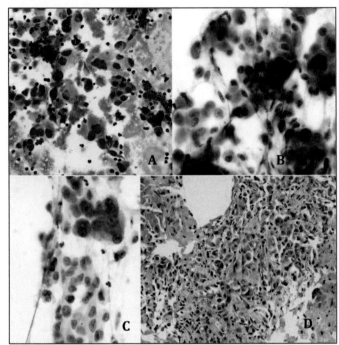

Figure: Diff-Quik stain (A), PAP stain (B &C), D: H&E, cell block). Translocation associated renal cell carcinoma are characterized by cellular specimens with pleomorphic cells with voluminous cytoplasm with the nuclei pushed towards periphery. They often exhibit prominent nucleoli. ©CytoAtlas

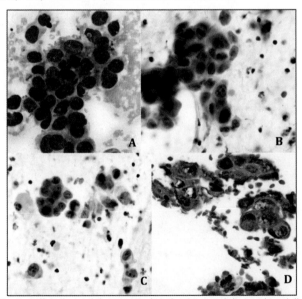

Figure: Diff-Quik stain(A), PAP stain (B&C), H&E stain (D). Renal Medullary Carcinoma are characterized by cellular specimens with markedly pleomorphic cells with high nuclear: cytoplasmic ratio, coarse chromatin, and prominent nucleoli. They are often associated with necrosis and present with metastasis. ©CytoAtlas

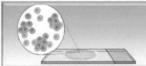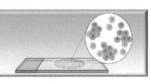

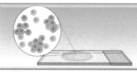

TUBULOCYSTIC RENAL CELL CARCINOMA
CYTOMORPHOLOGY
- Mixture of spindle and tubular cells
- Myxoid background
- Immunostains: Positive for EMA, AMACR and CK7
- Differentials: Metastasis from other sites, low-grade clear cell and papillary RCC

CLEAR CELL PAPILLARY RENAL CELL CARCINOMA
CYTOMORPHOLOGY
- Acinar, papillary, or tubular clusters
- Small columnar or round cells with clear cytoplasm, eccentric round to oval nuclei and smooth nuclear border and fine chromatin
- Immunostains: Positive for PAX-2, PAX-8, GATA-3, CK7 and CAIX in a cup-like fashion
- Differentials: Metastasis from other sites, low-grade clear cell and papillary RCC

UROTHELIAL CARCINOMA
CYTOMORPHOLOGY
- Sheets, papillae, or single cells
- Sometimes cercariform cells: neoplastic cells with long cytoplasmic tail and intracytoplasmic vacuoles can be seen
- High-grade lesions composed of more isolated cells with dense hyperchromasia and irregular nuclei
- Immunostains: Positive for GATA-3; Negative for PAX-8
- Differentials: Metastasis from other sites, RCC
- Very important to distinguish from RCC as urothelial carcinoma requires ureteral resection as well along with kidney

OTHER TUMORS
LYMPHOMA
- Usually, secondary
- Most common: B-cell lymphomas and diffuse large B-cell lymphomas

METASTASIS
- Most common: Lung
- Judicious use of immunohistochemistry helpful to arrive at diagnosis along with the clinical history
- Differentials: Metanephric adenoma, collecting duct carcinoma, mucin producing RCC, small cell carcinoma of kidney, primary lymphoma of kidney and urothelial carcinoma

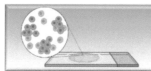
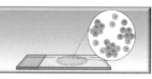

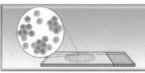
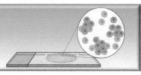
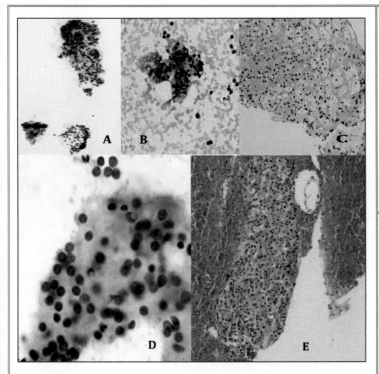

Figure: PAP stain (A & D) Diff-Quik stain (B), H&E stain (C & E). Normal adrenal gland (A,B and C) vs adrenocortical adenoma/hyperplasia (D and E). Normal adrenal gland in aspirate preparations is often difficult to differentiate from adrenocortical adenoma/hyperplasia. Normal adrenal glands are characterized by grape like vesicles tight 3-D clusters of both chief and clear cells (A, B and C). Adrenal adenoma/hyperplasia (D and E) are usually characterized by dominance of one normal cell type, chief cells in the figure, often indistinguishable cytomorphologically from normal appearing adrenal gland. ©CytoAtlas

WILMS TUMOR

CYTOMORPHOLOGY

- One or more of the three components: blastemal, epithelial (tubules) or stromal/mesenchymal
- Blastemal: Small, round cells with round to oval nuclei, coarse chromatin, frequent mitoses, and apoptotic debris, glomeruloid bodies
- Anaplasia: important for prognosis
- Immunostains: Positive for WT1 (nuclear); negative for CD57, retained INI1
- Differentials: Metanephric adenoma, papillary RCC, Rhabdoid tumors, mesoblastic nephroma (stromal predominant Wilms Tumor)

ADRENAL GLAND FNA

INDICATIONS:

- Infections: Tuberculosis, fungal infections
- Primary neoplasms: Cortical neoplasms: Adrenal cortical adenoma/carcinoma; medullary neoplasms: pheochromocytoma and myelolipoma
- Metastases: Adrenal gland is a common site for metastatic tumors

Specimen Collection and complications:

- Mostly if not all image guided: CT or USG
- Transhepatic approach: for right adrenal: benign hepatocytes; incidental finding
- Complications: Pneumothorax, episodic hypertension/ death from FNA of pheochromocytoma has been reported

Accuracy:

- Accuracy rate: 96-98%
- Very good NPV for lesions >3cm
- Non-diagnostic rate: 14%

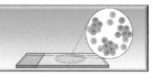

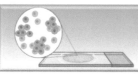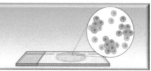
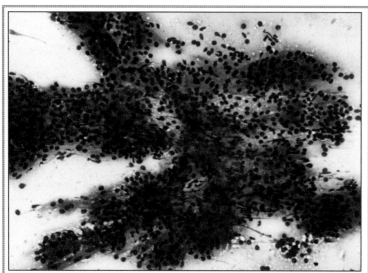
Figure: H&E stain. Adrenocortical adenoma. Courtesy Terrance Lynn, MD

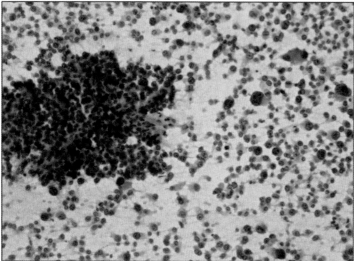
Figure: PAP stain. Adrenocortical carcinoma. Courtesy Terrance Lynn, MD

MYELOLIPOMA

CYTOMORPHOLOGY

- Fat and marrow elements
- Megakaryocytes, red blood cells and white blood cells precursor cells
- Differentials: Angiomyolipoma
- Immunostains: CD71 (Red blood cells precursors), MPO (myeloid precursors), CD61 (megakaryocytes precursors), Negative for: HMB45 and Melan-A

ADRENAL CORTICAL NEOPLASMS

CYTOMORPHOLOGY

- Numerous naked nuclei
- Frothy background
- Rare intact cells with granular cells and vacuolated cytoplasm
- Carcinoma preparations tends to be cellular, with moderate to marked nuclear atypia, mitoses, and necrotic debris

HIGH YIELD POINTS

- It's often very challenging to distinguish hyperplasia/ adenoma to carcinoma in cytology specimens
- Adrenal-cortical hyperplasia and adrenal cortical adenoma is indistinguishable by cytomorphology
- Differentials: Metastases from other sites
- Immunostains: positive for Inhibin, Melan-A, Calretinin, SF-1

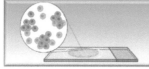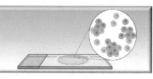

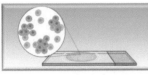

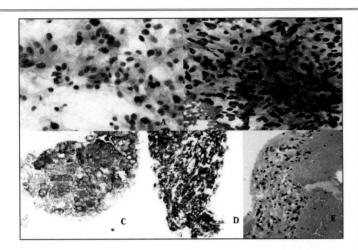

Figure: PAP stain (A), Diff-Quik stain (B), Chromogranin IHC (C), synaptophysin IHC (D) and H&E stain (E). Pheochromocytomas are characterized by cellular specimens with pleomorphic, oval to spindle cells arranged in sheets, and loose clusters. The cells show granular cytoplasm, ill-defined cytoplasmic borders and stippled chromatin. The neoplastic cells are positive for chromogranin (C) and synaptophysin (D). ©CytoAtlas

PHEOCHROMOCYTOMA

CYTOMORPHOLOGY

- Cellular specimens
- Cells arranged in loose clusters and singly scattered
- Can be associated with marked pleomorphism, small polygonal cells to spindled to epithelioid to plasmacytoid cells
- Naked nuclei
- Stippled chromatin, intracytoplasmic pseudo-inclusions, cytoplasmic granules seen in Diff-Quik type stains

HIGH YIELD POINTS

- Can resemble adrenocortical neoplasm
- Shouldn't perform FNA if clinically suspected pheochromocytoma: as rare incidence of death has been reported due to FNA procedure related hypertensive crisis by hormone secreting phaeochromocytomas
- Immunostains: Positive for Chromogranin and synaptophysin, S100 stain highlights sustentacular cells. negative for Inhibin, Melan-A, Calretinin, SF-1

METASTASIS

- Most common sites: lung, RCC, and melanoma
- Can be solitary or multiple
- Judicious use of immunostains and clinical history help clinching the diagnosis

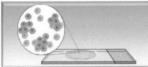
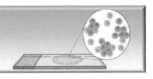

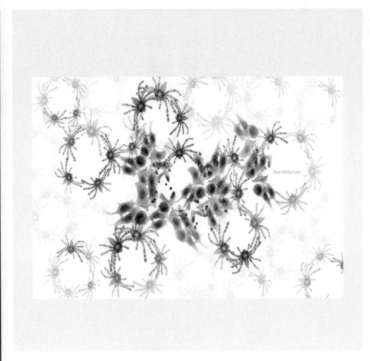

Chapter 17: Lab Management

Swikrity U Baskota, MD*

Terrance Lynn, MD

*Illustrations in this chapter made by Swikrity U Baskota, MD using BioRender

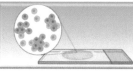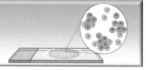
Regulations
  HIPAA
  CLIA
Procedure Manuals
Billing
Quality Control and Quality Assurance
  False Negative Pap Interpretations
  Annual Statistics
  Workload Limits and Records
  Competency Assessment
  Proficiency Testing
  Indicators of Performance
Safety and Exposure Control Management

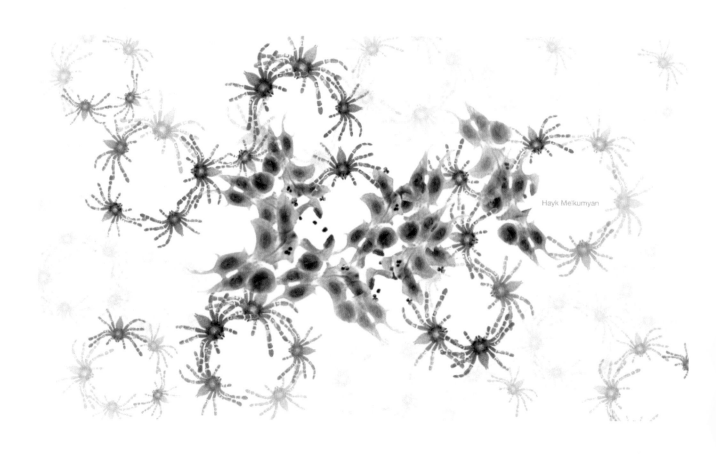

Hayk Melkumyan

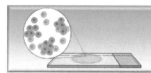

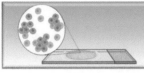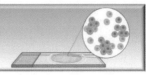

REGULATIONS

HIPAA

- Health Insurance Portability and Accountability Act of 1996
- Comprehensive law that regulates several aspects of health care that includes but not limited to health care coverage between job change and privacy of medical information
- DHHS published final rule: December 28,2000, and took effect: April 24,2001, requiring health care providers to comply by April 14,2003
- The rule applies to the use of individually identifiable health information to be used only for health purposes, unless permission is taken to be used for any other purpose
- The personal identifiable information includes medical record number, social security number, and/or accession number used in a cytology laboratory
- HIPAA also requires every provider to use same health care transactions, code sets and identifiers
- Code sets include CPT (current procedure terminology), Health Care Common Procedure Coding System (HCPCS) and others

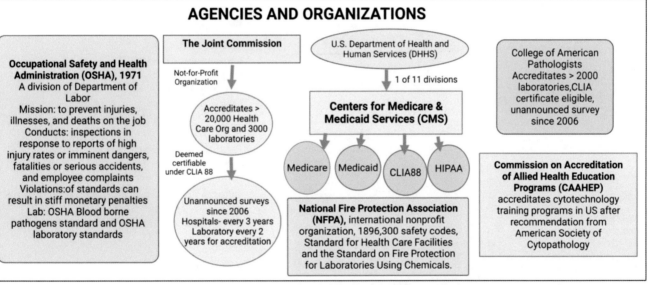
Figure: Agencies and Organizations in Laboratory Management

CLIA

- Clinical Laboratory Improvement Amendments (CLIA) of 1988

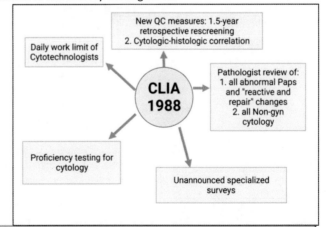

Figure: CLIA 1988 established regulations

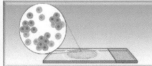

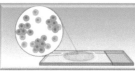 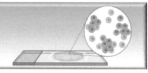
PROCEDURE MANUAL

TWO TYPES

- Client service manual
- Laboratory procedure manual

CLIENT SERVICE MANUAL: Policies must include

- ➢ Preparation of patients
- ➢ Specimen collection, labeling, and preservation
- ➢ Conditions of specimen transport

LABORATORY PROCEDURE MANUAL

- Must be dated/approved/signed by laboratory director
- Criteria for specimen collection, processing, or rejection

- Procedures for microscopic examinations
- Step-by-step description of procedure
- Electronic or paper manual acceptable but both should be readily available on-site and document controlled
- Any change in manual must be redated and signed including change in the laboratory director
- Manufacturer manual may be used but must be supplemented by the lab (whenever necessary)
- Any of the discontinued procedure should be kept for 2 years (at least)

WORKFLOW

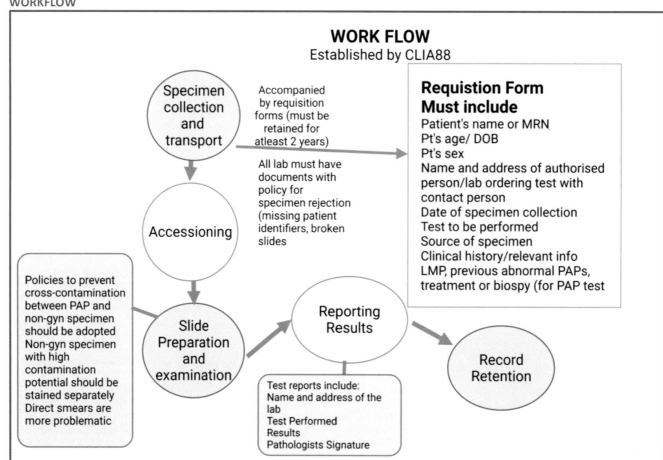

Figure: Workflow in a cytology laboratory

BILLING

- Billing codes either CPT (Current procedural Terminology) just numbers: 5 digits; with modifiers or HCPCS codes separate codes used for drugs, supplies and certain other services including pap tests

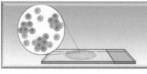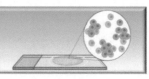
MOST COMMON BILLING CODES(CPT) USED FOR PAP TESTS					
PREPARATION TYPE	COMPONENT	MANUAL SCREENING	THINPREP IMAGER ASSISTED SCREENING	FOCALPOINT (INSTRUMENT ONLY)	FOCALPOINT (WITH MANUAL SCREENING)
Smear	Technical	88164	NA	88147	88148
	Professional	88141	NA	88141	88141
Liquid Based	Technical	88142	88175	88174	88175
	Professional	88141	88141	88141	88141

CPT CODES FOR NON-GYNECOLOGIC SPECIMEN			
PREPARATION	CPT CODES	PREPARATION	CPT CODES
Direct Smear	88104	**FNA PROCEDURE**	
Cytospin	88108	**Extraction by a pathologist without image guidance**	10021 and +10004 for each additional lesion
Enriched Prep (ThinPrep®/SurePath™)	88112	**Extraction by a pathologist with image guidance**	10005 and +10006 for each additional lesion
Cell Block	88305	**Adequacy assessment**	88172 (first episode) 88177 (additional episode/per lesion/site 88173 (Diagnosis)
Immunostain (qualitative)	88342(First) 88341 (additional)	**Touch Imprints**	88333 (First episode) 88334 (Additional episode)
Immunostain (quantitative)	88360 (first) 88361 (additional)	CONSULT	
Special stains for microbials	88312 (every additional +1)	**Outside slides**	88321
Other histochemical stains (like PAS/PAS-D)	88313 (every additional +1)	**Outside slides + H&E/other slides prep**	88323
In-situ Hybridization	88365, 88364x2	**Outside slides + additional many studies (includes review of medical record)**	88325
Stained Smear, other source	88160		
Unstained Smear, other source	88161		

QUALITY CONTROL AND QUALITY ASSURANCE

FALSE NEGATIVE PAP INTERPETATIONS RESULTS FROM:

- False-negative(FN) paps result from sampling, or laboratory (screening or interpretive) error
- Sampling error: either no lesional cells present in collection device or lesional cells not transferred from collecting device to the glass slides
- Laboratory error:
  - Screening: cases in which diagnostically abnormal cells were not detected either during computer-assisted screening or manual screening by the cytotechnologist
  - Interpretive: cases in which diagnostically abnormal cells were identified during screening but not interpreted as abnormal

ANNUAL STATISTICS

- CLIA'88 requires cytology laboratories to keep a record of annual statistics of at least but not limited to:
  - Total number of cytology cases
  - Total number of unsatisfactory cases
  - Total number of cases by specimen type
  - Total volume by diagnostic categories (unsatisfactory, negative, atypical)
  - Total number of pap tests with discrepancies
  - Total number of negative pap tests that were re-classified as abnormal
  - Total number of paps reported as HSIL, adenocarcinoma or malignancy with no histologic follow-up

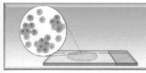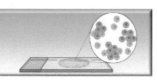

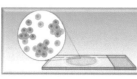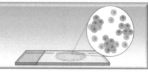
MEDICARE BENEFICIARY COVERAGE FOR PAP TEST- THREE CATEGORIES

SCREENING (ROUTINE) PAP TEST
No current sign, symptom, or complaint referable to the reproductive organs
No previous abnormal Pap
No high-risk factors for cervical or vaginal cancer

NO MORE THAN ONE TEST EVERY 24 MONTHS IS COVERED

Note: A laboratory can bill the patient directly, but only if it has a signed Advance Beneficiary Notice of Noncoverage (ABN) from the patient on file

SCREENING (HIGH-RISK) PAP TEST
Early onset of sexual activity (before 16 years of age)
Multiple sexual partners (five or more in a lifetime)
History of sexually transmitted disease (including human immunodeficiency virus [HIV])
Fewer than three negative Paps in the previous 7 years
Daughter of a woman given diethylstilbestrol during pregnancy
Abnormal Pap in the past 3 years (childbearing-age women only)

NO MORE THAN ONE TEST EVERY 11 MONTHS IS COVERED

THE DIAGNOSTIC PAP TEST
Previously diagnosed cancer of the vagina, cervix, or uterus
Pevious abnormal Pap
Current abnormal findings of vagina, cervix, uterus, ovaries, or adnexae
Significant complaint referable to the female reproductive system
Any sign or symptom that might be related to a gynecologic disorder

NO FREQUENCY LIMIT BUT TEST MUST BE MEDICALLY INDICATED

Figure: Medicare Beneficiary coverage for three different categories of Pap tests

CLIA 88 QC STANDARDS
PAP CYTOLOGY SLIDE RE-EXAMINATION REQUIREMENTS

PROSPECTIVE 10% RESCREEN
Some randomly selected negative Pap cases and others targeted usually with a h/o SIL
The laboratory must specify how the cases are selected
The rescreening must be carried out prospectively
Errors in diagnosis can be corrected before the report is issued
The rescreening must be done by a technical supervisor

RETROSPECTIVE LOOKBACK (5 YEAR RESCREEN)
All cases with a new diagnosis of HSIL or carcinoma with prior negative for last 5 years gets reviewed
The percentage of diagnoses reclassified as unsatisfactory (UNS), ASC, or worse ranges from 12% to 94%
If a significant discrepancy is found affecting patient care, ammended report should be issued and clinician should be infomed but instances exceedingly rare

CYTOLOGIC-HISTOLOGIC CORRELATION
All Paps reported as HSIL, adenocarcinoma, or other malignant neoplasms be correlated with subsequent histopathologic reports
The variables included are:
A. the time interval between the Pap test and the biopsy
B. the discrepancy note
C. the timing of the review
D. the individual(s) assigned responsibility for discrepancy resolution

Figure: CLIA'88 PAP cytology slide re-examination final requirements

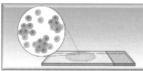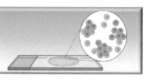

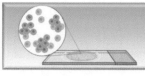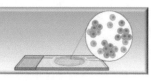
WORKLOAD LIMITS AND RECORDS

- Absolute limit to 100 slides/ 24 hours for primary screeners by CLIA 88 in US
- Primary screeners: can be cytotechnologist or pathologists
- Maximum time: 8 hours (12.5 slides/hour)
- Each cytotechnologist responsible for maintaining their own records of number of slides/times screened
- If working at multiple locations/laboratories, all should be accounted for
- 100 is absolute maximum, actual workload limit is set by technical supervisor based on performance evaluations every 6 months
- Smears counted as 1 slide:
  - Gynecologic ThinPrep® and SurePath™
- Slides counted as half are:
  - Cytocentrifuge preparations (e.g.: cytospins)
  - Cell block
  - Non-gynecologic ThinPrep®
  - Non-gynecologic SurePath™

COMPETENCY ASSESSMENT

- CLIA'88 requires documented competency assessment for all cytotechnologists, general supervisors, technical specialists
- Minimal requirements:
  - Direct observation of routine test performance (handling → testing)
  - Recording and reporting of results
  - Review test results and performance which includes prior analyzed specimens, internal blind testing samples, QC, proficiency tests, and preventative maintenance
  - Directly observed instrument maintenance and performance of maintenance
  - Direct observation of instrument function check
  - Direct observation and assessment of problem-solving skills

PROFICIENCY TESTING

- CLIA'88 requires proficiency testing for all cytopathology labs
- Only two approved vendors: College of American Pathologists (CAP) and American Society of Clinical Pathology (ASCP)
- Tests are announced >30 days in advance and are timed (2 hours to complete) and proctored

- Occurs annually and participants select pap preparation they are most accustomed to and evaluate 10 gynecologic slides
- Pathologists who examine paps after cytotechnologists prescreening may screen a set of test slides that are dotted by cytotechnologist
  - If prescreened slides are selected, cytotechnologists interpretation accompanies slides
- Each exam has 4 possible answer choices
  - Unsatisfactory for diagnosis
  - Negative (and includes organisms, reactive changes but does NOT include HPV effect)
  - LSIL
  - HSIL or cancer
- Exams are scored and participants must earn at least a 90% to pass
  - If participant fails, they may retake using a separate test set within 45 days of failure
  - If pass on second attempt, deemed "successfully participated" and do not need to be retested until following year
  - If a second fail occurs, participant must have documented remediation in area of failure (noted on letter of test results)
  - All paps screened by individual after notification of 2nd failure must be rescreened/reevaluated
  - To sit for a third examination, participant must then take a 4-hour test composed of 20 slides, if failure occurs, individual must stop examining pap slides upon notification of failure
  - To earn pap privileges back, individual must obtain 35-hours of formally structured education with specific focus on gynecologic cytology
  - Individual must then take a test composed of 20 slides and will repeat this step until pass
- Documentation of slide handling, proctoring, and entire testing process must be documented and maintained by laboratory director

INDICATORS OF PERFORMANCE

- Objective measurements can be obtained by various metrics
- Ratio of Atypical Squamous Cells to Squamous intraepithelial lesions is a performance indicator
  - As seen in Bethesda, a 3:1 upper limit benchmark for ratio

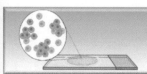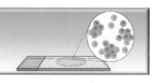

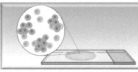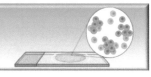

- ➢ Ratio is essentially a measurement of the degree of uncertainty in cytologic interpretation
- ➢ Atypical Squamous cells is defined as a "diagnosis of uncertainty" and Squamous intraepithelial lesion is defined as a "diagnosis of certainty"
- ➢ Applies to both cytotechnologist and cytopathologist
- ➢ If above, feedback can be provided to individual
- ➢ Little correlation with hrHPV rates to ASC:SIL ratio
- ➢ Cytology to Biopsy correlation is an indicator
  - ➢ Comparison of pap smear to biopsy is insightful because it can reveal over or under calling and comparison to peers
  - ➢ Positive cytology and confirmation by biopsy is a true positive and thus give a positive predictive value to a cytopathologist and their diagnostic call
  - ➢ If cytology positive and biopsy negative, this is an "overcall" (false positive), which will decrease PPV
  - ➢ Specificity, sensitivity, and likelihood ratio can also be calculated
  - ➢ Ideal performance metric would include both sensitivity and specificity → can plot a Receiver operator curve from this

SAFETY AND EXPOSURE CONTROL & MANAGEMENT

- ➢ Critical component of laboratory operations include having policies and procedures in place that keep staff safe
- ➢ Occupational Safety and Health Administration issued standards in 1991 which outlines methodologies and procedures to minimize/eliminate risks associated to exposures to substances (including infectious materials)
- ➢ OSHA revised standards in 2001 to include new standards after the Needlestick Safety and Prevention Act was passed into law in late 2000
  - ➢ OSHA standards require employers to select safe/safer needles and devices that reduce risk of accidental needle stick
  - ➢ It also requires that employers involve employees in the selection of these devices
  - ➢ Standard also requires employers to keep a record of needlestick/contaminated sharps injuries
- ➢ Exposure control plan is a written document and sets forth goals to reduce and/or eliminate occupation exposures
  - ➢ Must be updated annually

- ➢ Must include "determination of exposure" which details list of jobs for which has potential for such event
- ➢ Contains a written list of tasks and/or workplace procedures that carry risk of exposure
- ➢ Must include Compliance Methodology which includes
  - ❖ Universal precautions
  - ❖ Workplace engineering and practice controls
- ➢ Workplace engineering and practice controls must be provided to employee and include the following
  - ❖ Handwashing, facilities and receptacles for sharps disposal, storage and transport methods of contaminated objects & regulated waste disposal, safe laundry hygiene, and personal protective equipment
  - ❖ Sharps containers must be sealable, leakproof (specifically 'sides and bottoms'), puncture-resistant, labeled and/or color coded, easily accessible for disposal of sharp, secured upright, and replaced frequently to prevent overfilling
- ➢ Employers must provide immediate and confidential medical evaluation upon exposure
- ➢ Includes notification regarding exposure to vaccination against Hepatitis B and a post-exposure plan
  - ❖ Employers are required to offer free Hepatitis B vaccination to all employees who have risk of exposure
  - ❖ Exceptions are those who have medical contraindications or have been previously vaccinated and have appropriate antibody levels
  - ❖ Employees may decline Hepatitis B vaccination but must sign a declaration of declination
- ➢ Includes communication to employees about hazards and risk of exposures
  - ❖ Such communication is visible biohazard signs/symbols
  - ❖ Such signs/symbols must be fluorescent orange or red with opposing unrelated color (often black)
- ➢ All employees involved in jobs in which occupation exposure occurs/occurred must be provided training at time of employment regarding safety practices
  - ❖ Required to be free to employee

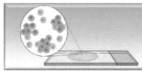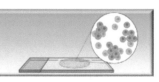

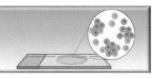

- ❖ Must be repeated annually
- ➢ Must include mention of documentation of exposures and documentation must have the following characteristics:
  - ❖ Employee's name and social security number
  - ❖ Post-exposure plan and appropriate follow-up
  - ❖ Vaccination status against Hepatitis B
  - ❖ Health care professional's written advice and/or medical opinion
  - ❖ Confidential and limited access to these records
- ➢ Potentially infectious agents/materials include the following:
  - ❖ Semen, vaginal secretions, cerebrospinal fluid, serous fluids from body cavities, amniotic fluid, saliva, and fluid with visible bloody contamination, any unfixed human specimens
  - ❖ In general, if unsure, treat as infectious/contaminated
- ➢ OSHA Laboratory Standard
- ➢ Specific standards that recognize the hazards and potential exposures in a lab setting
- ➢ All labs must have a list of hazardous chemicals utilized
  - ❖ Formally called a Chemical Hygiene Plan
  - ❖ Cytology labs have few chemicals, but these must be included
  - ❖ Laboratory director is charged with identifying hazardous chemicals that are present
  - ❖ This must also include Chemical name, health effects upon exposure, and procedures for identifying/quantifying level of exposure
  - ➢ Permissible Exposure Limits (PELs)
  - ❖ Time limits and/or time-weighted averages (TWA) of permissible exposure
  - ❖ 8 hours is considered 'long' TWA
  - ❖ 15 minutes considered 'short' TWA
  - ❖ Must have a set "action level" which triggers exposure monitoring (at minimum)
  - ❖ Xylene is often used in process of slide making and thus has a set defined PEL of 100 parts per million (ppm) for a TWA of 8 hours
  - ❖ Odor threshold of Xylene is significantly lower (~1 ppm) and thus is generally regarded as "adequate" warning to employees upon exposure

- ➢ Material and Safety Data Sheets (MSDS) are required to be on file for every hazardous chemical
  - ❖ All chemicals must be labeled with warning labels
  - ❖ Labels are brief synopses of main hazards
  - ❖ MSDS must detail PEL, as well as complete and detailed technical information and is much more expansile than labels on containers
  - ❖ Employees must be trained to recognize and read MSDS and labels on hazardous materials
  - ❖ Critical to understand how to protect themselves and what to do in case of accidental exposure or emergency
- ➢ Satellite accumulation areas are required for all laboratories which generate hazardous and/or regulated waste
  - ❖ SAA is a designated area for which hazardous items/materials are stored until removed for waste processing
  - ❖ Often this is a "biohazard" room, but can be a cabinet, fume hood or other safe location
  - ❖ SAA must have the words "Hazardous Waste" somewhere visible to all before entering
  - ❖ SAA required to list all chemicals as words as listing their chemical formula is deemed unsatisfactory and unsafe
  - ❖ SAA must delineate specific type of hazard (combustion, toxic, causes blindness etc.)
  - ❖ SAA must have a place for documentation of when container (or room) needs emptied
- ➢ Hazardous wastes must be disposed of properly
  - ❖ Cannot flush down toilet or rinse in sink
  - ❖ If placed in landfill, must have been "treated"
  - ❖ May be incinerated, but process and incinerator is subjected to approval by government (Environmental Protection Agency)
- ➢ Healthcare facilities must abide by the National Fire Protection Association Standards
- ➢ Formally known as NFPA 99 Standard
- ➢ Has specific emphasis on fire safety in healthcare facilities (including laboratories)
- ➢ Most important in cytopathology laboratory in which flammable or combustible chemicals are utilized
- ➢ NFPA 45 Standard sets forth standard for maximum quantity allowance of a chemicals with fire hazards

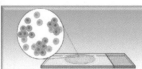 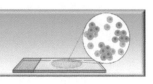

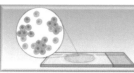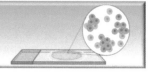
- "Fire Diamond" sign (placard) originated from the NFPA 704 standard which organized specific hazards that are present at time of exposure (spill, vapor release, fire, etc.)
- Organized by both color quadrants and a severity scale (see figure)
- Colors are standardized and have specific meaning and are located at same spot on every placard
- Red is located at 12 o'clock and represents flammability
- Yellow is located at 3 o'clock and indicates instability/reactivity

- White is special hazard and is located at 6 o'clock and are written as the following(W̶, Ox, and SA)
- W̶ indicates unusual reactivity with water
- Ox indicates chemical is an oxidizer
- SA indicates chemical is a simple asphyxiant (Nitrogen, helium, other Nobel gasses)
- Blue for health hazard and is located at 9 o'clock
- Severity of hazard is graded on a scale from 0 to 4
- Severity grading of 0 is considered minimal
- Severity grading of 4 is considered most severe

Figure: National Fire Association Standard on Fire Protection for Laboratories Using Chemicals

- All the biohazard chemicals in the laboratory should be labeled with biohazard label

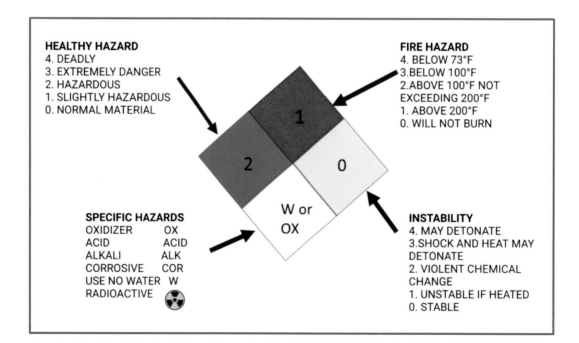

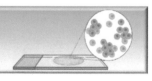

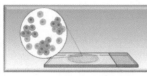 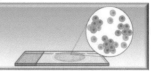

LABORATORY PERSONNEL

LABORATORY DIRECTOR
- Every high complexity testing laboratory under CLIA 88 regulations must have lab director
- Name must be listed in CLIA certificate
- May direct upto 5 laboratories
- Responsible for overall operation and administration including personnel employment
- Can also perform as TS/GS
- Must be licensed MD/DO
- Must be certified in AP,or if not technical supervisor(TS) must be certified in AP
- Must possess license as a lab director issued by the state in which the lab is located if/when applicable

TECHNICAL SUPERVISOR (TS)
- Pathologist: for scientific and technical supervision as CLIA 88
- Must be available as-needed basis
- Can also be GS/CT
- Responsible for QC, solving technical problems,monotring test results
- Personnel evaluation, biannual evaluation of cytotechs, workload limits for each, and reassessments
- Must be licensed MD/DO
- Must be certified in AP

CYTOTECHNOLOGIST(CT)
Responsibilites: documenting slide interpretation results
Recording no. of slides/no. of hours worked each day
Qualifications: Graduated for school of CT accredited by CAAHEP, and certified in CT by approved agency like American Society of Clinical Patholgoists (ASCP) or HEW

GENERAL SUPERVISOR (GS)
- Responsible for day-to-day oversight
- Can be both TS/GS
- Must be licensed MD/DO
- Must be certified in AP or Cytotechs with atleast 3 years of experience in last 10 years

Figure: Chart depicting laboratory personnel and their responsibilities

Federal Retention Requirements for Cytology Laboratory	
MATERIAL/RECORD	**PERIOD OF RETENTION**
Cell blocks	10 Years
Reports	10 Years
Non-gyn Slides (including (FNA)	10 years
Gynecologic slides	5 years
Immunohistochemistry controls	2 years
Test requisition, accession	2 years
Worksheets	2 years
QUALITY MANAGEMENT RECORDS	
Proficiency testing records	2 years
Instrument and equipment maintenance and function checks	2 years
Temperature monitoring (e.g. graphs, logs) of refrigerators, freezers	2 years
Policies and procedures	2 years following discontinuance
PERSONNEL	
Competency assessment records	2 years
Training Records	2 years

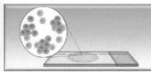 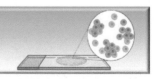

Chapter 18: Molecular Pathology

Terrance Lynn, MD
Aastha Chauhan, MD

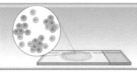

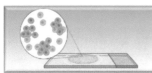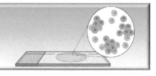

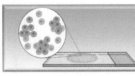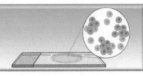
INTRODUCTION

- With the shift from large surgeries to minimally invasive techniques such as FNA and core biopsies, ancillary testing on such specimens has been rising
- Cytologic specimens offer several advantages for molecular testing due to preservative solutions and the direct smears (see table)
- Advances in molecular technology has allowed for large 500+ gene panels for expansive testing

- Smaller hospitals may utilize commercial labs which have potential downfalls
  - ➤ Longer turnaround times and higher costs
  - ➤ Patient insurance may not cover testing
  - ➤ Unable to perform quality control
  - ➤ Only receive final report
  - ➤ Do not get to analyze raw data and thus reduces ability to do research

PREPARATION	ESTABLISH ADEQUACY BY ROSE/ROSA	ABILITY TO DO IHC	FISH	PCR	NGS	NEED FOR SLIDE SACRIFICE TO DO NGS OR PCR?
Fixed slide	Yes	Yes, but requires additional validation by each lab	No	Best for low tumor volume	Best for low tumor volume	Yes, whole slide imaging and sacrifice slide by scraping off small tumor clusters
Air dried slide	Yes	No	Yes	Best for low tumor volume	Best for low tumor volume	Yes, whole slide imaging and sacrifice slide by scraping off small tumor clusters
Cell Block	No	Yes	Yes	Yes	Yes	No need to sacrifice slide
Core Biopsy	No	Yes	Yes	Yes	Yes	No need to sacrifice slide
Liquid based Preparation	No	Yes, but requires additional validation	Yes	Yes	Yes	Yes, if no additional tumoral DNA in preservative

Table: Versatility of cytologic specimen preparations for ancillary testing

PREANALYTIC CONSIDERATIONS

- Specimen characteristics and processing are important factors as they may affect testing by:
  - ➤ Quality of material (viability/necrosis)
  - ➤ Quantity of material (cellularity)
  - ➤ Configuration of tumor (thick clusters or monolayer of cells)
    - ❖ Affect reagent penetration
  - ➤ Intraprocedural triage of ancillary studies

- ➤ Collection and storage prior to testing
  - ❖ High temperatures cause RNA degradation (spontaneous)
  - ❖ Freezing specimens causes shearing of DNA from ice crystals
  - ❖ FFPE over time shortens amplifiable DNA → changes maximum storage time length due to hydrolysis → apurinic and apyrimidinic sites

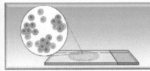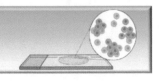

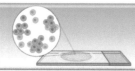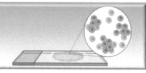
- ❖ Specimens submitted in hypertonic media → DNA helix denaturation
- ❖ Non-sterile collection media contaminated by bacteria → changes pH → depurination in acidic environments or denaturation in basic environments
- ➢ Specimen decalcification
  - ❖ EDTA preferred as it is less damaging to DNA than other decal agents

METHODS AND CELLULARITY FOR ANCILLARY TESTING

- In no way is all molecular testing created equal, therefore choosing wisely based on cytologic characteristics is key
- Immunocytochemistry:
  - ➢ Detects cellular proteins by antibodies
  - ➢ Preferred: cell blocks or core biopsies
  - ➢ Recommended: ~100 cells for detection in cell block but depends on developer/manufacturer
  - ➢ Can be problematic if scant tumor burden as it may not be present in sequential sections of CB preparation and may yield inconclusive or erroneous results
  - ➢ Can use liquid based preparations if:
    - ❖ Validated by laboratory
    - ❖ Cells are intact and free of artifact
    - ❖ Tumor can easily be distinguished from background cells

- ❖ Can etch location of tumor
- Fluorescence in situ hybridization (FISH):
  - ➢ Detects specific DNA (or RNA) sequences on a specific chromosome
  - ➢ Must know gene targets of interest
  - ➢ Must identify appropriate type of probe sets (see figure X)
  - ➢ Requires sufficient tumoral cellularity
  - ➢ Touch Preps, LBP, Smears, and CytoSpins preferred as there is no truncation of nucleus or loss of signal
    - ❖ FFPE cause nuclear truncation →artifactual signal loss
    - ❖ Can eliminate FFPE artifact if thick section → extracted nuclei and no need for architecture
    - ❖ Not appropriate for certain FISH studies (e.g., HER-2/neu)
  - ➢ Enumeration probes sets →detect deletions, aneuploidies, duplications, and amplifications
    - ❖ Use a centromeric-specific + locus-specific probe
  - ➢ Dual-Color Break apart probe sets → detects rearrangements based on physical separation of probes
  - ➢ Break-apart probes → best for detecting gene rearrangements with promiscuous partners
  - ➢ Fusion probes → most common for gene fusions with consistent partners

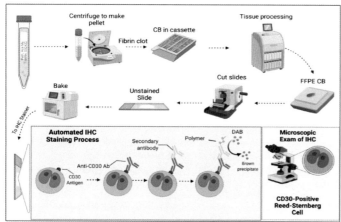

Figure: Cytology specimen in RPMI to creation of IHC stained slide. Created by Terrance Lynn, MD using BioRender.

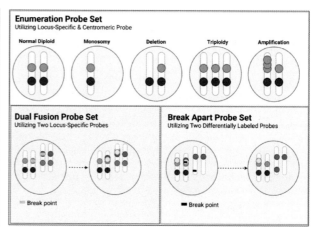

Figure: Different types of FISH probes and their function. Created by Terrance Lynn, MD using BioRender.

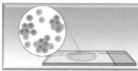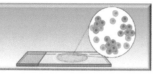

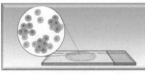
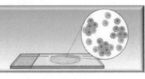

- PCR and NGS Methods:
  - ➢ Most important step is the preanalytical characteristics of specimen as result is not directly tied to morphology like IHC or FISH
  - ➢ Amount of input DNA is crucial for success and thus reliant on specimen cellularity
    - ❖ Single diploid cell yields ~6 pg of DNA
    - ❖ Extraction efficiency is dependent on method
  - ➢ To detect a 5% mutant allele frequency, it requires ~10% tumor cellularity
    - ❖ Low tumor burden → microdissection before extraction
  - ➢ DNA and RNA quality assessment occurs after extraction by any of following
    - ❖ Automated electrophoresis
    - ❖ Fluorometry
    - ❖ qPCR (most sensitive and specific)
    - ❖ UV Spectrophotometry
  - ➢ Perform amplification & library preparation → sequence
  - ➢ After sequencing → bioinformatics and data processing steps occur:
    - ❖ Assessment of raw data quality
    - ❖ Alignment of reads to a reference genome
    - ❖ Variant identification
    - ❖ Variant annotation
    - ❖ Data review
  - ➢ Read Depth ("Coverage")
    - ❖ Number of reads that overlap with alignment at specific locus of interest
    - ❖ Often expressed as a %
  - ➢ Variant allele frequency (VAF)
    - ❖ A measurement (in percent) of the sequencing reads observed that match a specific variant in DNA divided by the coverage at a specific locus
    - ❖ Essentially a surrogate marker for amount of DNA in original sample that contain variant
    - ❖ In diploid zygosity
      - o Heterozygous loci should have approximately 50% VAF
      - o Homozygous loci should have nearly 100% VAF
      - o Reference loci should be near or at 0%

  - o If any of the above are not close to these values → consider incorrect base calling or errors with alignment
  - ➢ Strand Bias
    - ❖ Measurement of how much variant reads deviate from the likelihood of sequencing plus and minus strands
    - ❖ A high SB is more indicative of an alignment process artifact than an actual true mutation
  - ➢ Variant quality (QUAL) scores
    - ❖ QUAL scores are generated during the calling of variants step
    - ❖ QUAL scores transformed into log scaled values (PHRED)
    - ❖ QUAL values vary between assays, methods of capture, and variant calling software
      - o Laboratories should independently assess performance of each assay
  - ➢ Interpretation and creation of report in context of cytomorphology & clinical
  - ➢ VAF and tumor cellularity are critical considerations
    - ❖ If VAF >> than expected → consider germline variant or loss of heterozygosity
    - ❖ If VAF << than expected → consider low tumor heterogeneity or false positive
  - ➢ Writing a molecular report requires knowledge of various reporting systems and use of appropriate terminology
    - ❖ The following is the best practice for writing or understanding a molecular genetic test report
    - ❖ Gene names are reported as defined by the HUGO Gene Nomenclature Committee
    - ❖ Copy number variations (CNVs) should be clearly defined and includes "gain" or "loss" terms
    - ❖ Single nucleotide variations (SNVs) and insertion-deletions should be reported in the p. and c. formats
      - o Protein level ("p.") amino acid sequences
      - o Coding DNA ("c.") reference sequences
      - o Insertion-deletion is often referred to the shorted name "indels"
      - o The transcript reference sequence should also be reported

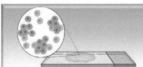
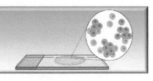

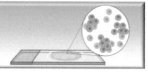

- o Transcript reference sequences are written in the "NM_000000.0" format
- ❖ There is a specific classification scheme of variants which is continuously updated based on new research and information
- ❖ American College of Medical Genetics and Genomics (ACMG) and Association of Molecular Pathology (ACMG-AMP System) is a variant classification system
- ❖ There are 5 tiers of classification
  - o Benign
  - o Likely benign
  - o Variant of unknown significance
  - o Likely pathogenic
  - o Pathogenic
- ❖ For somatic mutations, FDA standards and guidelines have an evidence-based categorization system which is based on diagnosis, prognosis, and potential therapeutics
  - o Tier I: Variants of Strong Clinical Significance (Therapeutic, prognostic, and diagnostic)
    - ▪ Level A Evidence: FDA-approved therapy exists
    - ▪ Level B evidence: well-powered studies with expert consensus
  - o Tier II: Variants of Potential Clinical Significance (Therapeutic, prognostic, and diagnostic)
    - ▪ Level C evidence: FDA-approved therapy for alternative tumor types or investigational therapies;

- Multiple small, published studies with some consensus
  - ▪ Level D evidence: Preclinical trials or few case reports, no consensus
  - o Tier III: Variants of Unknown Clinical Significance
    - ▪ Not observed at significant allele frequency in general or subpopulation database, or cancer database
    - ▪ No convincing published data/evidence of cancer association
  - o Tier IV: Benign or Likely Benign Variants
    - ▪ Observed at a significant allele frequency in general or subpopulation database
    - ▪ No existing evidence or published association of cancer
- ❖ Reporting of these tiers varies among laboratories as many opt to only report Tier I and II, other labs will include Tier III periodically
  - o Reports should be informative but concise (see figure)
  - o Molecular testing reports are "static" meaning no changes made even in setting of new associations or changes to variant listing in the tiers
  - o Reporting many Tier III results could reduce conciseness of report and lead to an overwhelming report for clinician → use best judgment and caution when choosing to report Tier III findings

Tier	Gene	Variant	Amino Acid Change	Nucleotide Change	Consequence	VAF	Read depth
I	*BRAF*	V600E	p.Val600Glu	NM_004333.6: c.1799T>A	Missense	42.3%	2022

Figure: Representation of concise reporting of a Tier I variant.

THYROID CYTOPATHOLOGY AND MOLECULAR TESTING

- Molecular testing of indeterminate thyroid lesions is critical as it assists in the next step of patient management as seen in Figure X.
- Cytopathologist run FNA and ultrasound guided FNA clinics offer several unique advantages for patients:
  - ➢ Image guidance to target lesion

- ➢ Ability to obtain diagnostic material
- ➢ Intraprocedural evaluation of adequacy
- ➢ Intraprocedural triage of specimen for ancillary studies
- ➢ Appropriate number of passes performed
- ➢ Rapid transport time to laboratory

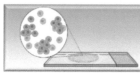

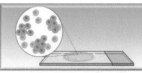 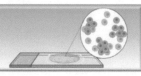

These clinics are not only effective, but demonstrate high-quality commitment to patient care
- NGS analysis in indeterminant thyroid nodules can be performed on the following:
  - Fresh specimen in preservative
  - Tissue sections from a cell block
  - Direct smears (Pap and Diff-Quik)
- NGS Molecular analysis of these lesions should include the following:
  - Gene mutations and gene fusions
  - Gene expression profile
  - Copy number alterations
  - Testing for medullary/C-Cells and parathyroid hormone

- Reporting of results if positive, will include alterations detected as well as a variant allele frequency (VAF)
- Thyroid molecular testing (ThyroSeq®) is performed using NGS
- When choosing a molecular test, examination of the positive predictive value (PPV), negative predictive value (NPV) gives an estimate of test performance
  - These are not fixed values and will vary based on disease prevalence in the population
- Ideally, the best tests aim for the highest NPV
- In addition to ThyroSeq®, ThyGeNEXT®+ ThyraMIR® and Afirma® Gene Expression Classifier are alternative commercially available molecular tests with various targets and methodologies

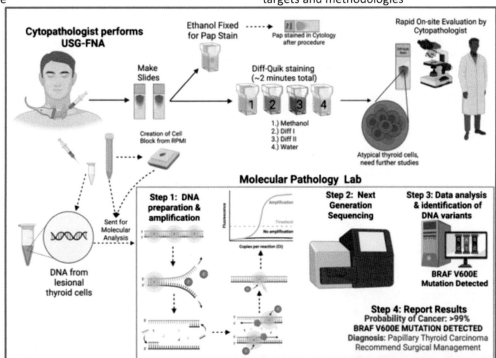

Figure: Thyroid FNA performed by cytopathologist and relationship to Molecular testing. Created by Terrance Lynn, MD using BioRender.

Genetic Component	DNA	microRNA	mRNA	Proteins
Methodology	NGS	RT-PCR	DNA Microarray; NGS	Immunocytochemistry
Detects	Point mutations & indels	Expression pattern of microRNA	Expression of mRNAs; Gene fusions	Protein expression
Relevant Tests	ThyGeNEXT, ThyroSeq	ThyraMIR	Afirma GEC, ThyGeNEXT, ThyroSeq	HBME1, PAX-8, TROP-2, Galectin-3, BRAF VE1, etc

Figure: Comparison of commercially available molecular tests for thyroid

 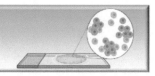

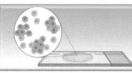 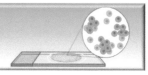

URINE CYTOPATHOLOGY AND MOLECULAR TESTING

- Urine sampling is a non-invasive, simple, rapid, and cost-effective methodology for screening and diagnosis of urothelial malignancies
- Urine cytology can be difficult to render a diagnosis, especially in the setting of degeneration or pelvic radiation for alternative malignancies
- There is fair sensitivity and high specificity for detection of HGUC by cytomorphology
- Urinary cytology is problematic for LGUN due to low sensitivity of detection
- Multi-target FISH can be applied to these difficult cases for further characterization of urothelial cells
- However, FISH in urine cytology utilizing UroVysion® is only FDA approved for voided urine with the following indications:
  - ➢ Initial approval: Monitoring recurrence
  - ➢ In conjunction with "standard diagnostic procedures"
  - ➢ Patients with hematuria in which bladder malignancy is in differential
- FISH results must be correlated with concurrent cytomorphology for accurate assessment

- Cytologically benign (NHGUC) or definitive malignancies (HGUC) have no role for FISH studies
- Steps to perform a UroVysion® Test (see figure X)
  - ➢ Specimen pretreatment
  - ➢ Denaturation and probe hybridization
  - ➢ Post-hybridization washes
  - ➢ Counterstaining with DAPI
  - ➢ Scoring and interpretation
- UroVysion® FISH examines the following:
  - ➢ Chromosomes 3,7, and 17
  - ➢ Locus-specific 9p21
- Positive UroVysion® test result is either:
  - ➢ 4 or more nuclei with polysomy in 2 or more chromosomes (3, 7, or 17) in same cell
    - ❖ 4 or more nuclei with >2 red signals in any of the two centromeric probe (red, green, aqua) signal
  - ➢ 12 or more morphologically abnormal nuclei that demonstrate homozygous loss of 9p21
    - ❖ No locus-specific 9p21 (no gold color) signal
- A negative test result is when none of the above are identified

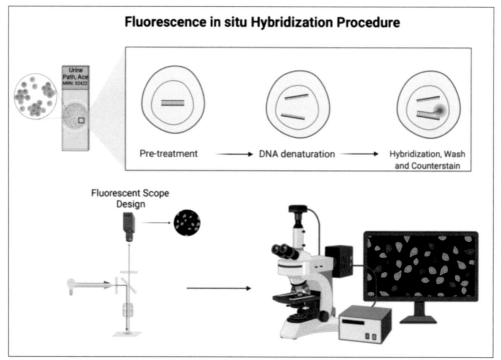

Figure: UroVysion® FISH procedure. Created by Terrance Lynn, MD using BioRender.

 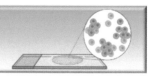

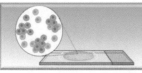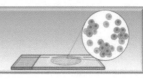
RESPIRATORY CYTOPATHOLOGY AND MOLECULAR TESTING

- Targeted agents for NSCLC and immunotherapy require accurate and reliable molecular testing prior to initiation
- College of American Pathologists, The International Association for the Study of Lung Cancer, and the Association for Molecular Pathology recommends testing *EGFR, EGFR T790M, ALK, ROS1, ERBB2, MET, BRAF, KRAS, RET, NTRK,* and *TP53* mutations in advanced stage lung adenocarcinomas
- IASLC/CAP/AMP guideline updated 2018 version accepts any cytology sample (including smears) with adequate cellularity and thus appropriate for molecular testing
- Cytology samples range from formalin-fixed, paraffin-embedded cell blocks and non-formalin fixed preparations such as smears, CytoSpins, liquid-based preparations, and fresh cells
- Cells from stained cytology smears can be removed from glass slides by scraping and collected in microcentrifuge tubes for extraction of DNA without the need for de-staining
- Cytology smears are optimal for microdissection or macrodissection for tumor enrichment
- Liquid biopsies using cell-free DNA (cfDNA) or circulating tumor cells can be used for molecular analysis
  - ➤ Sensitivity at this time is not high enough for recommendation as definitive test by IASLC guidelines
- Molecular Methodologies:
  - ➤ Next generation sequencing
    - ❖ Cytologic samples show comparable NGS results to their matched frozen pellets
    - ❖ Fixation and staining of cytologic specimens do not significantly alter nucleic acid quality
    - ❖ Due to its large gene panel and high sensitivity, NGS can detect alterations in a specimen for which was identified as wild type by single-gene assays
  - ➤ Fluorescence in situ hybridization
    - ❖ At least 50 evaluable tumor cells that are distinguishable from background cells and may be any of the following cytologic preparations
      - ○ FFPE Cell blocks
      - ○ Diff-Quik, Giemsa, or Papanicolaou-stained direct smears
      - ○ Liquid based preparations

- ❖ *ALK* and *ROS1* rearrangements can be identified using dual labeled, break apart probes
  - ○ Recently, *ROS1* can be performed by immunohistochemistry, however it is difficult to perform adequate validation due to rareness of cases
- ➤ PD-L1 Immunohistochemistry
  - ❖ National Comprehensive Cancer Network guidelines (2021) recommend PD-L1 testing in advanced NSCLC
  - ❖ Various assays/platforms are FDA-approved for use
    - ○ *PharmDx Dako PD-L1 assay (22C3 clone)*
    - ○ *VENTANA PD-L1 assay (SP263 clone)*
  - ❖ Can be performed on CB, direct smears, exfoliative samples, and liquid-based preparations
  - ❖ Cytology preparations are comparable to histology and require 100 viable tumor cells for evaluation
  - ❖ PD-L1 is scored using a Tumor Proportion Score (TPS)
    - ○ Defined as proportion of viable tumor cells showing partial or complete *membrane* staining regardless of intensity
      - ▪ TPS (%) = (#PD-L1 positive tumor cells / Total # of viable cells) x 100
  - ❖ Cytoplasmic staining does not count

PANCREATIC CYTOPATHOLOGY AND MOLECULAR TESTING

- Molecular testing is important in distinguishing non-mucinous cysts (with intrinsically low malignant potential) from mucinous neoplasms (IPMN) and mucinous cystic neoplasms (MCN)
- Molecular tests in pancreatic cyst fluid utilizes the following
  - ➤ Gene mutations (SNVs and Indels)
  - ➤ Gene fusions
  - ➤ Loss of Heterozygosity and copy number abnormalities
  - ➤ CEA expression
  - ➤ Neuroendocrine markers
- Single nucleotide variations and indels are examined in the following genes:

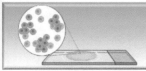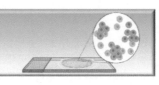

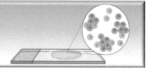
- ➤ AKT1, APC, BRAF, CTNNB1, GNAS, HRAS, IDH1, IDH2, KRAS, MEN1, MET, NF2, NRAS, PIK3CA, PTEN, STK11, TERT, TP53, TSC2, and VHL
- Loss of heterozygosity and copy number alterations are examined in the following genes:
  - ➤ SMAD4 (18q), RNF43 (17q), NF2 (22q), VHL (3p), TP53 (17p), and PTEN (10q) tumor suppressor genes
- Gene fusions are examined in the genes:
  - ➤ ALK and the following potential fusion partners:
    - ❖ EML4, TFG, CCDC149, GFPT1, GTF2IRD1, and STRN
  - ➤ BRAF and the following potential fusion partners:
    - ❖ MACF1, ZBTB8A, AGK, POR, SND1, AKAP9, BCL2L11, TRIM24, ZC3HAV1, CCNY, GORASP2, AGK, MKRN1, PICALM, and FAM114A2
  - ➤ ERBB4 and EZR
  - ➤ NTRK1 and the following potential fusion partners:
    - ❖ TPM3, IRF2BP2, SSBP2, SQSTM1, TFG, TPR, BANP, and ETV6
  - ➤ NTRK3 and the following potential fusion partners:
    - ❖ EML4, RBPMS, ETV6, and SQSTM1
  - ➤ ROS1 and CCDC30
  - ➤ RAF1 and AGGF1
  - ➤ PRKACB and ATP1B1 or DNAJB1
  - ➤ PRKCA and ATP1B1
- Gene expression of the following:
  - ❖ GUS, KRT7, KRT20, CHRGR, CEACAM5, and PGK1
- Benign/Likely Benign Interpretation → Absence of all the above → diagnosis of benign non-mucinous cyst
- Molecular markers seen in Intraductal Papillary Mucinous Neoplasm (IPMN):
  - ➤ More than 95% have one of the following
    - ❖ CTNNB1, RNF43, BRAF
    - ❖ GNAS codons 201 and 227

- ❖ Highly specific for IPMN
- ❖ KRAS codons 12, 13, and/or 16
- ➤ If advance dysplasia, there will be one or more of the following in addition to GNAS or KRAS
  - ❖ AKT1, PIK3CA, PTEN, or TP53
- Molecular markers seen in Mucinous Cystic Neoplasms (MCN):
  - ➤ Prevalence of the following is variable but seen in up to 50%
    - ❖ CTNNB1, RNF43, BRAF
    - ❖ KRAS
      - o Absence of GNAS mutations
      - o Association with high-grade dysplasia and/or early invasive ductal adenocarcinoma:
  - ➤ Presence of alteration in SMAD4, AKT1, PIK3CA, PTEN, or TP53 AKT1, PIK3CA, PTEN, or TP53
- Molecular markers seen in Serous Cystadenomas:
  - ➤ Nearly all have a mutation in VHL
  - ➤ Absence of GNAS and KRAS mutations
- Molecular markers seen in Solid-Pseudopapillary Neoplasms:
  - ➤ CTNNB1 mutations (exon 3)
  - ➤ Absence of GNAS, KRAS, VHL, RNF43, and BRAF mutations
- Molecular markers seen in Pancreatic Neuroendocrine Tumors (PanNET):
  - ➤ MEN1 and/or TSC2 mutations
    - ❖ Only seen in a proportion of lesions
  - ➤ VHL mutations
  - ➤ Copy number alterations → decreased disease-free survival
  - ➤ Absence of KRAS mutations
- Molecular markers seen in Pancreatic Ductal Adenocarcinoma:
  - ➤ SMAD4, KRAS, and/or TP53

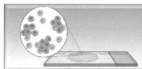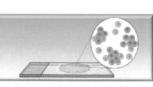

Bibliography and Suggested Reading

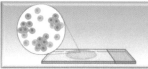
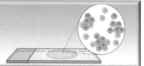

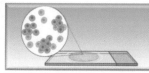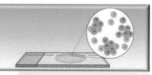
1. Cibas ES, Ducatman BS. Cytology: diagnostic principles and clinical correlates. Amsterdam: Elsevier; 2020.

2. Layfield LJ, Baloch Z. The Papanicolaou Society of Cytopathology System for Reporting Respiratory Cytology Definitions, Criteria, Explanatory Notes, and Recommendations for Ancillary Testing. Cham Springer International Publishing; 2019.

3. Martha Bishop Pitman, Lester James Layfield. The Papanicolaou Society of Cytopathology System for Reporting Pancreaticobiliary Cytology. Cham Springer International Publishing; 2015.

4. Ali SZ, Cibas ES. The Bethesda system for reporting thyroid cytopathology: definitions, criteria, and explanatory notes. Cham: Springer; 2018.

5. Rosenthal DL. The Paris system for reporting urinary cytology. Cham Springer; 2016.

6. Bongiovanni M, Faquin WC, Esther Diana Rossi. The Milan system for reporting salivary gland cytopathology. New York, Ny: Springer Science+Business Media; 2018.

7. Bardales RH. Cytology of the mediastinum and gut via endoscopic ultrasound-guided aspiration. Cham: Springer; 2015.

8. International System For Serous Fluid Cytopathology. S.L.: Springer; 2020.

9. Hoda RS, Rao R, Scognamiglio T. Atlas of thyroid cytopathology on liquid-based preparations: correlation with clinical, radiological, molecular tests and histopathology. Cham, Switzerland: Springer; 2020.

10. Khalbuss WE, Means M. Gynecological and breast cytopathology board review and self-assessment. New York: Springer; 2013.

11. Dey P, Springerlink (Online Service. Fine Needle Aspiration Cytology: 100 Interesting Cases. Singapore: Springer Singapore; 2020.

12. Demay RM. The art and science of cytopathology. Chicago: Ascp Press; 1996.

13. Kini SR, P Greensheet, Purslow MJ. Color atlas of pulmonary cytopathology. New York; London: Springer; 2011.

14. Xin Jing, Qing Kay Li, Siddiqui MT. Atlas of Non-Gynecologic Cytology. Cham: Springer International Publishing; 2018.

15. Swerdlow SH. WHO classification of tumours of haematopoietic and lymphoid tissues [Internet]. Lyon: International Agency For Research On Cancer; 2017 [cited 2019 Apr 30]. Available from: http://publications.iarc.fr/Book-And-Report-Series/Who-Iarc-Classification-Of-Tumours/Who-Classification-Of-Tumours-Of-Haematopoietic-And-Lymphoid-Tissues-2017

16. Cancer L. Digestive system tumours. Lyon International Agency For Research On Cancer; 2019.

17. Laffan TA, Horton KM, Klein AP, Berlanstein B, Siegelman SS, Kawamoto S, et al. Prevalence of Unsuspected Pancreatic Cysts on MDCT. American Journal of Roentgenology. 2008 Sep;191(3):802–7.

18. Fukuda A. Molecular mechanism of intraductal papillary mucinous neoplasm and intraductal papillary mucinous neoplasm-derived pancreatic ductal adenocarcinoma. Journal of Hepato-Biliary-Pancreatic Sciences. 2015 Apr 21;22(7):519–23.

19. Roy-Chowdhuri SV, ander Laan P, et al. Molecular Diagnostics in Cytopathology: A Practical Handbook for the Practicing Pathologist. Springer International Publishing; 2019.

Lynn TJ, Campbell A. (2021) Molecular Diagnostic Methods. In: Ding Y., Zhang L. (eds) Practical Oncologic Molecular Pathology. Practical Anatomic Pathology. Springer, Cham.

20. Zheng R, Zhang L. (2021) Lung Cancer. In: Ding Y., Zhang L. (eds) Practical Oncologic Molecular Pathology. Practical Anatomic Pathology. Springer, Cham.

21. Lin F, Prichard JW et al. Handbook of Practical Immunohistochemistry: Frequently Asked Questions. Springer Publishing New York; 2015.

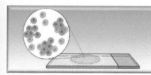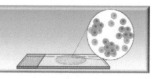

Made in the USA
Monee, IL
04 October 2023

43967757R00143